DEMOCRATIC CAPITALISM AT THE CROSSROADS

Democratic Capitalism at the Crossroads

Technological Change and the Future of Politics

Carles Boix

PRINCETON UNIVERSITY PRESS

PRINCETON AND OXFORD

Copyright © 2019 by Princeton University Press

Published by Princeton University Press
41 William Street, Princeton, New Jersey 08540
6 Oxford Street, Woodstock, Oxfordshire OX20 1TR

press.princeton.edu

Library of Congress Control Number: 2019930187
ISBN 978-0-691-19098-3

British Library Cataloging-in-Publication Data is available

Editorial: Eric Crahan, Bridget Flannery-McCoy, Pamela Weidman,
and Alena Chekanov
Production Editorial: Jenny Wolkowicki
Jacket design: Layla Mac Rory
Production: Erin Suydam
Publicity: Tayler Lord and Caroline Priday
Copyeditor: Maia Vaswani

This book has been composed in Adobe Text Pro

Printed on acid-free paper. ∞

Printed in the United States of America

10 9 8 7 6 5 4 3 2 1

To Carles, Enric, and Martí

CONTENTS

ACKNOWLEDGMENTS

This book grew out from my teaching a semester-long seminar on "The Politics of the Future" (later on renamed "Democratic Capitalism at the Crossroads") to students at the Woodrow Wilson School of Public and International Affairs in Princeton for several years. I am grateful to all of them for their good-humored willingness to engage with and challenge the readings we explored together. They provided me with a splendid venue to probe the ideas that I have eventually developed here. I also wish to acknowledge the support I received from the Princeton Institute for International and Regional Studies to run a monthly talk series on the "Future of Capitalism" where we enjoyed thought-provoking conversations with top scholars and practitioners on how our political and economic future may look.

The current text, either some of its chapters or in its entirety, has been presented in seminars at Harvard University, the Institutions and Political Economy Research Group (IPERG) at the University of Barcelona, MIT, Oxford University, Texas A&M University, Universidad Carlos III, the University of Nottingham, and Yale University. I thank all the participants for their comments, especially Alícia Adserà, James E. Alt, Cesc Amat, Benjamin Armstrong, Pablo Beramendi, Elissa Berwick, Pradeep Chhibber, Peter Hall, Dani Rodrik, David Stasavage, and Kathleen Thelen. Pau Vall provided invaluable research assistance. I completed the manuscript during a sabbatical year at the University of Barcelona partly funded by the European Research Council under the European Union's H2020 Program.

DEMOCRATIC CAPITALISM
AT THE CROSSROADS

1

Introduction

Politics in democratic countries is today in a state of turmoil. Trust in national institutions has reached a historical low. In advanced industrial economies, slightly over one in three people express confidence in their governments. Only twenty percent of Americans think that politicians care about their opinions—a number sharply down from almost four in five in the late 1950s. In France, Germany, and the United Kingdom, the proportion is even lower, at around ten to fifteen percent. Such a wave of disaffection has, in turn, given way to growing disengagement from traditional party politics. In Western Europe, electoral abstention has doubled since the 1970s, mainly among the youngest cohorts. Among those electors who vote, close to one-quarter are casting their ballots for far-right and far-left parties. Populist and nationalist alliances now govern a handful of European countries. And, in a context of increasingly polarized politics, in 2016 close to half of American voters elected a president intent on challenging, if not overturning, the very liberal democratic order of global cooperation and open economies that the United States designed and built after World War Two.

Not coincidentally, those political trends follow a set of momentous economic transformations across the world. Since the

1980s, the invention of the personal computer and, more generally, of modern information and communication technologies—as well as the globalization of trade and the offshoring of production, which have been fostered by those technological advances—have reshaped both the workplace and the overall structure of the labor market, intensifying the demand for highly educated individuals in the advanced world and the employment of manufacturing workers in emerging economies while reducing the number of blue-collar and white-collar jobs in North America and Europe. Salaries have behaved likewise. Over the two decades preceding the last Great Recession of 2007, the (household) per capita income of the richest ten percent in advanced economies rose more than sixty percent in real terms (that is, once we take into account changes in prices). The urban and rural middle strata of China and Southeast Asia saw their income grow by almost eighty percent in the same period. By contrast, the income of the bottom half of the income distribution in countries like Germany, Japan, and the United States has remained flat for close to four decades.

There is nothing to indicate that those economic transformations or the political turbulence that accompanies them will stop in the near future. If anything, the pace of technological and employment change may accelerate in the next few decades. According to some recent estimates, almost half of all current jobs may end up being automatized in the next twenty to thirty years. Most of that substitution by computer algorithms and robots will first affect the least qualified individuals. But it may not be limited to them, hitting, at some point in time, relatively creative, nonroutine jobs that today still appear hard to robotize.

Unsurprisingly, the extent and consequences of automation have become the object of a heated debate in the academic and political arenas. Technological pessimists foresee a brave new world where, once artificial intelligence makes its final breakthrough into the so-called "singularity moment," workers will become completely redundant or will draw, at most, a meager salary. Sitting at the top of a mass of unemployed and underemployed individuals, there will be a small creative class—a thin layer of inventors, top managers, and highly educated professionals—enjoying the benefits of automation and globalization. The system of democratic capitalism that has so far prevailed in the advanced world will crumble under the weight of so much economic inequality. Policy makers will not be able to reconcile free markets with representative elections and deliver both economic growth and a generous welfare state in the way they did during the better part of the twentieth century. The new technologies of information and communication invented in Silicon Valley will take us back to the contentious politics of nineteenth-century capitalism, finally vindicating Karl Marx, who, more than 150 years ago, predicted the eventual substitution of machines for workers, the immiserization of the masses, and the collapse of capitalism at the hands of a horde of angry men, armed with pitchforks and torches, marching down on the wealthy few—now huddled in their Manhattan and Bay Area mansions.

On the other side of the aisle, technological optimists concede that automation will disrupt the labor market and hurt the wages of the least educated, alienating them from politics and elections. Yet, they contend, those costs will be temporary—the transitory pangs associated with the birth of any new technological and social order. In due time, an overabundant economy will free the great majority or even all of us from both the bondages of work and ruthless interpersonal competition, and allow humankind to hunt in the morning, fish in the afternoon, and read poetry after dinner.

In this book, I take a different approach. The consequences of today's technological changes, I will claim, are not set in stone. They will work their way into the economy through their direct (although, at this point, still uncertain) impact on the demand for different types of labor and on the cost and ownership of capital. Yet they will also depend on the institutional and political strategies we follow in response to those technological transformations. During the last two hundred years, in their quest for profits and wealth, the entrepreneurs and industrial captains of modern capitalism have always pushed for the rationalization and automation of production. That "process of industrial mutation", to employ Schumpeter's renowned words, "incessantly revolutionize[d] the economic structure from within, incessantly destroying the old one, incessantly creating a new one"—modifying the relationship between capital and labor, the patterns of employment, and the distribution of income over time (Schumpeter 1950, 83). In doing so, it periodically generated a (changing) number of critical political challenges that were then met with a particular set of policy responses.

The same logic applies to today's technological innovations. Because they have already heightened economic inequality and may result in an even more extensive robotization of substantial numbers of (low- and semiskilled) jobs, they could put an end to the broad social consensus around democracy and capitalism that prevailed during most of the twentieth century—particularly in the advanced world. That does not necessarily mean, however, that they will—and that they will make us travel back in time to the nineteenth century, when the industrial capitalism invented in Manchester and its cotton factories turned out to be incompatible with the construction of fully democratic institutions. The reason is simple. The growing economic and political tensions we are witnessing today are happening in very affluent societies: their average per capita incomes are more than ten times higher than at the beginning of the first Industrial Revolution. So much wealth, jointly with the presence of stable democratic institutions and relatively well structured bureaucracies, should give us much more maneuvering room than any generations before us ever had to respond to the technological and economic challenges of today. Therefore, the task ahead of us is to think about how to harness those economic and institutional assets to the advantage of the many.

With that goal in mind, we should understand, first, how technology has shaped capitalism and, second, when and how the latter has coexisted, sometimes in a delicate, uneasy balance, with democracy. I explain this, necessarily in a sketchy manner, in this introduction by describing how modern capitalism has evolved in terms of its structure of production (i.e., the level of automation and the role of labor) and its relationship to politics—from the first Industrial Revolution born in Manchester through the twentieth-century capitalism invented in Detroit's assembly plants up to the new information era that emerged in Silicon Valley. In the rest of the book, I develop that argument more extensively, mainly focusing on the nature of twentieth-century democratic capitalism and, above all, on the challenges and opportunities brought about by today's technological revolution.

Richard Arkwright

The first Industrial Revolution, set in motion in Manchester by entrepreneurs such as Richard Arkwright, the designer of the spinning frame and one of the first businessmen to set up a modern factory, led to higher rates of economic growth than had been enjoyed by the old agrarian societies it replaced. Nonetheless, the newly generated wealth was anything but equally distributed. Putting an end to a system of production that had taken place in small artisanal shops, British industrialists reorganized the manufacturing process as a sequence of routinized tasks done in large factories, mechanizing them with the aid of a growing number of machines. The preindustrial skilled craftsman, who often made an entire product by hand, was replaced with unskilled individuals who were each in charge of a very specific action in the chain of production. Dragged by low factory salaries, overcrowded housing, and bad sanitation conditions, living standards experienced a sharp decline in the new industrial towns—at least for the first decades of the Industrial Revolution. By contrast, profits rose and capital accumulated steadily.

In that context of growing inequality, labor and the owners of industrial capital were locked in a protracted economic and political conflict. Businessmen as well as conservative and liberal politicians fretted about the potential entry of the masses into the political arena, the triumph of socialism, and the eventual abolition of private property. In the words of John Stuart Mill, Britain's foremost political philosopher of the nineteenth century, everyone may have had an interest in the "due representation" of the workers, but only "so long as [they were] not admitted to the suffrage so indiscriminately as to outnumber the other electors." Indeed, the introduction of "equal and universal suffrage" was, he warned, a "violent remedy" because it implied "disfranchising the higher and middle classes . . . who comprise the majority of the most intellectual in the kingdom" (Mill, "Recent Writers on Reform," quoted in Selinger and Conti 2015, 291). Full democracy, with its strictly egalitarian one-man-one-vote rule, looked incompatible with the philosophy of economic laissez-faire that defined nineteenth-century liberalism and with the inequalities generated by the first Industrial Revolution. At the opposite extreme of the political spectrum, support for some kind of political settlement that could reconcile democracy and capitalism was equally tenuous. Socialist unions and parties, growing in popularity since the end of the nineteenth century and loosely organized in an international cartel, rejected any form of "bourgeois democracy" as a political and economic empty shell. Instead, believing Marx's forecasts about the eventual collapse of capitalism, many of them advocated assaulting the state through revolutionary means, nationalizing the economy, and establishing a "dictatorship of the proletariat."

Henry Ford

As World War One was drawing to a close, one hundred years ago, few observers would have predicted that democracy and capitalism would reign uncontested a few years later. Just before World War One, parliaments elected by male universal suffrage were in place only in a handful of countries—and, even there, they were usually checked by unelected upper houses or powerful monarchs. Then, after the war armistice in the fall of 1918, a revolutionary wave, pushed by militant workers and demobilized soldiers, threatened to engulf Europe. Russia had already fallen under the control of Lenin and the Bolshevik faction of the Russian Social Democratic Labor Party a year before. In the first days of November 1918, the German and Austro-Hungarian monarchies collapsed. The Hungarian Communist Party took over the state a few weeks later. In Germany, the Spartacist movement attempted to proclaim a dictatorship of the proletariat in January of 1919. The latter's failure, however, marked a political turning point in the industrial world. With the support of a broad coalition including Christian democrats, social democrats, and liberals, Germany enacted one of the most democratic constitutions of the time. At around the same time, Britain, Belgium, the Netherlands, and the Scandinavian countries conceded the right to vote to all adult men. In turn, Western social democratic parties accepted elections as the means to allocate power and signaled their willingness to respect some regulated version of the market economy. A little over a decade later, Franklin D. Roosevelt's "New Deal" institutionalized the concept of a "mixed economy," according to which capitalism was to operate embedded in a regulatory framework aimed at stabilizing the market, and where the state was to protect its citizens from the poverty associated with unemployment, sickness, and old age.

The implementation of that new political and economic blueprint—often met with ideological skepticism, if not downright hostility—was at times riotous. In the United States, for example, Roosevelt threatened an uncooperative Supreme Court with a plan to expand the number of justices to almost double its size only to encounter considerable backlash from public opinion and the Congress. In continental Europe, interwar governments faced business lockouts, general strikes, and military unrest. Democracy collapsed in Austria, Germany, and Eastern Europe in the 1930s. In France, Left and Right came close to clashing violently just before World War Two. Over time, however, the institutional arrangements of democratic capitalism—that is, free markets, full democracy, and a generous welfare state—took root everywhere.

After the war, they did in France and Germany under the direct leadership of Christian democratic parties—the Mouvement Républicain Populaire and the Christian Democratic Union (CDU), respectively. Four decades later, they came into place in nations formerly controlled by the Soviet Union.

The United States and the United Kingdom extended the same logic of limited public intervention to the international arena after World War Two. In the Bretton Woods Conference, held in a hotel in New Hampshire in the summer of 1944, officials from forty-four nations, led by Harry Dexter White, a senior official at the US Treasury, and British economist John Maynard Keynes, reaffirmed their countries' commitment to the goals of currency stability and convertibility and to the principle of trade openness that had characterized the international system before 1914. At the same time, however, they agreed to design an international set of rules and institutions that could give enough autonomy to each country to respond to the particular economic and social demands of its voters. After reestablishing an international monetary system of fixed exchange rates, they called for the introduction of capital controls to enable governments to adjust their economies without sacrificing the goals of full employment and growth. In addition, they accepted the possibility of orderly currency realignments and, to minimize economic crises across the world, they provided for direct short-term financial support to domestic authorities from a newly created International Monetary Fund. Last but not least, the General Agreement on Trade and Tariffs restored a philosophy of open borders, nesting it within a framework of multilateral negotiations in which national governments had de facto veto power over trade policy.

The roots of that new political order, which implied the successful conciliation of the demands of democracy and the logic of capitalism, were economic. By the turn of the twentieth century, a sweeping wave of technical innovations had transformed the production system of Manchester capitalism, with momentous consequences for the economy and the labor market and, eventually, for politics. The invention of the assembly line and of mass-production techniques by Henry Ford and the Detroit car industry and their extension to a broad range of industries, resulting in the automation of whole parts of the manufacturing process, as well as the use of electricity and electric motors to power hauling and conveying operations, generated large productivity gains and fueled a period of unprecedented economic growth.

From 1900 onwards, the economy expanded on average at an annual rate of about 2.5 percent in the United States and almost 3 percent in Western Europe—a pace two times faster than in the previous century. Per capita income doubled in the forty years that preceded World War Two. It then doubled again during the Cold War. More crucially, labor markets changed in two fundamental ways. First, the demand for unskilled workers, whose brawn power had fed the first wave of industrialization, declined sharply. Instead, twentieth-century factories needed individuals capable of reading the operating instructions of machines as well as installing, repairing, and improving them. Second, a secular fall in communication and transportation costs, due to the invention of the telegraph and the railway and the naval application of the steam engine, led to the rise of global markets, the formation of large corporations, and, as a result, the growth of new layers of white-collar jobs needed to manage those firms. As semiskilled and skilled workers became central to the process of production—that is, as they replaced the very unskilled labor toiling in the Manchester factories to become the main type of labor complementary to machines and capital—wages grew across the board, particularly among middle social strata. Accordingly, the general distribution of earnings became more equal.

Growth and the equalization of labor and income conditions gave rise to a relatively affluent working class. The number of working households living under conditions of absolute poverty declined precipitously over the first half of the twentieth century. Buying food and clothing, which had absorbed two thirds of the budget of the average American family just after the Civil War, dropped to about a third of its expenditure on the eve of World War Two. The number of goods (from furniture to phones and automobiles) owned by a growing middle class expanded exponentially. By the 1960s, life expectancy had almost doubled with respect to that of the middle of the nineteenth century. Average height, which is a relatively good proxy of access to food and good health habits, rose by about four inches in Europe over the span of a century. The overall quality of health and lifestyle of seniors became extraordinarily high in developed countries. We only have to compare the photographs of forty-year-old men and women in poor countries with those seventy-year-old individuals in the United States or Europe to realize how much better off the latter are today.

Economic inequality is often measured through the Gini coefficient, developed by the Italian demographer Corrado Gini a century ago. In a perfectly equal society where everyone has the same income, the Gini index scores 0. In an economy where one person receives all the country's income, it reaches its maximum, 100. Figure 1.1 shows the evolution of the Gini index over the nineteenth and twentieth centuries for three major economies—the United States, the United Kingdom, and Japan. During the first stage of the Industrial Revolution, the Gini coefficient was high—at around 50—and rising. In both the United Kingdom, which spearheaded the Manchester model of capitalism, and the United States, which followed England closely, it increased until the last third of the nineteenth century. In Japan, a late industrializer, it rose until World War Two. Roughly coinciding with the expansion of Detroit capitalism, inequality declined everywhere throughout the middle decades of the twentieth century.[1] Other ways to measure the distribution of income tell a similar story. In England and Wales, the fraction of total income in the hands of the top ten percent of the population fell from slightly below fifty percent in 1914 to less than thirty percent in the late 1960s. In Australia, the United States, and France, to name just a few countries, it dropped by about fifteen percentage points to around thirty percent.

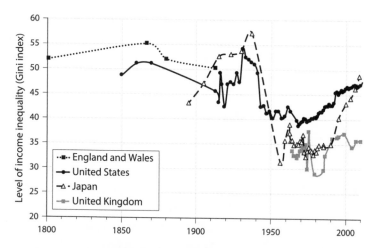

FIGURE 1.1 Two centuries of income inequality. Sources for the US data: for the nineteenth century, Lindert and Williamson (2016); for 1913–63, Plotnick et al. (1998, fig. 2); after 1963, Milanovic (2016). Sources for the United Kingdom: up to 1913, Lindert and Williamson (1983); after 1960, Milanovic (2016). Sources for Japan: before World War Two, Minami (2008); after World War Two, United Nations University-WIDER (2015).

Detroit capitalism, characterized by its efficiently run assembly lines and spotless factories, balanced power relations between corporate management and union bosses, and well-paid and well-fed employees, eventually tempered the politics of the twentieth century. The "red scare" of the end of World War One and the electoral contentiousness or outright civil conflict of the 1920s and 1930s gave way to the middle-of-the-road electioneering of the 1950s and 1960s. Moderating their electoral platforms to compete for the center of the political space, the mass parties founded at the end of the nineteenth century turned themselves into "catch-all" parties that strove to attract all kinds of voters, regardless of the latter's class or income. Liberal, Christian democratic, and conservative parties pivoted to the center first. Spearheaded by the German Social Democrats' decision to drop the use of Marxist doctrine in their Bad Godesberg party congress of 1959, socialist parties shifted to the right over the next two decades. Extreme, antisystem parties collected few votes in Europe, with the exception of post-war France and Italy, which had large communist parties. By the late 1960s or early 1970s, however, they had formally renounced the use of revolutionary violence. In that context, it did not take long for European left-wing intellectuals to deride democratic elections as meaningless events contested by politicians acting as Tweedledum and Tweedledee, the twins of Lewis Carroll's tale, or as a choice between "gin and tonic and tonic and gin."[2]

The combination of economic growth and the presence of stable democratic elections resulted in the construction of fully fledged welfare states. Even though the creation of an insurance system to cover industrial accidents and employment shocks and of modest pension schemes took place in several countries in the early decades of the twentieth century (Flora and Heidenheimer 1981), it was the traumatic experiences of the Great Depression of 1929 and World War Two that ushered in the construction of formidable social programs on both sides of the Atlantic. Roosevelt signed the Social Security Act in 1935, creating a broad old-age-pension system as well as unemployment insurance, old-age assistance, and programs of aid to families with dependent children. In Scandinavia, the union-business agreements of the 1930s opened the door to even more comprehensive welfare states. In Britain, the Beveridge Report, published in November of 1942, called for the extension of social rights to every citizen in the form of universal health care, a general pension scheme with compulsory retirement ages, subsidized public housing, and free schooling.

In Europe, socialist and Christian democratic parties set up most of those programs. Once in office, however, conservative and liberal parties maintained and occasionally expanded them. As a result, the role of government in the economy grew dramatically. In 1870, public spending was less than ten percent of the total economy in the United States and Europe—with most of it directed to the police and military. Transfers and subsidies accounted for less than one percent of the total economy. By the 1970s, public spending had risen to around forty percent of gross domestic product (GDP) in large economies and to over fifty percent in small countries—with half of the spending devoted to health, pensions, education, and labor-market programs. Although modern welfare states were mainly designed as insurance mechanisms to alleviate individual risks, such as the loss of employment or old-age infirmity, their impact on income inequality was substantial—reinforcing the wage-compression trends of twentieth-century capitalism. Before taxes, the Gini index of industrial democracies fluctuated around 40. After public transfers, it was less than 30 (Pontusson 2005).

Steve Jobs

What many have come to label the golden age of democratic capitalism started to unravel in the 1970s—as the big productivity gains spawned by the great inventions of the late nineteenth century and early twentieth century, from electricity to the steam engine and the assembly line, tapered off. The annual average growth rate in Organization for Economic Cooperation and Development (OECD) economies, which had reached 6.6 percent during 1945–60 and fluctuated around 5 percent until the mid-1970s, fell to about 2 percent afterward. Economic growth picked up in the 1990s, lifted by the invention of the personal computer and the democratization of its use thanks to entrepreneurs like Steve Jobs, the creation of internet, email, and mobile phones, as well as promising steps in robotics and biotechnology. But that improvement proved short-lived. By the 2000s, per capita income growth had fallen to 1.4 percent in the United States (Gordon 2014).

More fundamentally, those new information and communication technologies began to reshape the structure of employment—in a way reversing the effects that the second Industrial Revolution had on labor markets. In the big factories and large corporations of the first half of the twentieth century, capital and semiskilled labor had been complementary to each other. Now, the rapid diffusion of automatized processes—the result, in turn, of having extraordinarily fast microprocessors—was making a substantial fraction of qualified blue-collar workers redundant, in a way similar to what had happened to artisans in the early part of the nineteenth century. The number of US factory workers shrunk from a postwar peak of nearly 19.5 million in 1979 to about 12 million in 2014, even though total manufacturing output (in real dollars adjusted for inflation) roughly doubled in the same period of time.[3] Europe experienced a similar downward trend: manufacturing jobs accounted for over one-fifth of all employment in 1970 but less than one-tenth in the middle of the 2010s.

The impact of automation was not limited to industrial jobs. Complex software programs can now perform an increasing number of the routinary tasks that used to be part and parcel of a wide range of traditional white-collar jobs, from accounting and administrative support to travel agency. Routine occupations, that is, those jobs composed of tasks that imply following a well-defined number of procedures (and that can be reproduced by machines fed with appropriate rules and algorithms), employed almost forty-five percent of the working-age population in the United States until the mid-1980s. By 2014, that share had declined to around thirty-one percent (Cortes, Jaimovisch, and Siu 2017). By contrast, the number of professional and managerial jobs, which are low in routinized tasks and highly reliant on abstract, relatively creative thought processes, has risen steadily. In the United States, the share of high-skill occupations (managers and professionals) over total employment grew from almost twenty-eight percent of all civilian employment in 1980 to thirty-nine percent in 2010 (L. Katz and Margo 2014). Similar changes have taken place in Europe.

In combination with a sharp drop in transportation costs, the information and communication revolution globalized trade at a truly worldwide scale after the late 1970s, intensifying, as a result, the direct employment effects triggered by the invention of the personal computer. The rise of newly industrialized countries, such as the so-called East Asian Tigers, and the growing practice of job offshoring put an end to the international division of labor prevalent during the postwar period, characterized by a rich core of industrial economies, tightly interconnected through intra-industry trade, and a southern periphery specialized in exporting raw materials. An increasing number of American, European, and Japanese companies—from toy- and other consumer-goods makers in the 1970s to electronics companies in the 2000s—unbundled their production operations across the world, maintaining highly paid tasks in their national headquarters while moving low-wage jobs to developing countries. The hyperglobalization of the late twentieth century eroded the job status and wages of blue-collar industrial workers and the administrative middle class in advanced industrial economies. Recent estimates attribute about one-third of all employment losses in the last few decades to trade and the relocation of production abroad.

Those divergent trends in the structure of employment—with demand falling for manual and clerical positions and rising for highly educated individuals—translated into a wider wage structure and a more unequal distribution of incomes. Since the middle of the 1970s, median male earnings—that is, the income received by men at the fiftieth percentile of the earnings distribution—have remained stagnant in the United States—once we adjust them for inflation. In Japan and Europe, median salaries have performed slightly better, but they have still risen much less than the overall economy. Wages for those in the bottom quintile of the earnings distribution have done much worse—dropping in real terms in the United States and the United Kingdom and barely increasing in the other advanced economies. In the meantime, earnings have doubled for individuals with postgraduate education and grown by almost fifty percent for those holding bachelor degrees in the United States in the last half century. Less dramatic but similar wage dynamics have taken place in the majority of advanced industrial economies, so that by 2010 the earnings of an individual in the ninetieth percentile of the wage distribution were three to five times greater than the earnings of an individual at the tenth percentile of the same distribution. In those European countries where earnings inequality has remained unchanged, the cost has often been very tepid employment growth.

The unwinding of the Detroit economic model eventually shook the social and political consensus of the postwar period. Dissatisfaction with political institutions and the political establishment grew across almost all countries. In the United States, the share of people believing that government is run for the benefit of a few big interests doubled to over seventy percent in two decades (Dalton 2004, figs. 2.2, 2.3). In most European countries, the proportion of respondents trusting politicians dropped from about one-half in the early 1970s to less than one-third in the late 1990s. Much of the growing mistrust was concentrated among those most hurt by economic change. In 2012, almost forty percent of British respondents with no educational qualifications and a third of working-class respondents agreed strongly with the statement "people like me have no say in government"—more than twice the rate for university-educated respondents (R. Ford and Goodwin 2014). In the United States, individuals with a high-school diploma were (and are) much less likely to trust the federal government than those with a graduate or postgraduate education. Over time, political disaffection morphed into political disengagement. The rate of electoral abstention in Europe rose from seventeen percent in 1974 to thirty-three percent in 2016. Most of the drop in turnout took place among the social strata most affected by economic change. Abstention rates among low-income voters have become two to three times higher than among high-income individuals. Young cohorts, who have borne a good share of the costs of a changing labor market, are now abstaining at twice the rate of senior voters.

The political and electoral landscape has become more heterogeneous—marked by increasingly divergent interests between business owners (particularly those in high-tech firms with huge stock valuations and minimal workforces) and the rest of society, and between highly educated individuals, able to benefit from the spread of computational technologies and hyperglobalization, and the rest of the workforce. American politics has become much more polarized than in the past. The broad bipartisan consensus that was a feature of American politics in the 1950s and 1960s has given way to highly ideological and strict party-line voting behavior. In Europe, support for liberal, Christian democratic, and social democratic parties, who had dominated the political landscape since the interwar period, fell by twenty-five percentage points between 1975 and 2015—mostly to abstention. Then, in the wake of the Great Recession, the share of voters casting their ballots to either anti-immigration, anti–European Union right-wing platforms (mostly in northern Europe) or radical, populist left-wing movements (particularly in southern Europe) grew to almost one-quarter in 2015.

Machine Learning

The defeat in 1997 of Garry Kasparov, then reigning world chess champion, at the hands of Deep Blue, a powerful chess-playing machine developed by IBM, was hailed as the definitive sign that machines would replace humans in either all or a broad swath of intellectual and economic activities. The rise of robots could take several decades to happen—after all, the first person to suggest a "computing routine or 'program'" to play chess was the American mathematician Claude Shannon back in 1949 and the first chess-playing computer had been tried, with little success, in the Los Alamos National Laboratory in 1956—but, many claimed, it would eventually come to fruition.

Today's state of chess playing points to a less dramatic, even if still highly challenging, future in the relationship between machines and humans. Less than a decade after the victory of Deep Blue, the game was transformed by the invention of "centaur chess"—matches where human players team up with computers to exploit the latter's ability to retrieve and examine thousands of chess moves and countermoves. As it turned out, the combination of humans' creativity and strategic insights with machines' tactical acumen allowed simple amateurs to beat the strongest chess-playing machines—sometimes with more success than grandmasters, who often thought they knew better than computers.[4] Hence, if chess playing has any predictive value about the future of the economy in general, even though extremely sophisticated computational and information technologies (of the kind that are still in the making) may take over many of the jobs currently done by humans, they will be also likely to enhance our ability to work and produce. In other words, machines and humans will remain complementary to, rather than strict substitutes for, each other.

That complementarity will differ, however, across individuals. At this point in time, only a fraction of the labor force seems to enjoy the skills, talents, and flexibility to work with and take advantage of these new technologies—to succeed, as it were, in "centaur jobs." As a result, the process of employment dislocation and economic polarization that we are witnessing will probably accelerate in the medium term. If so, the democratic capitalist deal that defined a good part of the twentieth century could find itself at a major political crossroads—one where our societies could be torn apart between the employment and wage dislocations brought about by technological progress and the equalizing tendencies and demands inherent to a democratic system.

The rise of those political and social tensions does not imply, however, that there is a unique, predetermined social and political outcome ahead of us—one where the key institutions of twentieth-century democratic capitalism will buckle under the weight of mounting joblessness and growing wage inequality. Although Silicon Valley capitalism and Manchester capitalism may resemble each other in terms of their disruptive impact on employment, the stagnation of wages they brought to certain social strata, and their level of economic inequality, they differ, at the very least, on two critical dimensions: first, we are now much wealthier; second, fully democratic institutions and relatively capable bureaucracies have been in place in the richest parts of the globe for several decades.

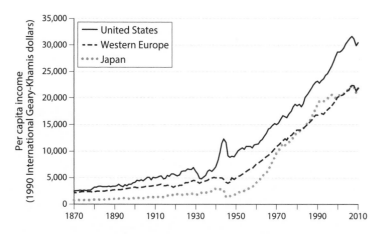

FIGURE 1.2 Per capita income, 1870–2010. Source: Bolt and van Zanden (2014).

As shown in figure 1.2, average income per person (reported in constant dollars of 1990) is about ten to fifteen times larger today than 150 years ago in North America, Europe, and Japan. It should therefore be possible to use our representative institutions to harness this massive buildup in wealth to smooth the technological transformations of the present and, in the process, to pursue the main collective objective—guaranteeing relatively equal life chances to all—that defined the middle and late decades of the twentieth century. That arguably calls for two types of interventions: firstly, providing everyone with the kinds of talents and skills that are complementary to the new technologies of production; secondly, compensating and protecting those individuals who may become underemployed or directly unemployable.

In the world of Manchester capitalism, formal skills were of little importance. All that counted was having cheap workers who could manipulate, in a mechanical way, rather rudimentary machines: children and illiterate adults. Neither businesses nor the state had much of an interest in "wasting" money funding educational schemes that were irrelevant to factory jobs. As a matter of fact, working families did not either: any year "lost" by their children attending school implied taking less money without any certainty that they would get better jobs and higher wages later on. By contrast, the diffusion of "Detroit" technologies coincided, for a good reason, with the expansion of school enrolment and the corresponding broadening of the American and European middle classes. States, corporations, and individuals had strong incentives to fund primary and high schools and/or vocational training institutions because Detroit capitalism led to the rise of occupations that required labor to have some basic literacy and numeracy competencies. In the future, as the Silicon Valley technological revolution progresses, the utility of some—the most basic and "routinizable"—skills will continue to decay, precisely because algorithms and computer programs are good at reproducing them. By contrast, other types of competencies, which are generally associated with relatively long educational processes and with "soft" abilities such as creativity or interpersonal skills, will rise in value. Investing in the generation of "centaur-like" aptitudes will be necessary to spread the benefits of the new technological revolution.

Producing that kind of human capital, however, may not be possible for everyone, or even sufficient in the long run. Up to this point, the process of automation has relied on feeding a computer (such as Deep Blue) with a program or set of strictly defined rules that imitate the actions and calculations of humans. Yet, in the last few years, programmers have developed new techniques, broadly defined as "machine learning," that allow computers to program themselves. After being instructed with the general rules of a game and/or fed with data, machines build up their own procedures to solve the problem at hand. In December 2017, for instance, the artificial-intelligence company DeepMind released AlphaZero, a generic algorithm that, with no chess knowledge at all, trained itself for a few hours, and went on to beat the world-champion chess program, Stockfish 8, in a one-hundred-game matchup. With these new technologies already succeeding at more complex games and tasks than chess, such as Go or image recognition, there is a distinct possibility that humans will become superfluous in a broader set of tasks at some point in the future. That, some claim, may involve reinforcing or setting up mechanisms to guarantee some basic income for the unemployed or unemployable. It may even entail "socializing" the ownership of those new technologies to ensure that their profits are shared as widely as possible.

Plan of the Book

Examining the challenges raised by technological change and its effects on employment, wages, and politics, as well as discussing how we may respond to them, requires exploring the interplay of economic and political institutions since the first Industrial Revolution. That is what I do in the rest of this book, which is structured as a kind of funnel—paying widening attention and space to those events, institutions, and problems that are closer to us in time. Although the chapters are organized, when we consider them together, to support the main claims of the book (about the impact of technological change on the structure of production and on the kind of labor that is complementary to machines, and, as a result, on wages, inequality, and political institutions), the reader should be able to read each one of them as a separate, self-contained piece of information on the puzzle of the interaction between democracy and capitalism for each one of the periods under analysis.

The next chapter, "Manchester," sketches in relatively broad strokes the nature of nineteenth-century capitalism and its relationship to its contemporary political institutions. As such, the chapter provides information about the new technologies of the first Industrial Revolution, their consequences on overall growth and the welfare of labor, and their ultimate political effects. Nevertheless, "Manchester" is mainly written as a conceptual exploration of the two building blocks of the book: modern (industrial) capitalism and representative democracy. With that goal in mind, the chapter often relies on the contributions of key intellectual witnesses of that historical period, such as Adam Smith, Karl Marx, and John S. Mill, whose ideas have come back in force in current debates about the future of both capitalism and democracy. More specifically, the chapter introduces the main narrative arc of the book to the reader: how industrial entrepreneurs, in their search for higher profits (the engine of capitalism), push for higher levels of automation in the production process; how a specific level of automation makes a particular type of labor complementary to the new technology of production and, therefore, especially sought after by businesses; how that complementarity affects, in turn, wages and living standards across the entire workforce; and how those changes give rise to a fresh set of political challenges. During the first phase of the Industrial Revolution, the growing mechanization of manufacturing and the creation of the factory resulted in the substitution of unskilled workers for a traditional class of craftsmen employed in artisanal shops. That complementary between machines and an illiterate or minimally educated labor informed, in turn, the low wages and poor living conditions of the working class. It was for that reason that conservatives and liberals, as well as socialist intellectuals and politicians, despaired of reconciling capitalism with democracy.

Chapter 3, "Detroit," examines, at much more length and with more fine-grained data than the previous chapter, the production revolution brought about by the assembly line and related technologies, its employment and income consequences, and the ways in which those changes laid the foundations for the triumph of the system of democratic capitalism during the best part of the twentieth century. As automation progressed, semiskilled and skilled individuals replaced unskilled workers as the main type of labor complementary to capital. The demand for lower-middle- and middle-class jobs, jointly with the expansion of secondary education, resulted in the formation of a broad affluent working class. In turn, fast economic growth and the relative equalization of incomes made social peace and universal suffrage possible. That new model was so successful, at least relative to Manchester, that many came to see democracy and capitalism as fostering, together, a virtuous political and economic cycle: capitalism produced the wealth that sustained political freedom and made governmental turnover at the polls acceptable to elections' losers; democratic states provided both accountable political institutions and a well-fed, healthy, and well-trained labor force—which together incentivized capital investment and more technological progress.

The core of the book, formed by its last three chapters, addresses the present and future of the emerging capitalism of the late twentieth and early twenty-first centuries. Chapter 4, "Silicon Valley," describes how the information and communication technologies of the last few decades, by making highly skilled labor the main complement of capital in the production process and fostering the current process of globalization, have broken the equalizing tendencies of Detroit and confronted governments in advanced economies with a growing trade-off between employment and inequality. Chapter 5, "Dire Straits," moves on to explore the electoral and political effects of those transformations. It provides fresh data on the rise of political disenchantment and electoral abstention among voters in advanced industrial economies. It shows the erosion of popular support for the old parties that constructed the democratic capitalist deal during the Detroit period. And it examines, employing simple but useful tools developed by current scholars of politics, the causes, nature, and prospects of so-called "populist" parties.

Chapter 6, "Robots vs. Democracy?," discusses the overall impact of future automation as well as the economic and political responses we should develop to exploit its benefits and tame its potential threats. I consider, in the first place, the effects of automation on the demand for particular types of labor and on our ability to meet those changes by training our workforce. I then reflect on its impact on the ownership of capital, mostly questioning a rather extended thesis that asserts that robotization will ineluctably result in the "hyperconcentration" of wealth in a few hands. Next, I consider the political consequences of the computer revolution. Contrary to some catastrophizing claims, I find little support for the idea that it will jeopardize democracy and holding regular elections per se. Still, I identify a potential decline in the level of political accountability of policy makers vis-à-vis public opinion, and I suggest, accordingly, a range of legal and political reforms to avoid it. Making sure that democratic institutions remain as representative and as close to citizens as possible will be crucial to ensure that governments administer the gains of the ongoing technological revolution to the advantage of the great majority. The policies that they deploy will depend on the (still uncertain) intensity of technological change—and will range from aggressive educational investment through antitrust measures to, exceptionally, some socialization of the ownership of capital. I close the book by warning about the future (not necessarily positive) effects of Silicon Valley capitalism on both newly developed economies and developing countries—the full automation of production may stop or even undo their recent economic growth—and on the evolution of globalization and transnational migration flows.

2

Prelude

MANCHESTER

Before the Industrial Revolution irrupted in full force in England at the turn of the nineteenth century, Britain—as well as continental Europe—was a predominantly agricultural economy. Parts of England, the Netherlands, and the territories along the course of the Rhine had a relatively higher concentration of midsized urban agglomerations than the rest of the continent. But, even there, the vast majority of the population lived off the land, clustered in villages or small towns, either farming their own piece of land or working as wage-laborers for the local landowner.

With agriculture mostly being a seasonal activity, a substantial number of men and women spent part of their off-season time occupied in some form of industrial work—spinning; weaving; manufacturing small iron products such as nails, horseshoes, or door hinges; and making baskets, brooms, or furniture. Over the course of the eighteenth century, so-called "putting-out" entrepreneurs— individuals who coordinated the production of workers by providing them with raw materials, collecting their output, and paying them a fixed rate per piece manufactured—increasingly organized that rural manufacturing sector. Yet even in the most sophisticated "put-out" networks, the economy remained of a traditional kind. Laborers worked in or near their homes, engaged in individual work or in very small teams normally composed of members of their own families. And their production was seasonal, constrained by the vagaries of geography and weather. Water was the main or only source of energy harnessed for manufacturing purposes. Heavy rains very easily made roads impassable and transportation all but impossible—holding down the size of markets and, with them, the scale of production units.

A few urban clusters were dotted with much bigger "factories," or concentrations of workers producing a similar good under the same roof: royal arms-making industries; manufacturing enterprises such as the Saint-Gobain company, a glass and mirror maker established by the French state in the late seventeenth century; and half a dozen factories in iron, silk, and brass making, employing hundreds of workers in mid-eighteenth-century England. Still, the bulk of industrial activity in towns remained in the hands of local workshops headed by a master craftsman, aided by a few apprentices, family members, and servants. As in the countryside, the urban manufacturing of goods was small in scale and heavily reliant on manual work—often of a very skilled nature.

That world—the world of any pre-Dickensian novel—changed as a string of technological innovations gradually mechanized the textile manufacturing process. In the 1760s, James Hargreaves designed the spinning "jenny," which twisted the yarn using rotating spindles that pulled the rovings from their bobbins, allowing a single cottage spinner to spin several threads at once. In turn, Richard Arkwright invented a watered-powered spinning frame that applied water energy to produce much stronger yarn. About a decade later, Samuel Crompton combined Hargreaves' spinning jenny and Arkwright's water frame into the famous "mule," which produced a high-quality yarn that outcompeted the finest handmade Indian muslins. Because the mechanization of weaving, the next production step that followed spinning in the cotton-making industry, proved much harder to achieve, the efficiencies introduced by the spinning mule fed a growing demand for handloom weavers for a few decades. However, once the power loom, first designed in 1785, was finally refined after 1815, cotton weaving became fully automatized and the demand for manual laborers plummeted dramatically.

Due to the physical properties of wool and linen, it took much longer to substitute machines for manual workers in those manufacturing sectors. By 1850, however, both branches of the textile industry had become fully mechanized. Likewise, industrialists and engineers, driven by the logic of competition and profit making, toiled to expand the application of machines to all branches of the economy—from transportation and energy extraction to all sorts of mechanical industries.

The development of new forms of energy beyond the traditional use of animal power then multiplied the efficiency gains brought about by mechanization. Water remained the main source of energy until the first third of the nineteenth century. In 1800, total horsepower in Britain was about 170,000—with about seventy percent generated by water. Thirty years later, total horsepower had doubled—with forty-seven percent coming from steam engines. Steam power, initially concentrated in textile factories, spread at a fast pace to the rest of the economy. By 1870, steam engines generated over two million horsepower—or almost ninety percent of all horsepower in the British economy.[1]

The Factory as a Mechanical Monster

In the wake of the mechanization of manufacturing, the factory became the central node of the new economy that had emerged in North Atlantic countries because it enjoyed a key advantage over other, alternative systems to organize production. The factory, "a large building," in the words of economic historian Joel Mokyr (2009, 338), "in which workers congregated every day to do their work, in fixed (and long) hours, usually in unpleasant, noisy, dirty, and often dangerous conditions," brought to perfection the application of the principle of the division of labor, according to which every worker was assigned to a specific task—coordinated by the engineer or manager in charge.

As early as 1776, Adam Smith had extolled the division of the production process into small tasks as a crucial way of increasing economic efficiency. By specializing in one particular task, the author of *The Wealth of Nations* argued, workers could become fully skillful at it. Moreover, splitting their actions into circumscribed parts should save them the time employed in switching between tasks. As the Scottish philosopher wrote in his renowned discussion of a pin factory, "a workman not educated to this business ... nor acquainted with the use of the machinery employed in it ... could scarce, perhaps, with his utmost industry, make one pin in a day, and certainly could not make twenty." However, once pin making "is divided into a number of branches" where "one man draws out the wire, another straights it, a third cuts it, a fourth points it, a fifth grinds it at the top for receiving the head; ... I have seen a small manufactory of this kind where ten men only were employed, and where some of them consequently performed two or three distinct operations. But though they were very poor, and therefore but indifferently accommodated with the necessary machinery, they could, when they exerted themselves, make among them about twelve pounds of pins in a day. There are in a pound upwards of four thousand pins of a middling size. Those ten persons, therefore, could make among them upwards of forty-eight thousand pins in a day. Each person, therefore, making a tenth part of forty-eight thousand pins, might be considered as making four thousand eight hundred pins in a day" (Smith [1776] 1991, bk. 1, ch. 1, para. 3).

A substantial part of the economy that preceded the British Industrial Revolution certainly operated under the principle of the division of labor. Banking, commerce, and transportation were conducted according to a rather refined system of specialization. In manufacturing, the putting-out system was based on the continuous flow of production through a network of independent specialists, such as carders, spinners, weavers, bleachers, and printers in the textile business, ultimately coordinated by an entrepreneur. Nevertheless, the factory system enjoyed a clear edge over those decentralized production processes already in place in protoindustrial regions. By concentrating all the steps of the production flow in one building, factories used energy more efficiently and reduced the time needed to move the manufactured good from one stage to the next. They allowed industrialists to monitor their workers' efforts and diligence quite directly—something that became more important as the costs of purchasing and maintaining increasingly sophisticated tools and machinery grew over time. Last, but not least, centralizing production in a factory plant facilitated the standardization of the final product and therefore the latter's sale.

The division of labor into small tasks or routinary actions had an additional—and equally crucial—advantage: it could be seamlessly integrated with the process of mechanization. Once tasks were split into elementary motions, engineers could construct devices or machines that performed those routines automatically, making human labor redundant. In 1830, the Manchester engineering firm of Sharp, Robert and Co. made a big splash when it marketed the self-acting mule across England, promising that it would allow firms to substitute unskilled machine operators for skilled spinners. Andrew Ure, a Scottish chemist who arguably became the first business consultant in Britain (and hence in the world), rushed to generalize that technical advance into a vision of industrial capitalism as a relentless march toward the substitution of machines (and cheap labor) for expensive artisans and craftsmen. In his tract *The Philosophy of Manufactures*, published in 1835, Ure defined the factory as "a vast automaton composed of various mechanical and intellectual organs, acting in uninterrupted concert for the production of a common object, all of them being subordinate to a self-regulated moving force," (Ure 1835, 13–14) and asserted that "the principle of the factory system then is, to substitute mechanical science for hand skill, and the partition of a process into its essential constituents, for the division or graduation of labour among artisans" (20). Emphasizing that "it is, in fact, the constant aim and tendency of every improvement in machinery to supersede human labour altogether, or to diminish its cost, by substituting the industry of women and children for that of men; or that of ordinary labourers for trained artisans" (23), he predicted that, whereas "on the handicraft plan [the old artisanal mode of production], labour more or less skilled was usually the most expensive element of production," in the modern factory, "skilled labour gets progressively superseded, and will, eventually, be replaced by mere overlookers of machines" (20).

Thirty years later Karl Marx would draw upon this account from Ure—whom he celebrated as "the Pindar of automatic industry," while attacking his work for "its undisguised cynicism, but also by the naïveté with which it blurts out the stupid contradictions of the capitalist brain"—as his point of departure to analyze the impact of capitalism on both the production process and the employment and wages of labor in *Das Kapital*. Taking over where Adam Smith had left off, Marx noted that each one of the minute human tasks or routines into which the process of production had been divided to make it more efficient could be (and indeed was being) replaced by a machine or "mechanism that, after being set in motion, performs with its tools the same operations that were formerly done by the workman with similar tools" (Marx [1867] 1906, 408). Each one of those machines and devices could be then integrated into a "collective machine, now an organized system of various kinds of single machines, and of groups of single machines" in which "the process as a whole becomes a continuous one, i.e. the less the raw material is interrupted in its passage from its first phase to its last; in other words, the more its passage from one phase to another is effected, not by the hand of man, but by the machinery itself." That continuous process would then culminate in "an organized system of machines, to which motion is communicated by the transmitting mechanism from a central automaton . . . a mechanical monster whose body fills whole factories, and whose demon power, at first veiled under the slow and measured motions of its giant limbs, at length breaks out into the fast and furious whirl of his countless working organs" (416–17).

The mechanization of industry would then transform the nature of work and of the workplace. The preindustrial system of production relied on the joint work and cooperation of craftsmen or specialized workers, who came together to produce each one of the specific parts of a given good. In Marx's own example, "a carriage . . . was formerly the product of the labour of a great number of independent artificers, such as wheelwrights, harness-makers, tailors, locksmiths, upholsterers, turners, fringe-makers, glaziers, painters, polishers, gilders, & c" (*ibid.*, 369). Even when they were working in the same building and under the control of a single capitalist, each one of those craftsmen was in charge of a particular (and relatively involved) step of the production process, such as assembling the body of the carriage, building the wheels, carving, gilding, etc., and then passing his finished part of the work to the next artisan. In the modern factory, by contrast, where the old structure of specialized artisans manufacturing relatively complex components of a final good had disappeared, the mechanization of production could proceed unimpeded. As soon as the work was split into minute tasks, machines started to replace human labor at a fraction of the latter's cost. And those workers that remained employed performed a different set of functions than before: operating machines mechanically, supplying them with the necessary inputs, and then moving the intermediate and final products within the factory and to external distribution points. As Marx (461–62) pointed out in a set of sharp comparisons, "in handicrafts and manufacture, the workman makes use of a tool, in the factory, the machine makes use of him. There the movements of the instrument of labour proceed from him, here it is the movements of the machine that he must follow. In manufacture the workmen are parts of a living mechanism. In the factory we have a lifeless mechanism independent of the workman, who becomes its mere living appendage."

For Marx, the triumph of the mechanized factory would then naturally push the economy toward a pure two-class structure, with capitalists on one side and unskilled labor on the other. In between the two, there may remain "a superior class of workmen, some of them scientifically educated, others brought up to trade . . . whose occupation it is to look after the whole of the machinery and repair it from time to time; such as engineers, mechanics, joiners." But at the end of the day, it would be "a numerically unimportant class of persons" (*ibid.*, 459). As the old class of craftsmen, who were highly skilled in the manual production of a particular good, were inexorably replaced by unskilled workers, paid to perform very specific tasks in front of a machine, factories would only employ the mass of uneducated laborers: fully fungible workers, who were easily movable across machines, factories, and even branches of production, and who, increasingly squeezed out by new and more efficient machines, would have to sell themselves by a shrinking fraction of their initial wage. To quote Marx again, "that portion of the working-class, thus by machinery rendered superfluous . . . either goes to the wall in the unequal contest of the old handicrafts and manufacturers with machinery, or else floods all the more easily accessible branches of industry, swamps the labour-market, and sinks the price of labour-power below its value. . . . When machinery seizes on an industry by degrees, it produces chronic misery among the operatives who compete with it" (470).

The Immiserization of the Working Class

The mechanization of industry proceeded at a slower pace than the one conveyed by Marx's fast and furious style of writing. In 1850, the use of mechanized factories was limited to cotton, a fraction of wool and worsteds, and iron forging in large blast furnaces. Small industrial workshops, often clustered in industrial districts— such as Lyon's silk industry, Solingen's cutlery and edge tools, or

Birmingham's metalworking companies—appear to have dominated the rest of the manufacturing sector well into the second half of the nineteenth century.[2] Nevertheless, the drive to mechanize production, economize on labor, and rationalize the flow of inputs into final goods proceeded in a relentless manner. Paper, glass, and pottery transited relatively early into the modern factory system. By 1870, all manual movements had been eliminated in the refinement of petroleum and the technologies employed there quickly spilled over to the distilling industry. Around the same time, metalworking industries started employing machines to cut and shape metal. Automatizing the manufacture of things such as bicycles, clocks, locks, sewing machines, or typewriters took much longer owing to their complexity. By the end of the nineteenth century, however, the factory system defined the entire industrial system in northwestern Atlantic economies. In Britain, less than one-third of industrial workers still worked at home in 1900 (Mokyr 2009, 339). In the United States, according to Carroll D. Wright, head of the Labor Commission, fourth-fifths of all people employed "in the mechanical industries of this country . . . [were] working under the factory system" in 1880 (quoted in Chandler 1977, 245).

The structure of employment changed accordingly. As was quickly recognized by Andrew Ure in the wake of the full mechanization of cotton making, "the effect of improvements in machinery, not merely in superseding the necessity for the employment of the same quantity of adult labour as before . . . but in substituting one description of human labour for another, the less skilled for the more skilled, juvenile for adult, female for male, causes a fresh disturbance in the rate of wages" (Ure 1835, 321). The introduction of the power loom in the first decades of the nineteenth century devastated British handloom weavers, whose numbers had doubled between the late 1780s (following the invention of the mule) and the end of the Napoleonic wars in 1815. Coetaneously, the demand for cheap unskilled labor, mostly in the form of women and children, peaked as machines were rolled out in the cotton industry. According to an 1834 Parliamentary Commission report, over fifty percent of all employees in the cotton industry were aged eighteen and under. Indeed, the effects of mechanization rippled across the world. As reported by Britain's governor general in India in 1834–35 (quoted in Marx [1867] 1906, pt. 1, ch. 15, 285), "The misery hardly finds a parallel in the history of commerce. The bones of the cotton-weavers are bleaching the plains of India."

Long-run data on the overall composition of the labor force over the course of the first Industrial Revolution are fragmentary. It seems clear, however, that as mechanization progressed, employment shifted away from artisanal occupations and toward barely qualified jobs. In trades not affected by automation—generally those that required finishing products—artisans were crucial and maintained their status as a labor aristocracy. By contrast, status and skill collapsed quickly in sectors such as the textile industry. As noted by economic historian Sidney Pollard, before the Industrial Revolution:

> The Lancashire muslin-weaver of the 1780s, of the type of Samuel Bamford's father, who "was considerably imbued with book knowledge, particularly of a religious kind; wrote a good hand; understood arithmetic; had some acquaintance with astronomy; was a vocal and instrumental musician, singing from the book and playing the flute . . .", or the well-known type of independent Yorkshire weavers . . . ["]who were able to make their cloth at home, and go to sell it in the market", or the Kirkintilloch hand weaver who "could ask from eighteen to twenty shillings a week, and that working ten hours a day, with now and then a holiday for digging in his garden, rambling in the country, or some merry-making . . . [were] the best educated, most reading, and most respectable of all the operatives of the north." (Pollard 1978, 119–120)

By the middle of the nineteenth century, unskilled workers had gained a predominant role in the new manufactures. According to calculations made by de Pleijt and Weisdorf (2017), in Britain the proportion of unskilled workers among all manual workers rose from 33 percent in the early eighteenth century to 43 percent in the first half of the nineteenth century. A closer examination of detailed data for several industrializing parishes shows that the change was accompanied by a distinct decline in craftsmanship and artisanal production. The American employment structure changed in similar ways. Within the manufacturing industry, the proportion of skilled workers fell from 39.4 percent in 1850 to 22.8 percent in 1910. Conversely, the share of unskilled workers rose from 57.5 percent to 65.4 percent in the same period.

A dearth of systematic statistics until much later in the nineteenth century has marred the collection and interpretation of data on wages, consumption, and the overall welfare of British workers. After rather protracted academic disputes, however, the consensus today is that the standards of living of the working class did not improve until the second half of the nineteenth century.[3] According to Feinstein's recent estimations, the weekly earnings in real terms (that is, once we adjust by the cost of living) of an average British manual worker rose by fifteen percent between the late 1780s and the mid-1800s, fell in the following decade, and, after experiencing some growth, shrank again in the 1830s and 1840s. In 1857, they were only one-third higher than eighty years before. Moreover, that meager growth in real wages was insufficient to make up for larger families. Higher birth rates raised the ratio of the dependent population of Great Britain to the number of working people from 2.61 in 1771 to 3.06 in 1821—and then remained stable for the next few decades. That demographic change probably reduced the standard of living of the average family by roughly ten percent, or about a third of the measured improvement in real earnings per worker between 1770 and 1857 (Feinstein 1998, 650).[4]

Such an increase in incomes was arguably not enough to compensate for the appalling work conditions in factories, well documented by parliamentary reports that led to the passage of successive Factory Acts, the agglomeration of the new working class in cities with poor housing, and the terrible public-sanitation infrastructure that affected the new industrial working class. Infant mortality, which had declined at the end of the eighteenth century, rose in urban areas between the end of the Napoleonic wars and the middle of the nineteenth century (Huck 1995; Wrigley and Schofield 1989). Adult mortality rates deteriorated sharply among urban and industrial populations after 1800 and did not recover to eighteenth-century levels until the 1870s (Szreter and Mooney 1998). In the 1850s, life expectancy was thirty-one and thirty-two years in Liverpool and Manchester respectively—versus Britain's national average of forty-one years. The evolution of human height, which is in part a function of nutrition and therefore a reflection of overall health conditions, tells a similar story. Average male height fell between the 1820s and 1840s. British men were shorter on average in 1850 than in 1760 (Floud, Wachter, and Gregory 1990, Komlos 1998).[5]

The decline in workers' living conditions contrasted with the fortunes of the owners of capital. The rate of return (net of depreciation) in the cotton industry fluctuated between nine and thirteen percent in early nineteenth century. The profit rate (in gross terms) of capital more than doubled from ten percent in the eighteenth century to about twenty-five percent in 1870 (Allen 2009). The distribution of national income across factors shifted accordingly. The share of national income received by labor fell from around sixty percent in 1800 to forty-five percent by 1845. By contrast, the share of national income in the hands of capital rose from twenty percent in 1770 to fifty percent one hundred years later.[6] Likewise, when we look at the overall distribution of individual incomes (coming from both capital profits and labor salaries), inequality peaked in Britain in the first half of the nineteenth century. The income share in the hands of the top quintile of the British population, which stood at around fifty-seven percent in the eighteenth century, went up to around sixty-three percent in 1801 and only declined very slowly over time—to fifty-eight percent in 1867.

Health outcomes mirrored those growing inequalities in economic fortunes. Until the middle of the eighteenth century, life expectancy was similar among British high nobility and the general population. Starting in 1750, it rose steadily among the former, so that one hundred years later the gap in life expectancy between aristocrats and commoners had grown to about thirty years. The most likely explanation is that, following the example of several members of the royal family, inoculation for smallpox, or variolation, spread rather quickly within the British political and economic elite. By contrast, the cost of that technique and of many other medical innovations ranging from quinine to the employment of midwives slowed down their extension to low-income social strata until much later in time (Deaton 2013). Height measurements point to similar differences. In the early nineteenth century, for boys at age fifteen, the London poor averaged 147 centimeters. The sons of the British gentry attending the Sandhurst Military Academy were already 163 centimeters tall (Komlos 1989, 95). In its final report of 1883, Britain's Anthropometric Committee reported the same gap between fourteen-year-old boys from industrial schools and those from private, fee-paying schools (Meredith and Oxley 2014, 141).[7]

At the end of the day, Marx's prediction about the immiserization of the working class did not come to pass. British wages rose in real terms between fifty and seventy-five percent between 1850 and the early twentieth century, driven by two factors: a downturn in real prices in the 1870s, and emigration to North America and the settler colonies (Feinstein 1998; Allen 2001). Hatton and Williamson (1998) estimate that, without emigration, the labor force would have been sixteen percent higher and real wages twelve percent lower in 1911. In any case, that wage growth, which marked a sharp break with the generally stagnant living standards of the preindustrial period and the first part of the Industrial Revolution, masked a wide gap between a "labor aristocracy" formed by engineers and skilled operators and an underperforming stratum of unskilled laborers and helpers. The latter's earning power experienced very little improvement. At the turn of the twentieth century, about two-fifths of the British working class still lived in poverty (Pollard 1978). In 1904 almost one in five working households reported insufficient income to meet minimum needs, according to data from the Board of Trade (Gazeley 2014). Inequality at the national level persisted well into the twentieth century. The share of national income received by the top quintile of the population only fell three points from fifty-eight percent in 1867 to fifty-five percent just before World War One. Health inequities were still rather substantial well into the twentieth century. For example, the life expectancy gap between the highest and the lowest social classes was 7.5 years in England and Wales in the early 1930s.

Improvements in living conditions were even more limited in the rest of Europe. According to economic historian Robert Allen, who has compiled wage series for skilled and unskilled construction workers in the leading cities in Europe from the second half of the fifteenth century until World War One, wages grew in real terms during the second half of the nineteenth century. Yet, even in large cities like Paris and Leipzig, the wages of laborers and craftsmen at the end of the nineteenth century were at most equivalent to the earnings of their British counterparts fifty years before (Allen 2001). A substantial part of wage growth was, once again, the result of migration to the New World and a corresponding reduction in the size of the European labor force (O'Rourke and Williamson 2001).

The Threat of Revolution

In light of the deterioration of living standards of British workers, most famously captured by Friedrich Engels's book *The Condition of the Working Class in England*, published in 1844, Marx predicted the end of capitalism as a result of a grand revolutionary outburst at the hands of an impoverished proletariat.[8] The German economist was looking back, like many other nineteenth-century observers of the Industrial Revolution, to a decades-long tradition of resistance among British artisans and manual workers against the mechanization of industry and the introduction of laborsaving machinery.

In the mid- and late eighteenth century, thousands of people had burned the first wool-shearing machine driven by water power, attacked Charles Dingley's new mechanized sawmill in Limehouse, and destroyed steam looms and other machines such as knitting frames and spinning jennies in several counties of central England.[9] A bigger wave of riots, known as the Luddite movement, broke out in the spring of 1811, smashing what a certain Ned Lud labeled as "obnoxious machines," making direct threats to their owners, and in a few cases murdering employers and local authorities. In Nottinghamshire, Derbyshire, and Leicestershire, workers wrecked hundreds of wide knitting frames (employed in the lace and stocking trades). A year later, the disturbances shifted to Lancashire and Cheshire, with Luddites raiding large cotton factories in the Manchester area that used steam-powered looms. In the first months of 1813, wool croppers broke gig mills and shearing frames on the Yorkshire Moors. Crushed by the deployment of thousands of British soldiers and swift mass trials such as the one held at York Castle in the spring of 1813, the Luddite movement eventually tapered off. Nonetheless, there was still a string of isolated incidents of machine smashing well into the fall of 1816.

Over the following years, labor turned away from opposing technological change to accepting it while demanding radical political and social changes. Prompted by the economic downturn that followed the end of the Napoleonic wars, several collective protests such as the London riots of 1815 and the Manchester Blanketeers March of 1817 culminated in a massive rally of tens of thousands of people in Manchester's St. Peter's square demanding electoral reform and the representation of the working man. A charge of the British cavalry to disperse it resulted in over a dozen dead and hundreds injured, sparking wide protests around England, a revolt in the Yorkshire West Riding, and a protracted general strike, mostly led by weavers' communities, in Scotland in the spring of 1820. A decade later, a wave of agricultural riots and a period of social unrest in the industrial and urban areas of the Midlands and the North of England prompted the House of Commons to pass a broad electoral reform suppressing dozens of medieval "rotten" boroughs with extremely small electorates, while giving direct parliamentary representation to new manufacturing cities such as Manchester and Leeds for the first time and doubling the number of enfranchised individuals in urban areas. Still, the franchise remained circumscribed to well-to-do property owners: only one in seven male adults had the right to vote after that reform.

Frustrated by such a restrictive franchise, six members of parliament and six delegates from working-class associations drafted a "People's Charter" demanding the introduction of universal suffrage, the secret ballot, and annual parliamentary elections. Their proposal quickly ballooned into the massive "Chartism" movement. Their first petition, presented to parliament in 1839, gathered 1.3 million signatures. Supported by a variegated coalition encompassing old-style radicals, trade unionists, Jacobin socialists, and self-styled modern socialists who had befriended Marx, the People's Charter held the promise of radical social improvements for the workers. As a Wiltshire member of the Chartist movement put it, their political triumph would bring "plenty of roast beef, plum pudding and strong beer by working three hours a day" (quoted in Rudé 1981, 180). A cycle of labor strikes accompanied the Chartist political movement. Large protests against the operation of the Poor Law of 1834 erupted in the northern manufacturing districts a few months before the publication of the Charter, and then became gradually embedded into the latter's political movement. In the summer of 1839, a set of strikes and riots broke out in Birmingham, Manchester, and the coalfields of Durham and Northumberland. Over the fall and winter of that same year, John Frost organized an armed march on Newport, and there were risings in Sheffield and the West Riding.

After parliament rejected the first petition following its condemnation by Lord John Russell, one of the main architects of the electoral reform of 1832, as a threat to property, three and a half million people signed a second one in 1842. In response to the House of Commons' refusal to take it into consideration, the Chartist newspaper the *Northern Star* wrote that "the 'House' has resolved they should not be heard! Three and a half millions of the slave-class have holden out the olive branch of peace to the enfranchised and privileged classes and sought for a firm and compact union, on the principle of EQUALITY BEFORE THE LAW; and the enfranchised and privileged have refused to enter into a treaty! The same class is to be a slave class still" (quoted in Charlton 1997, 34). The Chartist movement developed once more against a background of widespread social agitation, counteracted by governmental repression. "Plug-plot riots" hit the Midlands, Lancashire, Cheshire, Yorkshire, and the Strathclyde region of Scotland, with demonstrators marching from town to town and stopping work by pulling out the plugs from factory boilers. In response, the British government deployed troops to quell their actions and proceeded to incarcerate hundreds of individuals—transporting some of them to Australia. A third and final petition in 1848, supported by more than two million people, was again met by rejection, accompanied, in response to rumors about a potential Chartist uprising, by the decision to both ban public meetings and reinforce the penalties for sedition and treason.

Continental Europe witnessed even more tumultuous revolutionary movements in its urban centers. In February of 1848, a popular uprising in Paris led to the proclamation of the republic. A newly created Luxembourg Commission, formed by workers' representatives from all trades, was charged with the task of controlling all aspects of production, negotiating all work conditions with employers, turning private property into "associated property," and defending a new "democratic and social republic based on the sovereignty of labor" (Sewell 1986, 66–67). The Paris revolution sparked urban insurrections across Austria, Germany, and parts of Italy that led to the election of democratic parliaments and new liberal constitutions recognizing universal adult male suffrage.

Three years later, however, most countries had swung back to their previous political status. A nephew of Napoleon Bonaparte, Louis Napoleon, who had been elected first president of the new French republic, engineered a coup with the support of the military and the economic elites in December of 1851. After reasserting their rule, the Austro-Hungarian and Prussian monarchs restored the old political status quo across Germany and Italy.

Writing a year before Louis Napoleon's coup, Karl Marx concluded in *The Class Struggles in France, 1848 to 1850* that capitalism, based on the principle of private property, and full democracy, where the masses could vote to expropriate capital holders, were incompatible. Universal suffrage, he asserted, "withdraws the political guarantees of this [the bourgeoisie's] power. It forces the political rule of the bourgeoisie into democratic conditions, which at every moment help the hostile classes [the people] to jeopardize the very foundations of bourgeois society" (Marx 1934, 69–70). The Commune of Paris twenty years later seemed to confirm Marx's diagnostic. After Prussia defeated the French army in 1870, the National Guard, formed by militiamen, controlled the city of Paris. Following a soft coup in which its central committee superseded the authority of the mayor of Paris, new municipal elections in late March 1871 delivered a majority of seats to radical and extreme-left candidates. The new Parisian local government, or Commune, abolished military conscription, disestablished the Church, and passed a flurry of measures, such as the abolition of interest on debt, free public education, and the promotion of cooperatives, to create a "social republic" favorable to workers. As French troops moved closer to Paris, the Commune reintroduced the old Committee of Public Safety, created during the Terror period of the French Revolution, to jail all its enemies. In late May, the French army assaulted and eventually captured the city after a week-long battle in the streets of Paris. Close to six thousand Communards died in the barricades and in summary executions. At the end of the nineteenth century, Frederick Sterky, a leader of the Swedish socialist Left and first chairman of Sweden's trade union movement, wrote that "[if] the working class could send a majority to the legislature; not even by doing this would it obtain power. One can be sure that the capitalist class would then take care not to continue along a parliamentary course but instead resort to bayonets" (quoted in Tingsten 1937, 361).

Marx was not alone in his political diagnostic. Conservative and most liberal politicians shared it—anxiously. In his 1842 speech on the Chartism movement, the Whig politician and historian Thomas Macaulay declared:

> The essence of the Charter is universal suffrage. If you withhold that, it matters not very much what else you grant. If you grant that, it matters not at all what else you withhold. If you grant that, the country is lost. . . . My firm conviction is that in our country, universal suffrage is incompatible, not only with this and that form of government, and with everything for the sake of which government exists; that it is incompatible with property and that it is consequently incompatible with civilization. . . . I entertain no hope that, if we place the government of the kingdom in the hands of the majority of the males of one-and-twenty told by the head, the institution of property will be respected. If I am asked why I entertain no such hope, I answer, because the hundreds of thousands of males of twenty-one who have signed this petition tell me to entertain no such hope; because they tell me that, if I trust them with power, the first use which they will make of it will be to plunder every man in the kingdom who has a good coat on his back and a good roof over his head. (Macaulay 1842)

Twenty-five years later, Robert Lowe, a key figure in the electoral reform of 1832, rallied the moderate wing of the Liberal Party to defeat Gladstone's plan to expand the franchise to middle-class urban dwellers by emphasizing that the principle "on which all democracies are established . . . is the principle of numbers as against wealth and intellect. It is the principle, in short, which is contended for, and always will be contended for, by those who devote themselves to the advocacy of popular rights—the principle of equality. . . . You must look these matters in the face, for it is useless to suppose that, founding your institutions on democracy, you can go on legislating with a deference to established privileges and the rights of property" (R. Lowe 1867, 1540–43). In France, Jules Baroche, a liberal politician who had played a prominent role in the 1848 revolution, opposed "universal suffrage as it is presently organized" as "necessarily leading, sooner or later, to the triumph of those appalling ideas that are called socialism" (quoted in Kahan 2003, 79). As Adolf Thiers, who would became president of the Third Republic two decades later, put it in the constitutional discussions that took place in 1849–50, "everything must be done for the poor man, except however to let him decide the great questions which affect the future of the country" (quoted in *ibid.*, 82).

A Truncated Franchise

Throughout the nineteenth century, the staunchest antagonists of democracy consistently came from the ranks of the monarchical establishment and the old landholding elites, who had the most to lose from enfranchising propertyless rural laborers. Industrial capitalism's opposition to the expansion of the franchise was milder and conditional on economic growth. As the latter expanded the numbers in well-off urban strata, many governments granted them the right to vote. The British electoral reform of 1867 doubled the fraction of enfranchised male adults to thirty-two percent. The reform of 1884 doubled it again to sixty-four percent. Things were not that different in continental Europe. The franchise was highly restrictive across all of Europe at least until about the late 1840s— with less than ten percent of adult men having the right to vote except in Switzerland, the United Kingdom, and the United States. Then, throughout the second half of the nineteenth century, franchise requirements were loosened, resulting in the expansion of voting rights to, at a minimum, a majority of adult males.

TABLE 2.1. Political Representation under Manchester Capitalism

	Lower House (Franchise)	Upper House (Selection)
Belgium	Male universal suffrage after 1893 Weighted vote until 1919	Appointed
Denmark	Male universal suffrage after 1848	Fully appointed to 1864 Partly appointed after 1864
France	Male universal suffrage in 1792– 95 and 1848–49, continuously after 1871	Appointed until 1874 Elected afterward, with extreme rural over- representation
Germany	Male universal suffrage after 1870 with minor restrictions	Elected by federation units Dominated by Prussian parlia- ment (based on weighed vote by taxes)
Italy	Restrictive suffrage until 1912	Appointed
Netherlands	Male universal suffrage after 1918	Appointed
Norway	Male universal suffrage after 1900	Elected (a section of overall parliament)
Sweden	Male universal suffrage after 1911	Elected
Switzerland	Moderate restrictions until 1878, varying by canton	Initially chosen by cantons, gradually shifted to direct elections
United Kingdom	Male universal suffrage after 1918	Appointed/hereditary
United States	Highly restrictive in southern states Limiting conditions introduced by northeastern states in late 19th century	Indirect election by state legis- latures (until 1913 constitu- tional amendment)

Still, tax, income, or literacy requirements kept a substantial part of workers out of the ballot box. Column 2 in table 2.1 records the time at which male universal suffrage was granted in major European countries, as well as the franchise conditions in the United States at the turn of the twentieth century. Male universal suffrage was only introduced in Britain in 1918; on the eve of World War One, the franchise was still heavily skewed in favor of middle-class citizens. Whereas at most a tenth of the middle class were excluded from voting, about two-fifths of the working class did not have the right to vote. Male universal or quasi-universal suffrage was only granted in Belgium in 1893, Italy in 1912, the Netherlands in 1918, Norway in 1900, Sweden in 1911, and Switzerland in 1878.

In those places that did have universal male suffrage, constitutions included strong mechanisms to minimize the potential consequences of the one-person-one-vote rule. Column 3 in table 2.1 summarizes the selection procedures for upper chambers, which, at that time, had veto power over the legislation passed in (generally more democratic) lower chambers. Although France adopted male universal suffrage under the Third Republic, the conservative majority elected to the first national assembly after the abdication of Napoleon III in 1870 deliberately reshaped the French Senate into a chamber chosen by local councilors so that rural districts were dramatically overrepresented and could veto any revolutionary measures coming from the cities. In Prussia, the universal right to vote, recognized in 1848, was tempered by a three-class franchise system: after ranking individuals according to their tax payments, the richest taxpayers (those paying together up to one third of all direct taxes) had as many votes as the poorest taxpayers (those paying one third of direct taxes). The system, which was maintained to elect the Prussian parliament even after the German unification, created very stark inequalities in political representation: about three to five percent of individuals composed the top class and held as many votes as the lowest electoral class, which encompassed eighty to eighty-five percent of the population (Aidt and Jensen 2013; Kahan 2003, 76). In turn, Prussia maintained a thoroughly dominant position in Germany's upper house. Moreover, the German kaiser had veto powers, making the executive unaccountable to the Reichstag. In Belgium, Denmark, Italy, the Netherlands, and the United Kingdom the members of the upper house either were appointed by the monarch or inherited the right to a seat there.

In the United States, the franchise became extremely restrictive in the South after Reconstruction—in line with similar practices in European countries with high levels of landowning inequality. But, even in the North, the growing inequalities generated by the Industrial Revolution had some effects on the franchise. After the Civil War, half a dozen northeastern states approved the exclusion of paupers from the ballot box. The progressive movement, animated by professionals and middle-class reformers, pushed for the introduction of systematic registration procedures—the proportion of nonsouthern counties with personal registration procedures rose from thirty percent in 1900 to fifty-two percent in 1930 (Kleppner 1987)—as well as diverse mechanisms, such as the use of city managers, to shelter local administrations from elections. Although the progressives' main goal was to reduce electoral fraud, their measures were also directed at the consequences of universal suffrage, which was, in the words of one contemporary reformer, "another name for a licensed mobocracy" (quoted in Keyssar 2000, 99). Indeed, after the introduction of registration mechanisms, turnout declined by twenty percentage points in nonsouthern states between 1900 and 1925. The fall in participation was mostly concentrated among immigrants and the poor (Kleppner 1982; Piven and Cloward 1988). In the presidential election of 1908, whereas only seventeen percent of foreign-born men voted, seventy-eight percent of native men went to the polls in the northeastern states.

The prevalence of a truncated franchise and of strong constitutional constraints on parliamentary life had direct political consequences. With conservative and liberal parties hegemonic in the electoral arena, challenged only by Christian democratic movements, the principles of laissez-faire economics governed states and markets. Taxes were low. Governments balanced their budgets and tied their national currencies to the gold standard. Public programs to reduce poverty, subsidize unemployed workers, and provide health services to the infirm were small or completely absent.

Throughout the Manchester century, the socialist Left remained marginal in both votes and parliamentary seats. In spite of a growing industrial working class and mounting labor strife, support for labor and social democratic parties averaged less than fifteen percent across Europe around 1910. It was only the generalization of male universal suffrage, mostly happening at the end of World War One, that opened the doors to social democracy. In the interwar period, socialist and communist parties received about one-third of the vote—and over forty percent in several small countries such as Sweden. It was also at that time that capitalism, as understood in its classical form, and democracy seemed closest to collision with each other. The Russian Revolution and the social and human turmoil that followed at the end of World War One spread a "red scare" of strikes and revolutionary putsches across what Harvard historian Charles Maier has referred to as the European "bourgeois order" (1988). Barely ten years later, the Great Depression led to a dangerous polarization in French politics between the Right and the Popular Front, and to the complete breakdown of democracy in Austria, Germany, and Eastern and southern Europe.

3

The Golden Age

DETROIT

In 1906, after a few years devoted to the business of making medium-priced automobiles, Henry Ford concluded that the "greatest need today is a light, low-priced car with an up-to-date engine of ample horsepower, and built of the very best material . . . powerful enough for American roads and capable of carrying its passengers anywhere that a horse-drawn vehicle will go without the driver being afraid of ruining his car" (quoted in Hounshell 1984, 218). Two years later, in March 1908, his engineers announced the production of the *Model T*—a sturdy, durable, and light car that should not "require mechanical aptitude in the operator, and that may be run inexpensively" by the average American, and by the middle of that same year the directors of the company approved a $250,000 investment to build a new factory in the Highland Park section of Detroit to produce the new car cheaply and on a huge scale.[1] It would be there that in early 1914, following six years of intense experimentation, Ford engineers put together the quasi-automatized assembly line that made feasible the philosophy of mass production that had inspired them to start manufacturing the *Model T*, and that would almost single-handedly transform industrial capitalism in the twentieth century.

The Technology of Mass Production

Ford's production model resulted from combining into a single, fully integrated manufacturing system three production processes already employed separately by different companies around the country—making interchangeable components, using electricity, and placing machines in a sequential layout.

Probably following the suggestion of Walter Flanders, a Vermont mechanic who had worked in precision-machine-tool industries and who was hired as the overall production manager of the Ford Motor Company in 1906, Henry Ford embraced the idea of organizing production around the principle of interchangeability of parts and materials. To maximize both speed and accuracy in the mass production of specific components such as wheels, axles, or cylinders, each machine was to perform a single function and to make "interchangeable parts that fit smoothly together without the need for any last-minute sanding, filing, or polishing" (Nye 2000, 24). With all those parts becoming as similar or standardized as possible, their assembly could take place quickly and precisely, resulting in automobiles that were both reliable and cheap. In the middle of the nineteenth century, both Samuel Colt and federal arsenals had already implemented the strategy of employing interchangeable parts to produce gunlocks and firearms, with considerable success. Nonetheless, the high cost of making components as closely alike as possible had marred its application to other manufacturing sectors for several decades. It was only the invention of electricity—and, particularly, of reliable electric motors in the 1890s that reduced the oscillation and the variation in speed of mechanically driven shafts—that made the production of fully standardized components affordable across the board.

The use of single-function or single-purpose machines making identical components had a logical—and crucial—effect on their spatial disposition. It drove plant engineers to rearrange the location of machines not according to type, as had been the norm in the first car factories, but according to the specific flow of the production process needed to create a particular part and, indeed, the whole automobile. As Ford's machine-tool expert, Oscar Bornholdt, wrote, "at the Ford plant, the machines are arranged very much like the tin-can machines"—one right after the other (quoted in Hounshell 1984, 229). With the machines placed in a sequential manner, it was possible to save time and to make manufacturing faster and more efficient. Once again, electrification turned out to be a key precondition to make the new factory layout feasible. In steam-powered factories the engine was located at the center of the plant, generally in an elevated position, and power was transmitted employing gears, shafts, and belts. As a result, most machines had to be "arranged in straight lines beneath the drive shafts" (Nye 2000, 21). By contrast, as soon as machines were each propelled by their own electric motor, their spatial disposition could be structured with a sole preoccupation in mind: increasing the speed and quality of throughput.

Arranging single-purpose machines in a continuous production process eventually culminated in the assembly line. The concept of an assembly line was already well known—it had been invented in Chicago in the late 1860s, where slaughterhouses had animals moved through a chain to be disassembled—but its full application was only feasible in conjunction with electrically powered, single-function machines producing standardized parts. Even so, the development of an integrated assembly line in the Highland Park factory emerged in a piecemeal, unplanned fashion over the course of a full year. In the spring of 1913, some of its engineers developed a sub-assembly line of flywheel magnetos. Their ideas then spread to the production of transmission systems and of parts of the engine. In August of that same year, there was a first attempt at organizing the assembly of chassis as a moving line— with a rope attached to the cars and pulled using a windlass, and with a team of assemblers walking with the vehicle and installing the different parts distributed along the way. By November, Ford managers had succeeded in setting up a single assembly line for the engine. Eventually, in early 1914, a chain, powered by an electric motor, replaced the manual system employed to push the cars along what was now a fully integrated assembly line.

The impact of those changes was dramatic. The labor time employed in producing one *Model T* automobile fell from twelve hours and eight minutes in 1909 to two hours and thirty-five minutes by the end of 1913, and then to one hour and thirty-three minutes by the spring of 1914 (Chandler 1977, 280). A year later, the price of the car in real terms was, at $448.60 (in 1910 dollars), half its cost in 1910. By 1921, it had again dropped by half to $214. By the middle of the 1910s, Highland Park employed about eighteen thousand workers and Ford was selling over a third of all automobiles in the United States.

The production model invented—or, perhaps more precisely, epitomized—by Detroit spread quickly across America in two ways. First, it led to the mechanization, mostly driven by electrification, of most handling operations—that is, transporting and moving materials outside and within the factory. Second, it implied the automation of a considerable number of processing or strictly production tasks within the factory.

According to *Mechanization in Industry*, a book written by statistician Harry Jerome in 1934, almost half of all laborsaving changes introduced in US industry during the first third of the twentieth century resulted from the mechanization of handling systems. Horse cars and manual hauling methods were replaced with industrial locomotives and trucks, as well as cranes, monorails, and continuous conveyors (which was Ford's decisive contribution), across all sectors—from mining companies to iron plants, and from the brick industry and pulp and paper makers to automobile producers. In 1879, only one-third of all manufacturing establishments used horsepower generated by steam engines or electric motors. By 1929, ninety-two percent did. The use of generated horsepower per worker quadrupled between 1869 and 1929 (Jerome 1934, 215).

The automatization of processing or strictly defined production tasks within the factory was equally sweeping. After being adopted by other automobile companies, the quasi-automatic assembly-line system designed in the Highland Park factory spread to the manufacturing of household appliances (from refrigerators and washing machines to radios, irons, vacuum cleaners, and television sets) in the 1920s and 1930s. In a way, steel production in the Carnegie Steel Corporation, later the US Steel Corporation, partook in the same manufacturing philosophy. Andrew Carnegie designed an integrated system to roll the unloaded ore to blast furnaces to make iron, and then to Bessemer converters to produce steel, using mechanized rails and minimum labor interference. Iron and steel production experienced productivity gains similar to those enjoyed by car manufacturers. The average daily output of crude iron and semifinished steel per mineral blast furnace rose from 54 tons in 1884 to 584 tons in 1930. The output of pig iron per worker increased tenfold from 170 tons per year in 1884 to 1,700 tons per year in 1929. The annual production per worker of finished steel multiplied by four from about 30 tons in 1880 to 138 tons in 1929. Assembly-line principles were also applied to fruit canning, bread making, and cow milking and, albeit with mixed success, to construction. As David Nye wrote in *America's Assembly Line*, "in 1931 the Empire State Building was completed in less than two years with the use of assembly-line principles. Interchangeable parts sped up the installation of windows, for example, and stone was delivered pre-cut in standardized sizes.... Temporary narrow railroad tracks were installed on the perimeter of each floor, and huge hand carts, each the size of eight wheelbarrows, expedited the delivery of parts" (Nye 2000, 62).

The drive for mechanization and labor substitution behind the automatized assembly line was identical to the one that had led many manufacturers to develop the so-called batch-production or continuous-processing machines. The specific technological solution followed in each case was different, however. In the assembly line, many machines were integrated in a sequential process to make a product. In the batch-production system, a single machine did everything, integrating all the processes of production into a fully automatized mechanism and therefore confining workers to the functions of supplying materials into the machines and supervising the latter's motions.

Bonsack's cigarette-making machine, patented in 1881, is perhaps the most famous example of a batch-production machine. Operators fed it with tobacco, paper, and packaging material at different entry points and the machine churned out the finished product—a sealed and fully labeled cigarette box—ready to be dispatched to retailers. Its impact on production was dramatic: output rose from four cigarettes per minute and worker to two hundred. By that time, continuous-process machines were already common in a few industrial sectors and were spreading to many others. Soap makers had adopted them in the 1850s. By 1870, all manual movements of petroleum had been eliminated in large refineries. Batch-production machines were in place in wheat- and flour-processing plants in 1879, and in food-canning factories and match-making companies in the early 1880s. Eastman employed a similar technology in the production of photographic material in 1884. The rotary press, invented in 1896, revolutionized the printing industry, more than tripling output per hour. Whereas printing and folding a four-page newspaper had taken seventy-one employees working for nine hours in the early 1890s, it only required twenty-five people working seven hours thirty years later (Jerome 1934). Similar developments in the early years of the twentieth century reduced the proportion of handmade window glass from one hundred percent of all production in 1899 to two percent by 1926. Meanwhile, the proportion of glass bottles blown through automatic processes rose from less than half before World War One to ninety percent in 1924 (*ibid.*).

The efficiency gains experienced across almost all economic sectors translated into impressive and sustained productivity gains, measured as output per hour worked, for the whole economy during the twentieth century. The top panel of table 3.1

TABLE 3.1. Productivity Gains

| | ANNUAL PERCENT CHANGE IN GDP PER HOUR WORKED | | | |
	1870–1913	1913–50	1950–73	1973–90
United States	1.92	2.48	2.77	1.52
Western Europe	1.55	1.56	4.77	2.29
Japan	1.99	1.80	7.74	2.70

| | GDP PER HOUR WORKED (IN DOLLARS OF 1990) | | | | |
	1870	1913	1950	1973	1990
United States	2.25	5.12	12.65	23.72	30.10
Western Europe	1.61	3.12	5.54	16.21	24.06
Japan	0.46	1.08	2.08	11.57	19.04

Source: Maddison (2001, tables E-5, E-7).
Figures for Western Europe are a weighted average of Austria, Belgium, Denmark, Finland, France, Germany, Italy, the Netherlands, Norway, Sweden, Switzerland, and the United Kingdom.

displays the annual percentage change in GDP per hour worked (in real terms; that is, once we adjust for inflation) in the United States, Western Europe, and Japan for the historical periods of 1870–1913, 1913–50, 1950–73, and 1973–90. The bottom panel of table 3.1 reports the level of GDP per hour worked (in constant dollars of 1990) for the initial and final years of each period. Output per hour rose every year by almost 2 percent in the United States at the turn of the century. Despite the Great Depression and two world wars, its growth rate accelerated to more than 2.5 percent per year until 1973. By the law of compounded interest, that meant that output per hour worked more than doubled between 1870 and 1913—from $2.25 to $5.12. It rose more than twofold to $12.65 by 1950, and it then doubled again to $23.72 by 1973.

Productivity grew at a slower pace in both Western Europe and Japan during the first half of the twentieth century. In Western Europe, the annual growth rate averaged 1.5 percent—or about one whole percentage point less than in the United States. The productivity of a European worker in 1950 was still equivalent to the productivity of an American worker in 1913. Japan's labor productivity growth, at around 1.9 percent yearly, was closer to the US rate. However, because Japan's point of departure was lower, in 1950 its output per hour still remained below that of the United States in 1870.

Although the destruction caused by World War Two explains part of Europe's and Japan's lower average growth rate up to 1950, their economies lagged behind the United States' arguably mostly because their industries failed to incorporate America's mass-production technologies during the interwar period. The story of the automobile sector tells this fact pointedly. In the interwar period, the ratio of horsepower to operative in the British car industry was four to five times lower than in the United States. Still, by 1935, American manufacturers were turning out three times more cars per worker than their UK competitors. The use of mass-production techniques to manufacture cars was almost completely absent in both Germany and, with the exception of Citroën, France (Landes 1969, 445–47). In 1929, motor-vehicle production and registrations in Europe were one-eighth and one-fifth of the US levels, respectively (Gordon 2004, 23).

The Allied victory of 1945 inaugurated a period of rapid diffusion of the Detroit model overseas—and a corresponding process of economic catch-up with the United States. Coinciding with both the modernization of the European industry and the experimentation of Japanese firms with new production processes, such as the just-in-time manufacturing procedure directed at improving standard assembly-line systems, the annual rate of change in labor productivity jumped to 4.77 percent in Western Europe and to 7.74 percent in Japan—two and three times the American growth rate respectively.[2] Whereas after World War Two American workers were two times more productive than European workers, by 1973 they were only 50 percent more productive. In turn, while American workers produced six times greater output per hour than their Japanese counterparts in 1950, two and a half decades later the former were only twice as productive as the latter.

The Affluent Worker

Ford's assembly line and the batch-production machine responded to the same logic of mechanization, driven by the quest for efficiency and profit maximization, that had spawned the first Industrial Revolution in Manchester. The introduction of single-purpose machines making standardized components reinforced the kind of fine-grained division of labor envisioned by Adam Smith. Jobs were subdivided into small, repetitive operations that, according to a study conducted by Ford Motor Corporation in 1952, lasted between one and two minutes on average (Nye 2000, 23). Machines were designed to be operated by workers performing simple tasks who could be easily trained on the spot. The standardization and automatization of the assembly line reinforced the capacity of factory engineers to control and adjust the time of production to maximize efficiency. In short, factories such as Highland Park seemed to exemplify the epitome of the factory as a "vast automaton," to employ Ure's expression again—a place where capital was supposed to render labor completely marginal.

And, yet, the production model embodied by Detroit marked a fundamental turning point in the history of industrial capitalism. In the world of Manchester capitalism, unskilled workers operating machines had replaced an old class of artisans and highly skilled operators. That transformation, in conjunction with a large supply of labor, had pushed wages down while raising capital profits and the share of income in the hands of capital to soaring levels. By contrast, in the world of twentieth-century capitalism, the automation, mostly driven by electrification, of most handling operations (again, those that involved transporting and moving materials outside and within the factory) and of a considerable number of processing (or, in other words, strictly production) tasks had rather different (and often opposite) consequences in the structure of employment. First, it reduced the need for unskilled workers. Second, it raised the demand for semiskilled workers capable of repairing and devising machine tools. Finally, by encouraging the formation of large corporations, it led to the expansion of new layers of white-collar, relatively well paid jobs—from accounting departments to car dealerships.

The mechanization of handling operations depressed the need for unskilled workers, who had previously been indispensable for hauling and carrying materials and components to and inside the factory, while boosting the demand for semiskilled individuals capable of driving trucks, operating electric conveyors, and so on. Exact data on the number of unskilled and skilled workers by industry in the United States before World War Two remain fragmentary, because it was only after 1940 that the census of population recorded the educational attainment of American workers by sector and occupation. However, it seems clear that the demand for unskilled workers declined markedly after the turn of the twentieth century. In key industries such as iron and steel, "the proportion of common laborers was cut approximately in half from 1910 to 1931" (Jerome 1934, 63).

The automation of strictly production tasks had a double-edged effect on skilled workers. It continued to displace skilled operators in those industries that had been less affected by the technological innovations of Manchester capitalism—such as the glass industry, sanitary ware, or cigar and cigarette making. But the reduction in direct demand for craftsmen was mitigated, and indeed overturned, by three key developments associated with the very process of automatization. First, most skilled workers were kept in the factory—most likely in response to the large expansion in total output, due to falling prices and the rise of mass consumption, that took place during that period.

Second, the demand for trained technicians increased as planning and engineering units needed more employees to organize, supervise, maintain, and repair a growing number of factory machines. As pointed out by labor economists Claudia Goldin and Lawrence Katz in their groundbreaking work on technological change and education in the United States, companies now sought high-school graduates for blue-collar positions "because they could read manuals and blueprints, knew about chemistry and electricity, could do algebra and solve formulas, and, we surmise, could more effectively converse with nonproduction workers in high-technology industries" (Goldin and Katz 1996, 19). The share of manufacturing employment in "technologically forward industries" (defined as those where more than one-third of the young male blue-collar workers had a high-school diploma in 1940) grew from 20.7 percent in 1909 to 26.7 percent in 1929. The proportion of manufacturing employment in the top five industries by education (petroleum, chemicals, electrical machinery, printing and publishing, and scientific instruments) rose from 10 percent in 1910 to 16 percent in 1940 (*ibid.*, 24). The 1940 population census shows that the more capital-intensive industries, which had grown at the fastest pace in the previous decades, employed the highest numbers of educated workers. In industries with the highest capital-to-labor ratio or highest use of purchased electricity— such as aircraft, printing, office machinery, petroleum refining, or electrical machinery—more than 40 percent of male blue-collar workers aged eighteen to thirty-four had a high-school diploma. In relatively non-capital-intensive sectors—such cotton, logging, or sawmills—the proportion stayed below 15 percent (*ibid.*).

Finally, the growth of machine-producing industries raised the demand for skilled individuals at the economy-wide level. Excluding transportation-equipment manufacturers, the number of wage earners working in the machine-tool sector in the United States grew from 414,000 in 1899 to slightly over one million in 1929. As a proportion of all manufacturing wage earners, this implied an increase from 8.8 percent to 12.4 percent during the same period of time.

Besides the effect of automation in both handling and production operations at the factory level, the structure of employment in twentieth-century capitalism was shaped by an additional crucial transformation: the formation of large corporations. Before the introduction of steam power, the transportation of goods was slow and expensive, and, except for a few products, markets remained relatively small. The completion of railroad and telegraph networks, the invention of the long-distance steamship, the birth of a national press and advertising market in the second half of the nineteenth century, and, later in time, the layout of fully integrated phone lines resulted in the creation of large markets, both domestically and at the international level. In turn, the introduction of batch-production machines and assembly lines, making it easier for manufacturers to exploit the economies of scale associated with bigger markets, gave a few companies a dominant position in the production market: James Duke's American Tobacco Company in cigarette making, Carnegie in steel, Procter & Gamble in soap making, Ford and General Motors in car making, and Standard Oil in the refinery business, to name just a few examples.

The distribution market was affected by similar transformations. Department stores, such as Marshall Field's, Macy's, or Lord & Taylor, started to appear in the 1860s and 1870s in the largest American cities and then became national brands in the following decades. Some of them, such as Sears, Roebuck and Company, doubling as mail-order houses, placed a significant part of their sales through catalogs and rail or mail delivery. Then, at the turn of the century, chain stores, led by Woolworth, spread throughout the United States, selling low-priced goods in small department stores. Over time, several companies engaged in a process of vertical integration of both the production and the distribution business: firms would control the entire sequence that led from the supply of materials to their transformation into a particular product and then down to the latter's marketing and selling.

These increasingly larger firms required growing numbers of white-collar employees to manage many of their production and distribution tasks, from accounting to sales. Consider, as an example, the case of the Ford Corporation. By 1915 it already employed, in addition to thousands of blue-collar workers in its Detroit plants and its headquarters' management and administrative staff, about twenty-six thousand car dealers throughout the United States. The expansion of white-collar jobs became a generalized phenomenon across the country. In 1899, nonproduction workers made up 7 percent of all the jobs in the manufacturing industries. The proportion doubled in ten years to 14 percent in 1909, reaching 21 percent in 1924 (Goldin and Katz 2008, 172). According to L. Katz and Margo (2014), the proportion of white-collar employees in the manufacturing sector rose from 14.8 percent in 1920 to 23.5 percent in 1950 and then to 30.5 percent by 1970.

The growing complementarities between capital and semi-skilled or even skilled labor ushered in by Detroit capitalism led to the formation of a broad strata of what, at least relative to Marx's nineteenth-century proletariat, were affluent workers. Once again, Ford led the way, paying his employees much higher wages than other companies. Following a twofold increase in productivity brought about by the changes designed in Highland Park, Ford doubled wages to $5 a day in 1914. The average annual wage in the whole automobile industry rose from $594 in 1904 to $802 in 1914 and exceeded $1,600 by 1924 (Nye 2000, 53). Technologically advanced industries paid higher salaries than traditional manufacturing sectors. Jerome (1934) reports a strong correlation between annual wages and the volume of generated horsepower used per wage earner. In 1927, the average annual earnings of an employee in the US machine-tool industry was twelve percent higher than in the manufacturing sector as a whole.

The effects of strong productivity gains and the shift in the composition of employment toward a more skilled labor force rippled throughout the whole US economy. Figure 3.1 shows the evolution of mean and median earnings (adjusted for inflation) as well as of labor productivity (output per hour worked) of commerce and industry workers in the United States from 1913 to 1975—normalized to their value (expressed as 100) in 1937. Output per hour worked, growing at an average annual rate of 2.5 percent, rose by almost 80 percent between 1913 and 1937, and by 250 percent from 1937 to 1975. Average earnings of commerce and industry workers essentially tracked productivity throughout the

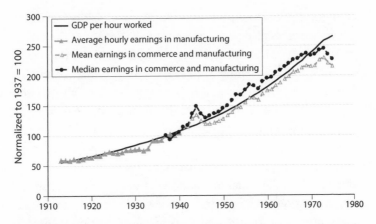

FIGURE 3.1 Evolution of labor productivity and real earnings in the United States, 1913–75. Output per hour worked is derived from table 4.2 through linear interpolation. Data on earnings up to 1937 are from Mitchell (2013), and from Kopczuk, Saez, and Song (2010) for the period afterward. All data are normalized to a base index that equals 100 in 1937.

whole period—growing by 69 percent between 1913 and 1937 and by 215 percent from 1937 to 1975.[3] For median earnings—that is, the earnings of a worker located in the middle of the whole earnings distribution—we only have data starting in 1937. During the period under analysis, it grew slightly faster than average earnings, pointing to a process of wage equalization that I examine in more detail later on.

Figure 3.2 displays the evolution of both labor productivity and average earnings in France, Germany, and the United Kingdom between 1920 and 1973. Owing to the type of earnings data available, figure 3.2 reports data on productivity and earnings trends for the whole economy in Germany and the United Kingdom, and for the industry sector in France.[4] This implies that we cannot make direct comparisons between the French and the German and British data. Productivity gains were small before World War Two (with the exception of France) and only grew steadily in the postwar period: by 300 percent in France, 259 percent in Germany, and 180 percent in the United Kingdom.[5] Average earnings tracked labor

FIGURE 3.2 Evolution of labor productivity and real earnings in Europe, 1920–73. Data on output per hour worked for Germany and the United Kingdom are for the whole economy and come from Broadberry (2006). Data on earnings are also for the whole economy, and come from Mitchell (2013). The French data on both labor productivity and earnings are for the industry sector and are from Boyer (1978). All data are normalized to a base index that equals 100 in 1937.

productivity very closely in both France and the United Kingdom. In Germany they did so with a ten-year lag.

Falling Inequality

The diffusion of the Detroit model of capitalism, with its shift in employers' relative demand from unskilled to semiskilled and skilled workers (and, as I will consider later on, an increase in the supply of the latter kind of labor), was accompanied by the equalization of wages and overall distribution of income in twentieth-century industrial economies. Figure 3.3 approximates the evolution of the distribution of earnings in the United States for the whole century by looking at three different data series. The first one shows the wage ratio between skilled and unskilled workers in the building trade from 1907 to 1947. The second displays the hourly wage ratio of railroad machinists to laborers from 1922 to 1952. These two first series are plotted on the left-hand

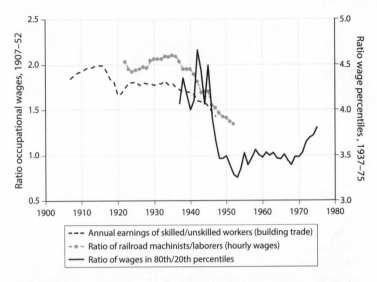

FIGURE 3.3 Evolution of wage ratios at different occupations and percentiles in the United States, 1907–75. Earnings of skilled/unskilled workers in the building trade and railroad machinists/laborers are plotted on the left-hand vertical axis; wages in the 80th/20th percentiles are plotted on the right-hand vertical axis. Sources: annual earnings of skilled/unskilled workers (building trade), Ober (1948); railroad machinists/laborers, Goldin and Margo (1992); wages in 80th/20th percentiles, Kopczuk, Saez, and Song (2010).

vertical axis. The third series reports the ratio between the wages of employees in the manufacturing and commercial sectors in the eightieth and twentieth percentiles of the earning distribution during the period 1937–75. The range of the series is displayed in the right-hand vertical axis.

Beginning in the 1910s, wage dispersion declined. An average skilled worker (in the building trade) earned two times the wage of an unskilled worker before World War One, but only seventy percent more in the early 1920s and slightly over forty percent more after World War Two. The wage ratio between machinists and laborers in the railroad industry displays similar trends. After peaking during the Great Depression, it began to fall in the late 1930s. Finally, according to the Kopczuk series, a worker in the eightieth percentile of the earnings distribution earned

4.3 times more than an employee in the twentieth percentile in 1938. Ten years later the ratio had fallen by a fourth to 3.4, and stayed put until 1970. This process of wage compression took place throughout the whole earnings structure. The earnings ratio for the eightieth to fiftieth percentile, which is not shown here, fell from 1.7 to about 1.5 in the early 1950s—and then grew again slightly to 1.6 by the mid-1970s. Wage compression was stronger and more persistent in the lower half of the wage distribution. The ratio for the fiftieth to twentieth percentile fell from around 2.5 in the 1940s to 2.2 by the early 1970s.

Unfortunately, there are no full time series on the distribution of earnings (or, at least, on earnings at different percentiles in that distribution) available beyond the United States for the early and middle decades of the twentieth century. An alternative to measure the evolution of earnings inequality starting in the early twentieth century consists in using data on the share of total income in the hands of the top percentile and the top decile of the income distribution in the World Top Incomes Database.[6] In line with the work of Ken Scheve and David Stasavage (2009), I calculate an "earnings inequality ratio" as the ratio between the proportion of the national income in the hands of the top ten percent of the income distribution (excluding the top one percent) and the proportion earned by the bottom ninety-nine percent. Excluding the top one percent makes sense because wages and salaries (labor income) are generally a minor fraction of the income of the top one percent of the income distribution. By contrast, labor income represents between seventy and ninety percent of the income of those individuals within the top ten percent but below the top one percent of the overall income distribution, and basically all of the income earned by the bottom ninety percent of the income distribution. The earnings inequality ratio works out as a good measure of wage dispersion: for those countries and years for which we have data, the earnings inequality index is very strongly correlated with the ratio of the earnings of the ninetieth and tenth percentile of the earnings distribution.[7]

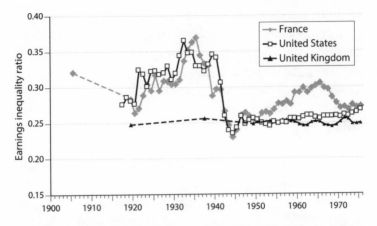

FIGURE 3.4 Earnings inequality ratio between top income (99th–90th percentile) and bottom (1st–99th percentile), for France, the United Kingdom, and the United States, 1900–1975. Dashed lines connect periods for which there are no continuous yearly data. Source: World Top Incomes Database.

Figure 3.4 reports the earnings inequality ratio in France, the United Kingdom, and the United States from the earliest available year in the twentieth century up to 1975. (Dashed lines connect periods for which there are no continuous yearly data.) The US earnings inequality ratio fluctuated at around 0.3 in the early interwar period. It then jumped to 0.36 in 1932. In other words, right before the Great Depression, the sum of all the income received by the top decile of the population (excluding the top one percent) was thirty-six percent of the total income received by the bottom ninety-nine percent. In the 1940s, however, the earnings distribution became much narrower. The earnings inequality ratio had fallen below its 1917 level by 1942, and it continued to drop, reaching 0.25 by the late 1940s. In France, the evolution of the earnings inequality ratio essentially tracked the American one until the mid-1950s. After climbing quickly in the Roaring Twenties, it declined after the Great Depression and throughout the war to 0.25. Afterward it rebounded, albeit moderately. Interwar data for the United Kingdom are scarce. But, overall, the British earnings inequality ratio fluctuated at around 0.25 until the 1970s.

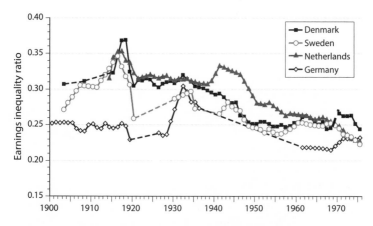

FIGURE 3.5 Earnings inequality ratio between top income (99th–90th percentile) and bottom (1st–99th percentile), for Germany and three small European countries, 1900–1975. Dashed lines connect periods for which there are no continuous yearly data. Source: World Top Incomes Database.

Figure 3.5 reports the same ratio for Germany and three small European countries—Denmark, the Netherlands, and Sweden. Inequality shot up during World War One, particularly in the small economies, but returned quickly to prewar levels (at around a ratio of 0.35). The Danish, Dutch, and Swedish earnings inequality ratios fell gradually throughout the interwar period and the first decades of the Cold War. The German decline, which was also rather slow paced, was mostly concentrated in the postwar period. As in the Anglo-American economies, by the late 1950s the top decile (excluding the top one percent) received a total income equivalent to about twenty-five percent of the income in the hands of the bottom ninety-nine percent of the distribution.

What was the main driver of the great wage compression between the interwar period and the 1970s? Did it result from great political and economic upheavals, from the shocks of two world wars and the Great Depression? Was it brought about by the formation of powerful trade unions throughout the twentieth century? Or was it the outcome of the technological innovation we have just examined in conjunction with a growing pool of relatively educated workers who could be hired by the new emerging firms and industries of Detroit capitalism?

The Scourges of War. An influential strand of the literature has recently portrayed war as the main economic equalizer of our contemporary age. In *Taxing the Rich*, political scientists Ken Scheve and David Stasavage identify a dramatic rise in the top-income- and inheritance-tax rates in the aftermath of the two world wars across the advanced world. Before 1914, the average tax rate on top incomes of future participants in World War One was identical to the average top rate among those countries that remained neutral during the conflict. By 1920, war participants had a top-income-tax rate about thirty percentage points higher than noncombatants on average. Likewise, their average inheritance tax rates, which had been similar before the war, differed by sixteen percentage points ten years after the end of the conflict. In countries that mobilized for war, tax rates were arguably raised on top incomes to spread to capital owners the sacrifices—in terms of lives, time, and income lost—borne by the general population. In introducing the 1916 budget into parliament, the British finance minister claimed that as "in time of war many businesses and industries . . . for one reason or another are able to maintain profits above the average return to capital in time of peace, . . . it is just that a portion of their advantage should be appropriated to the benefit of the state" (quoted in Scheve and Stasavage 2016, 166). Besides changing the tax system, wars have been seen also as reshaping the distribution of wealth and income through much more direct channels. As pointed out in Thomas Piketty's *Capital in the Twenty-First Century*, military combat and the budgetary and political shocks brought about by both world wars destroyed a considerable part of existing European wealth, from buildings and factories to infrastructure. In addition, investors suffered large losses in foreign assets as a result of expropriations due to revolutions and, in the second half of the twentieth century, the process of decolonization. Private savings were "largely absorbed by enormous public deficits" incurred to fund the war effort and by massive hyperinflationary runs in defeated nations (Piketty 2014, 149).

Two world wars and the Great Depression of 1929 certainly devastated wealth owners. Capital as a proportion of national income shrunk markedly in Europe during and immediately after World War One. The share of income in the hands of the top one percent, who received most of their income from capital, fell very sharply around the time of the two wars—from about twenty percent of national income in 1913 to fifteen percent by 1920, and then from slightly below fifteen percent in 1939 to ten percent in 1945—but remained flat before and after the two wars.[8]

Nonetheless, wars did not play the same role for labor income in leading to the progressive equalization of earnings across the entire distribution. Figure 3.6 displays the average earnings inequality ratios of both war participants and war nonparticipants separately, before, during, and after each world war. The evolution of the earnings inequality ratio, which by construction excludes the top percentile of the income distribution, was not correlated with war participation in any systematic way. Contrary to what the war hypothesis suggests, it actually rose among war combatants between 1913 and the mid-1920s, while dropping quite markedly among neutral states. During and after World War Two, it fell slightly among war participants, but also among noncombatants. The generalized decline simply continued a trend that had started before the war. All in all, the convergence in ratios across both types of countries by 1945 suggests that the decline in inequality responded to other structural factors.

Corporatism. A second (and probably more influential) academic line of thought has attributed the double outcome of wage growth and wage compression to the emergence of powerful trade unions after World War One. An extensive literature in economics has shown that, even though the forces of supply and demand operating in the labor market place strong bounds on the level of wages, the relative bargaining power of employers and employees shapes workers' earnings as well. We also know that in countries

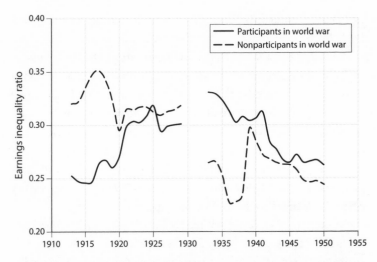

FIGURE 3.6 Evolution of the earnings inequality ratio among participants and non-participants in the two world wars. The participants in World War One included in the estimations are Australia, Canada, France, Germany, New Zealand, the United Kingdom, and the United States. The nonparticipants included are Denmark, Japan, the Netherlands, Norway, Portugal, Spain, and Sweden. The participants in World War Two are Australia, Canada, Denmark, France, Germany, Japan, the Netherlands, New Zealand, Norway, the United Kingdom, and the United States. The nonparticipants included are Ireland, Portugal, Spain, Sweden, and Switzerland. Source: Kinder and Hilgemann (2003).

with wage-bargaining negotiations taking place in a centralized manner at the industry or national level, trade unions insisted on narrowing wages at the factory level and reducing wage differentials within industries (Wallerstein 1999).

Labor unions grew in membership and militancy across the industrial world in the first half of the twentieth century. The United States underwent a spell of strong union activism, with widespread factory occupations in Akron's rubber industry in 1935 and in car plants the following year, which led to the recognition of the United Auto Workers (UAW) and the Steel Workers Organizing Committee (SWOC) by General Motors and US Steel respectively in 1937. Protected by the passage of the National Labor Relations Act of 1935, union membership grew to encompass almost a third of the

American workforce by the mid-1940s. Perhaps more decisively, almost seventy percent of the production workers in the major US manufacturing industries were covered by union contracts (Piore and Sabel 1984, 80). The structure of unions also changed. The craft-based unions of the past, federated in the American Federation of Labor (AFL), gave way to encompassing organizations (the Congress of Industrial Organizations (CIO) and the new AFL after 1937) that integrated both unskilled and skilled workers by industry. The European trade union movement also grew in membership and bargaining power over the interwar and postwar periods. In 1913, between fifteen and twenty percent of all employees belonged to a trade union in Germany, the Netherlands, and the United Kingdom. In the rest of Europe, union membership averaged ten percent. In 1960, almost forty percent of the German workforce and between a half and three-quarters of all employees in small European countries were affiliated to a trade union.

In response to the crash of 1929 and a spike in labor disputes, several countries moved to establish centralized wage-bargaining institutions, in which national employer and union committees negotiated, often with the presence of government representatives, employment conditions for the whole labor force. Denmark's national union federation and employers association signed a national collective bargaining agreement in 1934. Four years later, the Swedish business federation and the trade union confederation agreed in the Saltsjöbaden Accord to solve labor disputes at the national level. Austria, the Netherlands, and Ireland moved to adopt similar schemes in the postwar period. Germany and Japan developed a semicentralized wage-bargaining system in which labor negotiations were carried out at the industry level. However, the main manufacturing unions determined the pace and nature of wage and employment conditions across the country. Typically, wage negotiations across all German industrial sectors followed, in timing and content, the agreement reached by the metalworkers' union IG Metall and the engineering employers' organization, which represented the main exporting industries in the country.

FIGURE 3.7 Evolution of the earnings inequality ratio as a function of the wage bargaining system, 1913–90. The countries included are Australia, Canada, Denmark, France, Germany, Ireland, Japan, the Netherlands, New Zealand, Norway, Portugal, Switzerland, Sweden, the United Kingdom, and the United States. Source: Scheve and Stasavage (2009).

In Japan, wage bargaining took place during the spring (wage) offensive, or shunto. In that annual bargaining round, all settlements were formally negotiated at the company level between the firm's management and the company union. However, those agreements were mainly shaped by the decisions made by a small number of the largest corporations grouped on an industry or multi-industry basis, following extensive discussions between large firms across industries and between business and the Japanese government (Soskice 1990).

There is little evidence, however, that having stronger unions and centralized agreements was the cause of much wage compression during our period of analysis. Figure 3.7 shows the evolution of the average earnings inequality ratio in countries with decentralized wage-bargaining systems (i.e., those countries where wages were determined at the factory or individual level) and in economies with semicentralized and fully centralized wage-bargaining systems (i.e., where wages were set at the industry or at

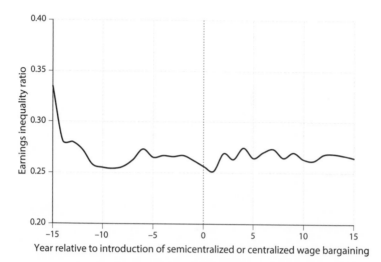

FIGURE 3.8 Wage-bargaining structure and evolution of the earnings inequality ratio. Year 0 is when labor-market institutions changed from a decentralized to a semicentralized or centralized wage-bargaining system. Source: Scheve and Stasavage (2009).

the national level) between 1913 and 1990. Starting just after World War One, both show very similar downward trends. If anything, the earnings inequality ratio was lower and then fell sooner, in the 1940s, in decentralized economies. By the 1960s, semicentralized and centralized wage-bargaining systems had a lower earnings inequality ratio on average. But the difference, of about 0.02 points, is almost negligible. It was only in the early 1970s, just as the dominance of Detroit capitalism was coming to an end, that both systems started to diverge as a result of an explicit equalization strategy pursued by unions in centralized regimes, and with economic consequences that I will discuss mainly in the next chapter.

Figure 3.8 dwells on the relationship between earnings inequality and wage institutions by calculating the average earnings inequality ratio of all those countries that moved from a decentralized wage-bargaining system to either a semicentralized or a centralized regime, fifteen years before and fifteen years after they switched the bargaining system. In that time series (of averages), it is not possible to identify any discontinuity in the earnings inequality ratio at the time labor-market institutions changed (marked by a dotted vertical line at year 0). If anything, the decline in wage dispersion seems to have preceded, in a fairly smooth manner, the change in wage-bargaining institutions—corroborating recent work by political economists Pablo Beramendi and David Rueda (2014). In short, labor institutions and the nature of wage bargaining cannot explain, at least on their own, the generalized process of wage compression that took place in the middle decades of the twentieth century.

It is true that we cannot discard altogether the hypothesis that trade unions were instrumental in securing higher wages, because their membership and power grew everywhere (albeit at different rates) in the middle of the twentieth century. Still, their success depended on the increasing efficiency with which goods and services were produced—as conveyed by two types of evidence. First, wage increases were tied to labor productivity gains across most sectors and economies. In 1948, General Motors and the UAW finally agreed to a wage-setting system that linked annual wage increases to changes in labor productivity and the price index—a solution that spread quickly to other mass-production industries and was informally followed by the remaining sectors of the US economy (Piore and Sabel 1984). Likewise, similar negotiation agreements, linking wages and labor productivity, prevailed across Western Europe (Marglin and Schor 1990).

Second, any wage deviations above productivity changes, such as were experienced in several European countries in the early 1970s, always proved short-lived. The evolution of the Swedish labor market provides a pointed example in that regard. Following an economic plan developed by two trade union economists, Gösta Rehn and Rudolf Meidner, Sweden made "solidaristic pay" in wage negotiations a key feature of economic policy in the 1960s and 1970s. Introducing a solidaristic wage norm, which implied paying the same wages to employees with similar jobs regardless of the employers' ability to pay, had two main goals in mind. On the one hand, in line with Swedish trade unions' strong commitment to equality, it was aimed at attaining a more compressed income distribution. On the other hand, it was conceived of as a tool to speed up the structural transformation of the Swedish economy by forcing the closing or rationalization of low-productivity firms, which could neither deliver high salaries nor bear "solidaristic" wage structures. To make wage solidarity possible, that economic strategy was accompanied by an active labor-market policy to re-train workers and by a restrictive fiscal policy to build up public savings that could be used to subsidize particular (ideally more dynamic, better-paying) economic sectors.

After the introduction of the Rehn-Meidner plan, Sweden ex-perienced a process of strong wage equalization—at a faster rate than other industrial economies—across companies and indus-tries. In 1970, wages in the top decile of the wage distribution were 56 percent higher than those in the bottom decile. By 1980, that figure had fallen to 34 percent. By way of comparison, it was 210 percent in the United States. However, during the same period, the profitability of the Swedish manufacturing sector dropped more strongly than abroad, and productivity growth lagged behind all other Western European economies (Pontusson 1992; Erixson 2010). Eventually, falling profits as well as mounting opposition among qualified workers to excessively compressed wage scales led to the unraveling of the Rehn-Meidner model. In the early 1980s, Swedish businesses decided to withdraw from the central-ized wage-bargaining system that had been in place for almost half a century, prioritizing instead wage flexibility and regulatory reforms. In short, after deploying measures that, at least for some sectors, broke the connection between wage growth and produc-tivity gains, Sweden had to realign its policies with economic fun-damentals. To put it more broadly, the Swedish experience shows that the production structure and productivity trends govern the processes of wage growth and wage compression, rather than in-stitutional factors, in the medium to long run.

Technology and Education. Having discarded war shocks and trade unions as the primary engines of wage equalization, we can go back again to assess the role that the innovations brought about by the new model of industrial capitalism played in shaping the distribution of income. As discussed earlier, by shifting the demand from poorly paid, unskilled jobs to semiskilled blue-collar and white-collar positions offering higher wages, Detroit curbed the inequities of Manchester capitalism. However, the rise of a wide layer of affluent workers hinged on an additional development: an abundant supply of individuals capable of operating, maintaining, and repairing fairly complex machines, and capable of performing the administrative and managerial functions required in modern corporations. In other words, it is likely that if the number of relatively well-trained individuals had remained low, the spread of new automation technologies would have proceeded haltingly, benefiting only a fraction of the population.[9]

The diffusion of the Detroit model coincided with the expansion of high-school education in the advanced industrial world. In the United States, enrollment rates in secondary education jumped from about twenty percent in 1900 to over seventy percent in 1960. In countries as diverse as France, Germany, Sweden, and the United Kingdom, they rose from less than five percent to more than fifty percent over the same period of time. As a result of this effort, about half of Americans aged between fifteen and sixty-four had some education beyond the primary level in the 1950s. In Europe, which lagged behind the United States in pushing its young population through high school, the proportion ranged from one-tenth in France to one-third in Scandinavia and the United Kingdom.

As more individuals completed primary education and advanced to secondary education, therefore acquiring the kinds of skills valued by businesses, the productivity gains of Detroit capitalism could be shared across the workforce more widely, pushing inequality downward. That pattern is apparent in figure 3.9, which plots the earnings inequality ratio in its vertical axis and the stock

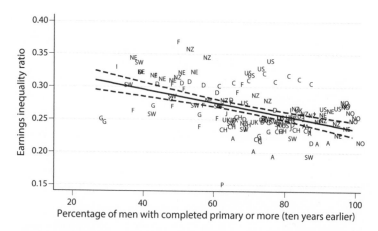

FIGURE 3.9 Education and wage inequality, 1900–1980. Abbreviations on the graph represent data points for different countries and time periods. *Solid line*, estimated relationship; *dashed lines*, 95% confidence interval. Data from Barro and Lee (2015).

of human capital in its horizontal axis. The data refer to advanced industrial countries from 1900 to 1980. Each abbreviation indicates a country and time period. The stock of human capital is measured as the percentage of men between fifteen and sixty-four years who had completed primary education—and therefore had secured the kind of skills required for the type of production systems in the Detroit model. The data, available every five years, are drawn from Barro and Lee (2015). To assess the claim that as the new model of capitalism unfolded, it was education that led to a drop in inequality, the stock of human capital is measured ten years before the earnings inequality ratio. For example, the observation closest to the lower-right corner of the graph, represented by "SW," corresponds to Sweden's human capital stock of 1970 (with 84.5 percent of men having completed at least primary education) and that nation's earnings inequality ratio of 1980 (about 0.2).

Wage inequality and education are strongly correlated in figure 3.9: the higher the percentage of educated men, the flatter the income structure. Figure 3.9 also displays the statistically estimated relationship (or functional form) between both variables with a solid line. Moving from a minimally educated to a fully educated workforce is associated with a fall in the earnings inequality ratio from around 0.31 to 0.24. This is a very substantial effect because two-thirds of all our actual observations fall within that range.[10] The relationship between education and inequality during this period of time works both for all the countries and for each country individually. Every nation trends downward—in terms of inequality—and rightward—in terms of education—at the same time. Take the case of the Netherlands, denoted by the letters NE: at the turn of the twentieth century, almost forty percent of men had completed primary education and the earnings inequality ratio was 0.35; by 1980, almost all Dutch men had at least primary elementary education and the ratio had fallen to 0.25.

Why did both school enrollment and the stock of human capital rise over time? And why did their expansion coincide to a large extent with the diffusion of the new production model? The answer to these questions lies in two sets of causes—economic and political. From an economic point of view, the transformation of twentieth-century capitalism gave both employees and employers strong incentives to invest in education, individually and collectively. In light of rising returns to education, in the form of a growing divergence between the salaries paid to semiskilled and skilled jobs (such as foreman, machine operator, engineer, or manager) and the wages earned by unskilled manual workers, individuals enrolled at higher rates in vocational training and secondary schools. Detroit-style corporations had a stake too in the expansion of schooling—they needed sufficiently well-trained individuals to run the machines in their factories and process the paperwork in their administrative offices. Henry Ford, for example, invested heavily in training his workers—from how to run a machine to, more controversially, how to behave in their social lives. Besides establishing a Ford English School to teach English and American values to recently arrived immigrants, he set up a Sociological Department, with about two hundred employees, to ensure that the family lives and overall behavior of his factory workers did

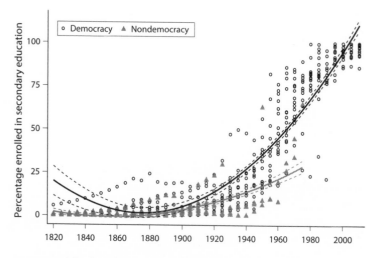

FIGURE 3.10 School enrollment under different political regimes. *Black open circles,* countries with male universal suffrage; *gray triangles,* countries without male universal suffrage. *Solid lines* indicate the estimated evolution of school enrollment rates under each political regime; *dashed lines* show the 95% confidence interval. Sources: for school enrollments, Barro and Lee (2015); for regimes, Boix, Miller, and Rosato (2013).

not deviate from a clear set of norms such as thriftiness, continence, and basic hygiene. Beyond this more anecdotal evidence, economic historian Peter Lindert has shown that American and German industrialists played an important role in promoting the expansion of education in the late nineteenth century and early twentieth century (Lindert 2004).

Figure 3.10 plots the percentage of young people in their official school age group enrolled in secondary education in advanced economies from 1820 to 2000. Each dot represents that level for a particular country, with the data reported at five-year intervals. Secondary enrollment rates were systematically low during the nineteenth century, except in the United States, which corresponds to the line of open circles that rises toward twenty-five percent in the last quarter of that century. By the interwar period, enrollment rates were taking off everywhere. After World War

Two, and coinciding with the diffusion of Detroit production systems, they rose exponentially in Japan and Europe, resulting in a catch-up process with the United States, which had been leading the world with enrollment rates over fifty percent in the first half of the twentieth century.

The rise of schooling responded also to political considerations. Spending money to educate unskilled workers is equivalent to transferring resources from those who are already educated to those who are not. Hence, it will only happen (or it will only be likely to happen) if the uneducated have some say over the policy-making process. Accordingly, the extension of the right to vote to all individuals regardless of their economic or educational status should push governments to make access to primary and secondary schooling universal (Ansell 2010).

To assess the impact of democracy, figure 3.10 divides observations into two categories. Black open circles indicate school enrollment in countries with male universal suffrage. Gray triangles represent school enrollment percentages in countries without male universal suffrage. Additionally, the continuous black line portrays the relationship, estimated mathematically, that best represents the temporal evolution of enrollment rates in those cases where all men had the right to vote. In turn, the solid gray line shows the temporal trend that fits most closely the evolution of school enrollment in countries without universal male suffrage.

A comparison of the distribution of these two types of observations indicates that political institutions mattered in terms of the educational effort made by each country. This was, however, conditional on the type of economy in place. In the nineteenth century—that is, before the rise of Detroit capitalism—the (few) democracies in place (Switzerland after 1848, France after 1870, and the settler colonies of Australia and New Zealand) had very low secondary enrollment rates. The only exception was, as noted before, the United States, where secondary-school enrollment rates were (particularly outside the American South) slightly higher. Indeed, the general trend in democracies (represented by the black line) hardly differed from the trend in nondemocracies (gray line). After World War One, there was a general process of democratization in Europe—as can be appreciated by noticing the multiplication of open circles after 1920 in figure 3.10. More importantly, that process interacted with the diffusion of the new production model. In democratic countries, there was a distinctive break with the past: enrollment rates in secondary school climbed to about fifty percent by 1960. By contrast, secondary schooling was much more tenuous in nondemocracies. By the middle of the twentieth century, on average democracies had twice as many people in secondary education than did nondemocracies.[11]

The End of Ideology

In January of 1912, two years to the day before the assembly line was fully operative in Highland Park, Frederick W. Taylor, the inventor of the doctrine of "scientific management," gave testimony before a special committee of the House of Representatives convened to assess the economic and social significance of the use of his new managerial techniques in the factory. For the American engineer, who had just published the book *The Principles of Scientific Management* the year before, the implementation of his methods held the promise of transcending the capital-labor struggles that had defined the nineteenth century. As he stated in the hearings, "the great revolution that takes place in the mental attitude of the two parties [capital and labor] under scientific management is that both sides take their eyes off the division of surplus as the all-important matter, and together turn their attention toward increasing the size of the surplus until this surplus becomes so large . . . that there is ample room for a large increase in wages for the workmen and an equally large increase in profits for the manufacturer" (quoted in Maier 1987, 26).[12]

The Detroit model of production eventually delivered the politics that Taylor imagined and had sketched before the US government representatives. Its efficiency in manufacturing new goods as well as its rising salaries fueled unprecedented increases in the level of consumption and material welfare of Americans. By 1940, ninety-six percent of all US urban homes had wired electricity, ninety-four percent enjoyed clean running piped water, eighty-three percent had interior flush toilets, seventy-three percent used gas for heating and cooking, and fifty-six percent owned mechanical refrigerators. About eighty percent of all households were in possession of a radio, and there was about one motor vehicle registration per household. Such an economic boom came hand in hand with a sharp increase in life expectancy and leisure time. Life expectancy at birth rose by around fifteen years from 1900 to 1940. The average number of working hours per week fell from sixty in 1870 to fifty-five in 1900 to forty by 1940 (Gordon 2016). In turn, these rapidly improving standards of living resulted in a wider and deeper commitment to the ideas of capitalism and democracy across all social strata. The episodes of political radicalism and agitation that had characterized Manchester capitalism grew scarcer and more short-lived over time. In electoral politics, the ideological stance of Republicans and Democrats became more moderate over a few decades.

The presidential elections of 1896 witnessed the rise of probably the last large populist movement in the United States against the economic and political establishment. Relying on the impoverished cotton and wheat farmers of western and southern states and fighting, in an effervescent campaign, the monetary policies supported by industry and, in the words of its candidate, William Jennings Bryan, "the idle holders of idle capital" (quoted in Dickinson 1896, 233), the Democratic Party gathered forty-seven percent of the popular vote—only to fizzle shortly after Bryan's electoral defeat. Nearly two decades later, in the presidential elections of 1912, the American Socialist Party polled six percent of the vote—a level of support similar to that of Britain's Labour Party before World War One—but it quickly fell into oblivion after Woodrow Wilson introduced several prolabor measures, such as workmen's compensation, child-labor legislation, a progressive income tax, and measures to shelter unions from court injunctions.[13]

As in Europe, trade unions grew smartly during World War One—doubling their membership to over four million people. Driven by the demobilization of American troops and the dismantlement of the War Labor Conference Board, where representatives of management and trade unions had worked together to solve labor disputes, labor unrest peaked right after the end of the European conflagration. In 1919 alone, more than four million workers participated in over 3,500 strikes. A general strike paralyzed Seattle for four days in February. Cleveland's May Day resulted in two people dead and dozens injured. In the fall, the Boston police walked out, and the trade unions launched wide-ranging strikes in the steel and coal industries, involving several hundred thousand men. Even then, however, labor unrest proved to be much milder than in Europe. In the period 1919–26, an average of four percent of all workers (employed in nonagricultural sectors) were involved in strikes in the United States every year. This was half the percentage of German workers and a third of the fraction of British employees participating in industrial disputes over the same period of time.[14]

In the presidential elections of 1924, an independent Progressive Party, led by Robert La Follette, endorsed by the American Federation of Labor, the Socialist Party, the Minnesota Farmer-Labor Party, and other left-wing forces, and calling for the public ownership of railroads and electric utilities and strong pro–trade union measures, polled one-sixth of the popular vote. Yet, as had happened in the aftermath of the 1896 and 1912 campaigns, La Follete's antiestablishment, radical political platform soon faded away from the American electoral scene.

The crash of 1929, by putting an end to the Roaring Twenties and apparently halting all the economic progress that had taken place in the previous decades, seemed to herald a return to more contentious politics. A year after the election of Franklin D. Roosevelt to the presidency, the senator and former governor of

Louisiana Huey Long launched the "Share Our Wealth" movement to advocate for a cap on personal fortunes, a sharply progressive income tax, and the federal funding of a minimum basic income, reaching a membership of over seven million. Nonetheless, it collapsed after the politician's assassination the following year, leaving the Democratic president free to govern from the political center.

In response to the Great Depression, Franklin D. Roosevelt turned to construct, over the following years, a new regulatory regime that, while guaranteeing the operation of a free-market system, stabilized the economy and expanded federal support to the unemployed, the poor, and the retired. Even though Roosevelt's New Deal met with the resistance, in part or as a whole, of key sections of American society, such as the Southern Democrats and a fraction of the Republican party, it ended up embodying a broad social consensus around the reconciliation of democratic demands and the operation of free markets. By the late 1930s, the first surveys launched by Gallup and Roper revealed "widespread opposition to repeal the New Deal, but a preference for incremental modification rather than broad further advances" (Schickler and Caughey 2011, 181) among the American public. Public opinion also embraced similar middle-of-the-road positions when asked about specific policy issues. Public support for social security rose twenty percentage points to ninety percent from 1936 to 1938. By contrast, the percentage of respondents in favor of socializing utility companies and banks fell from seventy and fifty percent respectively in 1938 to about forty percent in 1940 and thirty percent in 1946 for both sectors. More generally, support for both democracy and capitalism was widespread. In December of 1939, only five percent of respondents agreed with the statement that "private capitalism and democracy are breaking down" and supported the idea of finding a "new form of government." Despite the experience of war mobilization and the war performance of the Soviet Union, the number was still less than ten percent ten years later.

The specific nature of the political compromise built by Roosevelt seems to have been rooted in a process of ideological moderation that had been at work in the United States since the turn of the twentieth century. Nolan McCarty, at Princeton University, and his colleagues have measured the historical evolution of the ideological position of members of the US Congress on a liberal–conservative scale using roll-call voting records (McCarty, Poole, and Rosenthal 2006). Some of their results are summarized in figure 3.11.

The figure shows the average score (in that dimension) of the Republican and the Democratic Party (the entire party and, separately, just its Southern delegation) in the House of Representatives from the forty-seventh (1881–82) to the ninety-sixth (1979–80) Congress. A higher score indicates a more conservative policy stance. Democrats and Republicans were rather far apart from each other at the turn of the twentieth century—at −0.41 and 0.46 respectively in the liberal–conservative spectrum. At around World War One, the Democratic Party moved toward the political center—slowly at first and then quite rapidly in the 1920s. Some, but not all, of that moderation came from the Southern Democrats. Likewise, Republicans evolved toward more moderate positions fundamentally during the interwar period. In the seventy-third Congress, elected in 1933, the average ideologies of Democrats and Republicans were −0.17 and 0.30 respectively. In short, their ideological distance had dropped by half from 0.89 in 1895 to 0.47 in 1933. The New Deal accelerated a process of political convergence that had preceded the crash of 1929. In 1947, when the Republican Party briefly regained control of the House of Representatives, the distance between the two parties had fallen to 0.39—the lowest level since 1825. It would trend upward in the following decades, but only slightly. In 1977, the difference in party means was about 0.49, or half of what it had been one hundred years earlier.

Speaking at Yale University's commencement in 1962, President Kennedy summed up that golden age of economic affluence and political moderation in a way that harked back to Frederick W.

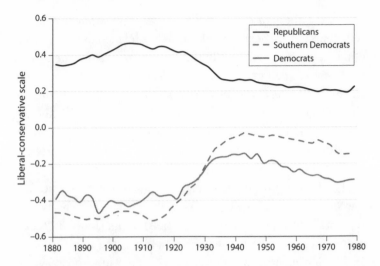

FIGURE 3.11 Ideological party means in the US House of Representatives, 1881–1980. Source: McCarty, Poole, and Rosenthal (2006).

Taylor's remarks before the House of Representatives exactly half a century before. "The central domestic issues of our time," Kennedy stated, "relate not to basic clashes of philosophy or ideology but to ways and means of reaching common goals." The great partisan clashes, the "grand warfare of rival ideologies" of the past had become "matters of degree." Indeed, "keeping a great economic machinery moving ahead" demanded "technical answers, not political answers." Economic problems, he declared, "cannot be solved by incantations of the forgotten past," but only when faced as "technical problems without ideological preconceptions" (Kennedy 1962).

Consolidating Democracy in Europe

In contrast to the United States, the experiment of democratic capitalism proved impossible in much of interwar Europe. Following the armistice of 1918 and the precipitous collapse of the Central Powers, labor unrest became rampant across the continent and would soon be met with radical force from the conservative side of the political spectrum. Left-wing members of the German Social Democratic Party, led by Karl Liebknecht and Rosa Luxemburg, staged two revolutionary uprisings in November of 1918 and January of 1919. The Hungarian communists established a revolutionary government in 1919, which was ferociously repressed the following year after a military coup. In the fall of 1922 Mussolini took over the Italian government. The following year brought about Hitler's failed putsch in Bavaria and two successful coups in Bulgaria and Spain. By the mid-1920s, Lithuania and Poland were under a right-wing authoritarian regime. The Great Depression then led to Hitler's election; right-wing coups in Austria, Estonia, Latvia, and Greece; the Spanish Civil War; and a highly polarized French election of 1936, which resulted in the victory of the Popular Front, an alliance of communists and socialists, and widespread labor agitation and a general strike that same year.

A similar level of ideological polarization seemed to be still in place in the immediate aftermath of World War Two. In a BBC broadcast in November of 1945, the English historian A.J.P. Taylor asserted that "nobody in Europe believes in the American way of life—that is, in private enterprise; or rather those who believe in it are a defeated party and a party which seems to have no more future than the Jacobites in England after 1688" (quoted in Maier 1987, 153). Indeed, in May of that same year, only thirty-five percent of the British public were in agreement with the statement that "the best way to provide jobs is by private enterprise and removing all government controls," and between fifty and sixty percent called for the nationalization of land, coal, transportation, electricity, and heavy industries (Gallup 1976). In the German zone under American control, where the US Army polled public opinion quite intensively, the sum of respondents ready to support either a communist or a Nazi government totaled sixty-six percent in the fall of 1945. In the winter of 1949, it was still forty-eight percent. In January of 1948, forty-nine percent of Germans living in the American zone supported the nationalization of heavy

industry (Merritt and Merritt 1970). During the few months following liberation from Nazi occupation, both France and Italy
were confronted with the sparks of a potential civil war between
communist and pro-American partisans. Open civil wars actually
broke out in Yugoslavia and Greece.

Defying expectations, however, Western Europe quickly became "Americanized"—at least in its economic structures—after
World War Two. The presence of US troops, first to de-Nazify
Germany and then to deter the Soviet army, stabilized the continent. Growth, and with it the adoption of the mass-consumption
patterns that had spread among American society before World
War, did the rest. During the first fifteen years after the end of
the war, European economies grew at the rather furiously paced
rate of 6.6 percent every year. By 1949, the United Kingdom had
reached its prewar per capita income. France and Italy did so in
1950. West Germany had regained its 1939 economy by 1953. The
number of privately owned cars (per thousand people) in Britain
rose from 43 in 1940 to 209 in 1970. In France private car ownership increased from 46 to 252 and in Germany from 7 to 227 over
the same period of time. The proportion of households with clean
running water went up from about eighty and fifty percent in Britain and France respectively after the war to almost one hundred
percent by 1990. The percentage of households with at least one
bathroom rose from sixty-two in Britain and ten in France to over
ninety-nine during the same period.[15] The expansion of the economy also transformed social expectations about future income and
employment prospects. By the early 1960s, around ninety percent
of Norwegians and British and about three-quarters of Belgians
and Germans agreed that capable individuals had good chances
of rising socially in their respective country (Lipset 1964, 284).

As the American sociologist Daniel Bell wrote in "America as
a Mass Society"—a paper he delivered at an international conference on "The Future of Freedom" convened in Milan in 1955
under the sponsorship of the Congress for Cultural Freedom, an
academic network intent on opposing the hegemony of Marxist

ideas in the academic world—the class-based politics of the past had been fueled by "resentment, [which], as Max Scheler once noted, is among the most potent of human motives; . . . certainly that in politics." But growth of the kind witnessed in the middle of the twentieth century was fast unmaking it. It was now apparent that "in the advanced industrial countries, principally the United States, Britain, and northwestern Europe, where national income has been rising, where mass expectations of an equitable share in that increase are relatively fulfilled, and where social mobility affects ever greater numbers . . . extremist politics have the least hold" (Bell 1988, 31). Bell's claim about an emerging social and political consensus in postwar Europe resonated with some other influential participants in the same conference, such as American political sociologist Seymour Martin Lipset; French sociologist Raymond Aron; and Anthony Crossland, a British politician who would go on to write influential tracts in favor of moderating Labour's program.[16] In *L'opium des intellectuels,* a book published that same year and explicitly directed against his former colleague Jean-Paul Sartre, Aron pronounced the ideology of the revolutionary Left dead, noting that "imperfect and unjust as Western society is in many respects, it has progressed sufficiently in the course of the last half-century so that reforms appear more promising than violence and unpredictable disorder. The condition of the masses is improving. The standard of living depends on productivity—therefore, the rational organization of labor, of technical skills, and of investments. Finally, the economic system of the West no longer corresponds to any one of the pure doctrines; it is neither liberal nor planned, it is neither individualist nor collectivist" (Aron 1957, xv). Mirroring Bell's and Aron's ideas, Lipset would become highly influential in linking democratization to economic development.

Figure 3.12 explores the relationship between economic affluence and the stability of democracy. The horizontal axis shows income per capita (in constant dollars of 1996), in $2,000 intervals. It then locates the specific countries and years where the collapse of democracy took place in Europe—from the poorest case (Portugal

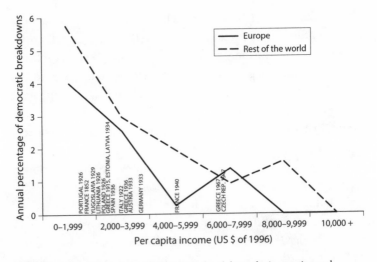

FIGURE 3.12 Annual percentage of democratic breakdowns by income interval, 1800–2000. *Solid line*, annual probability of democratic breakdown for each per capita income segment, calculated for European states between 1800 and 2000; *dashed line*, probability of democratic breakdown among non-European democracies. Data from Boix, Miller, and Rosato (2013).

in 1926) to the wealthiest instance (Czechoslovakia in 1947). Cases are clustered among low- to mid-low-income countries (relative to today's living standards). Excluding four cases (the French Republic in 1852 and 1940, and Greece and Czechoslovakia after World War Two), all breakdowns took place in the interwar period: they correspond to all those nations that experienced some transition to democracy, mostly as a result of the shock of World War One and the triumph of the Allies and the diffusion of Wilson's ideas, but could not hold to it owing to their domestic economic and social conditions.

Showing that a majority of democratic breakdowns happen in relatively poor countries does not tell us for certain that income matters for the stability of democracies. The distribution of democratic collapses could simply mirror the underlying distribution of all countries. To show it is otherwise, figure 3.12 also graphs, using a continuous line, the annual probability of democratic breakdown for each per capita income segment in Europe between 1800 and 2000. The probability of democratic breakdown is calculated as the number of democratic breakdowns divided by the number of democratic country-years within each per capita income segment. The probability of a democratic breakdown declines with income. Among European countries with a per capita income below $2,000 (in US dollars of 1996), there is a 4 percent chance of a transition to authoritarianism in any given year in Europe. The probability drops by half for European countries with per capita incomes between $2,000 and $4,000, and becomes close to 0 for richer countries. The proportion of democratic breakdowns rises exceptionally at around $6,000, driven by the cases of Czechoslovakia in 1947 and Greece in 1967. Without the former case, where Soviet intervention arguably led to the suppression of democratic institutions, the probability of democratic collapse would have been around 0.7 percent. The relationship between development and democratic stability is not exclusive to Europe. The dashed line reports the probability of experiencing a democratic breakdown among non-European democracies. That probability is higher at low income levels and then declines with growth.

Catch-All Parties

In 1958, while collating all his essays at Palo Alto's Center for the Advanced Study of Behavioral Sciences into a volume entitled *The End of Ideology*, Bell wrote a blunt epilogue in which he concluded that "the old ideologies have lost their 'truth' and the power to persuade" (Bell 1988, 402). Instead, he pointed out, "in the Western world, there is today a rough consensus among intellectuals on political issues: the acceptance of the Welfare State; the desirability of decentralized power; a system of mixed economy and of political pluralism" (402–3). Announcing that, at least in the industrial world, "the ideological age has ended," he noted that, at least "among the intellectuals, the old passions are spent" (404).

Indeed, a few years into the Cold War, not only had democracies become more stable, but party politics had also moved decisively toward the center. Extreme right-wing parties disappeared in northwestern Europe. In Germany, Christian democracy, represented by the Christian Democratic Union (CDU) and the Christian Social Union (CSU), almost doubled its vote share from 1949 to the mid-1960s—mainly absorbing the support for fringe conservative and authoritarian parties. In Italy and France, middle-class reactionary movements such as the Ouomo Qualunque and Puojadisme collapsed quickly. The Italian fascist party MSI remained marginal. Gaullism and moderate Christian democratic parties now occupied most of the French and Italian conservative electoral spaces.

The Left experienced quite symmetrical transformations. In Britain, Hugh Gaitskell, the successor of Prime Minister Attlee in the Labour Party's leadership, launched a campaign to drop Clause Four, calling for the nationalization of industry, from the party platform. In their party congress held in Bad Godesberg in 1959, the German Social Democrats scrapped from their party program any reference to orthodox Marxism as an instrument of analysis or guide to action, rejected their label as a "[working-]class party," and reasserted their commitment to democracy and peaceful reform. Socialist parties in Austria, Belgium, the Netherlands, and Scandinavia lost "nearly all traits of doctrinaire Marxism"—to use the words of Herbert Tingsten, a Swedish political scientist and participant in the Milan meeting of 1955 (Tingsten 1955, 145). All that was left was a strong commitment to the combination of a market economy and the kind of social insurance programs developed under Roosevelt's New Deal. Only France and Italy saw large, combative communist parties. But, even there, moderation ended up winning the upper hand. It did not take long for Italian communists to question Lenin's doctrine in favor of a one-party dictatorship and to enter into collaborative deals with business elites at the municipal level.

The process of programmatic moderation among political parties eventually affected their internal composition and electoral support. In an influential essay written in the mid-1960s, the German jurist and political scientist Otto Kirchheimer pointed out that "the ideologically oriented nineteenth-century party" had given way to the so-called "catch-all party," an electoral machine directed at maximizing votes by focusing on noncontroversial issues, stressing the competence of leaders, and de-emphasizing the interests of a particular social class (Kirchheimer 1966, 183). Catch-all parties were akin to large brands competing in standard consumer markets—interested in developing enough name differentiation to be recognizable by buyers (voters) but also in avoiding any excessive differences that could turn their (moderate) supporters away. Up to the middle of the twentieth century, one of the main lines of party competition pivoted around the division and confrontation between middle- and working-class voters. However, economic growth and increasing social mobility softened the class cleavage to such an extent that parties had started to play this down in elections.

Just as the old class-based allegiances to parties were thawing, a disciple of Seymour Lipset, the American sociologist Robert R. Alford, developed what would become an influential index of class voting to measure the extent to which the support received by left-wing parties differed across different social strata. The Alford index equals the difference between the percentage of manual workers voting for left-wing parties and the percentage of nonmanual workers voting for those same parties. An index of 100 indicates a society where party vote is perfectly aligned with class position—one where all manual voters choose left-wing candidates and all of the nonmanual voters support right-wing parties. An Alford index of 0 describes an electorate where the probability of voting for left-wing parties is identical across manual and nonmanual workers.[17]

Figure 3.13 shows the evolution of the Alford index since the interwar period in two separate sets of countries, grouped together according to whether economic (and class-based) policy issues have determined the vote alone or in combination with other policy issues. Figure 3.13A reports the Alford index in Australia, Denmark, Great Britain, and Sweden, where class and

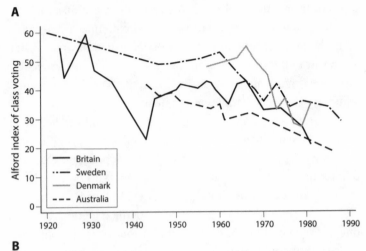

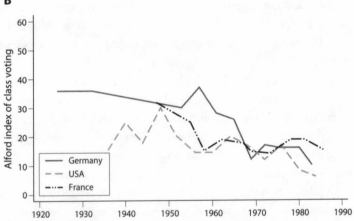

FIGURE 3.13 Class voting, 1920–90, (A) with one political cleavage; (B) with two or more cleavages. Interwar results from statistical estimations reported in Boix (2012). For the period after World War Two, direct survey data. Sources as follows. Australia: 1943–61, Alford (1963, table B-2); 1967, Aitkin (1982, table 8.8); 1980, Western et al. (1991, table 14.6). Denmark: Andersen (1984, table 1). France: Dalton (1988, table 8.2). Germany, 1924–32: Boix (2012, table 5). Great Britain: 1918–35, Boix (2012, table 1); 1943–62, Alford (1962, 422); 1964–83, Dalton (1988, table 8.2). Sweden: 1920, Boix (2012, table 6); 1946–76, Stephens (1981, table 3); 1976–88, Oscarsson and Holmberg (2015, fig. 27). West Germany, 1953–87: Dalton (1988, table 8.2). United States: 1936–60, Alford (1963, table B-3); 1964–84, Dalton (1988, table 8.2).

redistributive conflict defined in a fundamental way, and to the exclusion of most other issues, the terms of partisan competition at least since (and sometimes before) the introduction of universal suffrage. In the Swedish elections of 1920, seventy-five percent of manual voters cast their ballot for the Social Democratic Party, but only fifteen percent of nonmanual workers did—a historically high Alford index of 60. In the British elections of 1923, whereas sixty-six percent of manual workers voted Labour, only eleven percent of nonmanual workers did—an Alford index of 55. The extent of class voting declined slightly in the following years but it was still high in the first decade after World War Two—above 50 in Sweden and around 40 in Australia and Great Britain. In the 1960s, as mass consumption kicked in and baby boomers started to vote, class voting declined rather sharply everywhere. By 1980 the Alford index had fallen to 20 in Australia, 27 in Great Britain, and 35 in Denmark and Sweden.

Figure 3.13B displays the evolution of the Alford index in those countries where politics pivoted around other policy issues besides social class and the economy: for example, in France and the Catholic regions of Germany, elections turned around the status of religion in education and the public sphere as much as around the state of the economy and inequality. As a result, a fraction of the middle class favorable to a strict separation between state and church voted for left-wing (normally, anticlerical) parties. By contrast, church-going workers, affiliated to powerful Christian trade unions, leaned toward parties programmatically committed to the principles of Catholic social thought. In the United States, where race played a critical role in elections, the Democratic Party accommodated the working class of the industrial North and Midwest and, at least until the later 1960s, both rich and poor white voters in the American South. Compared with the countries in figure 3.13A, the Alford index was much lower to start with. In the German elections of 1924, it was 36.[18] After staying put throughout the 1950s, it declined systematically, reaching a nadir of 9 just before reunification. In the United States, the Alford index remained rather low until the late 1940s—mostly because support for the Democratic party was high among both manual and nonmanual workers. In 1936, for example, sixty-seven and fifty-two percent of manual and nonmanual voters respectively cast their ballot for Roosevelt. Over the following years, the Democratic vote among manual voters remained steady, while falling to less than forty percent among nonmanual voters. Accordingly, the Alford index inched up to about 30 in 1948. Yet, four years later, the Democratic vote share among manual workers started to decline and, with it, the Alford index. The behavior of French voters tracked the American pattern. In 1947, at the height of the strength of the socialist and communist parties following liberation, the Alford index stood at 32. Twenty-five years later it had dropped to less than half of that.

As Daniel Bell had stated, in a somewhat wry way, in his essays on the end of ideology, "politics offers little excitement," (Bell 1988, 404) at least compared with the passions and conflict that had ravaged Europe in the first half of the twentieth century. Indeed, the party may have lost much of its fun by the 1950s. But democracy and capitalism had finally learned to dance together.

4

Transformation

SILICON VALLEY

In October of 1952, William Shockley, the leader of the team that had invented the transistor at Bell Labs and a soon-to-be Nobel laureate in physics, wrote a single-page memo entitled the "A.T.R. Project," urging Mervin Kelly, the president of Bell Labs, to support the development of an "automatic trainable robot" that would "comprise 'hands,' 'sensory organs,' a 'memory,' and a 'brain,' which [would] coordinate the information furnished by the sensory organs with the memory in order to perform desired operations," and that could "be readily modified to perform any one of a wide variety of operations." Echoing *Automation: The Advent of the Automatic Factory*, a book published that same year by John Diebold, a Harvard Business School student, Shockley stressed that "the importance of the project described below is probably greater than any previously considered by the Bell System" because it had the potential to alter the foundations of industry completely. By the time he was writing, the (semi)automated factory had replaced human work only partially—it still relied on the implementation of critical tasks by semiskilled and skilled workers along the assembly line—and moving forward to achieve the full "substitution of machines for men in production" required devising robots that incorporated both the dexterity and perception of humans " (quoted in Brock 2012, 383).

With Kelly uninterested in creating an automatic trainable robot, Shockley decided to take a leave from Bell, working first at Caltech and then for the Pentagon. A few years later, having secured the financial backing of Arnold Beckman, the founder and CEO of Beckman Instruments, a leading firm in electronic instrumentation, he quit his position at Bell Labs for good to set up the Shockley Semiconductor Laboratory to manufacture silicon transistors for the mass market. Beckman, who had chosen the slogan "machines liberate men" as the opening sentence of his first report to shareholders in 1952 (quoted in *ibid.*, 387), was a strong believer in the future of automation. Beckman Instruments' annual report of 1954 endorsed the idea of building a "completely automatic factory" in which "instruments will take over many of the burdens of management and operators," and then went on to assert that "the ideal automatic factory will have a 'brain,' i.e. an electronic Computer" (388).[1]

In November 1955, Shockley opened his laboratory at the border of Mountain View and Palo Alto, where he had grown up as a child and his mother still lived, and where he could easily recruit researchers from Stanford University and benefit from a dynamic financial, military, and high-tech manufacturing region. However, Shockley's authoritarian managerial style and his decision to abandon the diffused silicon transistor in favor of an invention of his own, the four-layer diode, led eight of his main researchers to break away from the company and establish Fairchild Semiconductor about a mile away two years later. Unable to manufacture his prototypes, Shockley eventually closed his company and joined Stanford a few years later.

Although Shockley's foray into industry ended in personal failure, his decision to move to Palo Alto gave birth to what soon came to be known as Silicon Valley. The "traitorous eight," as

Shockley allegedly called the team that had left him, succeeded in manufacturing the diffused silicon transistor. Led by Robert Noyce, they would invent and develop the integrated circuit, or chip, based on the "planar process," a breakthrough manufacturing technology that allowed circuits to be chemically printed in silicon substrates. In the next two decades, Fairchild's spin-offs— including Intel, which had been started by two of the founders of Fairchild and which would pioneer the production of memory chips and microprocessors—and related start-ups multiplied into the hundreds in the region. In addition to being a manufacturing platform, Silicon Valley became an innovation hub in information and communication technologies—ranging from the concept of hypertext links and the networking of computers (eventually leading to the Internet) to the development of robotics and machine learning—and overall spearheading a fundamental transformation in industrial capitalism.

The Power of Information and Computation

The concept of an electronic digital computer to speed up the task of computing vast arrays of data had started to take shape by the end of World War Two. Following the development of high-speed calculators and considerable progress on servomechanisms during the war, the US Navy devised Mark I, an aircraft simulator for fighter aircraft, in 1944. A year later, the mathematician John von Neumann published a report outlining what would amount to the basic architecture of the computer to this day. In 1946, the first electronic automatic computer, the ENIAC, was developed to compute army ballistic tables. In 1950, the first general-purpose stored-program computer, Atlas I, went into full operation— followed by a commercial version, the ERM 1101, the year after. Nonetheless, it was the invention of the silicon transistor, its use in computers, and its eventual mass production that acted as crucial factors in accelerating the information-gathering and information-processing capabilities of computers needed to make progress toward the implementation of the full-automation move-ment envisioned by people like Shockley, Diebold, or Beckman.

In an ingenious paper on the evolution of computing, Yale economist William Nordhaus has estimated that just before World War Two the best electromechanical calculators were between ten and one hundred times faster than manual or human calculators. The ENIAC increased the calculation speed to five thousand times the speed of manual calculations. However, it would be later, once the transistor was incorporated in the early 1950s, that computa-tional speed grew at an exploding rate, roughly doubling every two years—in a pattern that has become widely known as Moore's law. By the late 1960s, the IBM360 was one hundred million times faster than manual calculators. And in the early 2000s, the Multiprogram-matic Capability Resource (MCR) Linus Cluster in the Los Ala-mos National Laboratory was one quadrillion (or 1×10^{15}) faster (Nordhaus 2007). With increasing speed, prices came tumbling down. Nordhaus has calculated that the cost of executing a set of standard computational tasks (defined as one million computations per second) fell from $500 (in 2006 prices) to half a dollar with the ENIAC. In the late 1960s, the cost had declined to a tenth of a cent. By the early 2000s, it equaled one-billionth of a cent.

As costs declined, financial services and company departments such as accounting, payroll, and inventory control, which pro-cess information quite intensively, began to use mainframe com-puters. IBM, which had taken the lead in the development of large, general-purpose computers for nonmilitary ends—such as the 701, 650, and 702 in the early 1950s and the series 7000 in 1958—sold about twenty thousand units of its series 1401 in 1960. By the early 1970s, there were between sixty and seventy thousand mainframe computers in the United States (Bresnahan 1999). Total revenue in the computer industry grew from about $500 million in 1960 to about $15 billion fifteen years later (Chandler 1997).

Nonetheless, the true expansion of the computer only hap-pened in the mid- and late 1970s. Early that decade, computing companies started to design software specifically targeted to the needs of customers. The proliferation of computers and a con-comitant increase in the demand for semiconductors, peripher-als, and other related products, reduced, in turn, their production costs and market prices. More fundamentally, the invention of the first microprocessor by Intel in 1971 spawned the development of microcomputers. The release of Apple II in 1977 inaugurated the mass market for personal computers, forcing IBM, which had to that point enjoyed a quasi-monopolistic position in the industry, to build its own IBM PC. In 1982, *Time* magazine put the personal computer on its cover as "Man of the Year," and by 1984 the annual sales of Apple and IBM personal computers together amounted to around $6 billion.

Computers became ubiquitous throughout the economy in a few years. According to data from the Bureau of Labor Statistics, twenty-five percent of all American workers and forty percent of all white-collar workers reported using a computer keyboard at work in 1984. In 1993, the proportion had risen to forty-seven and sixty-eight percent, respectively (Autor, Katz, and Krueger 1998). Capital investment in computers grew exponentially in the last third of the twentieth century. According to Nordhaus (2007), in 1950 there was one unit of (manual equivalents of) computer power available per hour worked in the American economy. By 2005, it had increased to one trillion units of computer power per hour worked.

The computer revolution would turn out to have momentous employment and income effects—reshaping the nature of available jobs, and therefore the structure of the labor market, and polariz-ing the distribution of earnings. As Alfred Chandler, an economic historian at the Harvard Business School, penetratingly put it: "Few other modern industries ever grew so fast or became such a powerful agent of transformation. The motor vehicle industry during the 1920s provides the closest historical parallel. An infant industry in 1900, it grew from middle size by 1915 to the nation's largest by 1935, in terms of revenues, value added in manufac-turing, and wages, and the third largest in employment. Motor vehicles transformed their industries—oil, rubber, glass, metals, chemicals, and modes of transformation. Computers did even more during the late 1960s and 1970s in transforming the ways of providing and processing information, which in turn revolutionized the processes of production and distribution" (Chandler 1997, 52–53).

Computer Algorithms and the Evolution of Employment

Just a few months after William Shockley had moved to Palo Alto, John McCarthy, a recently minted PhD in mathematics from Princeton teaching at Dartmouth College, coined the term "artificial intelligence," and convened a summer workshop to explore its possibilities. Research in that new field should proceed, according to McCarthy's proposal, "on the basis of the conjecture that every aspect of learning or any other feature of intelligence can . . . be so precisely described that a machine can be made to simulate it" (quoted in Markoff 2015, 114). That is the operational principle that, up to present day but with the exception of the field of machine learning, defines what computers do: following a precise set of rules, an algorithm in mathematical language, developed by programmers to reproduce or "simulate" as faithfully as possible the tasks, work actions, and decision-making procedures performed by humans.

As the costs of computing fell, McCarthy's insights would have formidable employment consequences—particularly for *routine* jobs—that is, tasks that follow explicit, identifiable rules and that can therefore be replicated by a particular computer program or set of algorithms. Taking advantage of the acceleration of computational speed and the invention of the personal computer, firms ranging from the automotive and chemical sectors to the food and beverage industry systematically substituted computers for manual workers engaged in repetitive production tasks to complement the flow of an assembly line.

Likewise, computers began to displace standard routine (or "routinizable") cognitive or nonmanual jobs in the service sector—those clerical and administrative jobs involving things such as bookkeeping, billing, auditing, and sorting and storing structured information. The impact of the new information and communication technologies (ICTs) on the telephone and banking industries is fairly well known. In the 1950s, AT&T employed several hundred thousand operators to manage its telephone switchboards and connect callers. Four decades later, all telephone routing systems had been automatized. The remaining fraction of telephone operators worked only in organizations such as hospitals and hotels that had large transient populations of patients and clients, and where personalized calls were too critical and too hard to transform into routinized processes. Similarly, the introduction of automated teller machines (ATMs) and optical reading devices in the banking system led to a decline in the proportion of employees working in very mechanical tasks, such as check verification or money transfers. Overall, however, the changes prompted by ICTs transcended any particular company or business sector. Less than a generation ago, midsized company managers, engineers, and university professors relied on intensive secretarial support to type and retype their correspondence, operational reports, laboratory results, or research papers; to file them; to schedule their meetings; to purchase airline tickets; and even to call a cab. Today, a laptop and a decent connection to the Internet have made a substantial part of the old administrative staff redundant, squeezing it out from the labor market.

By contrast, computers have hardly replaced nonroutine jobs—that is, those tasks that are accomplished employing some kind of tacit knowledge (a type of knowledge for which we have been unable, so far, to lay out clear procedures or rules that can be, in turn, programmed). To date, as MIT economist David Autor has put it, computerization has had a low impact on manual jobs "requiring situational adaptability, visual and language recognition, and in-person interaction," such as "food preparation and serving jobs, cleaning and janitorial work, grounds cleaning and maintenance, in-person health assistance by home health aides, and numerous jobs in security and protective services" (Autor 2015, 12). Similarly, computer programmers have not been able to develop software codifying nonroutine tasks that involve more abstract activities such as problem solving, creativity, or persuasion. Still, ICTs have had two important effects—one direct and the other indirect—on jobs, mostly managerial and professional occupations, that rely heavily on abstract thought processes.

Firstly, computers and computer software (such as computer-aided design [CAD] and related programs for engineers and architects, desktop publishing for marketing and communications experts, or databases and statistical packages employed by scientists and researchers) have directly raised the demand (and salaries) for the highly educated individuals capable of operating them.

Secondly, computers have prompted the transformation of the workflow and organizational structure of most companies, indirectly raising the demand for highly qualified individuals. As pointed out by Timothy Bresnahan at Stanford University, white-collar work can be separated into the "back office"—"an industrialized data-handling shop that turns information into machine-readable data"—and the "front office," where personnel mostly deal with customers and other people outside the organization (Bresnahan 1999, F405). Computers have had a simultaneous effect at both ends of the company—supplanting workers and their routine jobs in the back office, while at the same time increasing the value of people skills and the level of autonomy in decision-making processes in the front office. As a result, managers and professionals have assumed a much more influential position in any firm. With the support of computer databases, marketing managers can determine "what customers want," calibrate the computerized production system to fulfill their demands, and in fact develop new marketing systems to attract new customers. Likewise, those managers in charge of the accounting and control units can apply the newly gained computerized information to restructure the incentive systems that define the activities of salespersons and low-level managers, as well as the behavior of suppliers and customers. By both changing managerial skill requirements and making bureaucracies flatter, the new information flows have reinforced the centrality of managers and raised the demand and wage premium for those individuals who, besides having the proper quantitative or analytical skills, excel in the traditional interpersonal skills needed to motivate and coordinate workers.

In short, and very much in the same way the Detroit production system reshaped Manchester's labor markets by depressing the demand for unskilled workers and increasing the demand for semiskilled operators and technicians, the Silicon Valley economy has transformed the existing structure of employment. It has reduced the demand for routine jobs, both manual and nonmanual, generally filled by moderately skilled workers. Between 1979 and 2014, the share of routine manual occupations dropped from 23.2 percent of the working-age population to 15.1 percent in the United States. The share of routine cognitive jobs fell from 19.6 percent of the working-age population in 1989 to 16.1 percent in 2014. By contrast, the share of nonroutine jobs rose from 29.9 percent in 1979 to 40.5 percent in 2014—two-thirds of the increase happening in cognitive jobs and the rest in manual tasks.[2]

Taking a much longer temporal perspective, figure 4.1 reproduces the change in the share of employment of different occupational groups in the United States in the periods 1910–50, 1950–80, and 1980–2010. The different groups are displayed according to their average level of skills: from those with a low qualification content (industrial laborers) to those generally linked to high educational requirements (professionals). Between 1910 and 1980, and in line with the capital-labor complementarities of the Detroit model, unskilled jobs declined as a share of total employment by over seven percentage points, the share of blue-collar jobs remained flat—growing before 1950 and falling afterward—and both

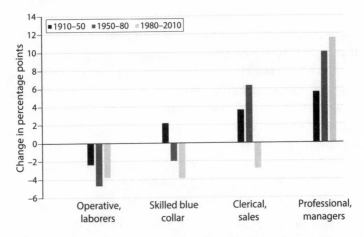

FIGURE 4.1 Change in employment share of nonagricultural occupations in the United States, 1910–2010. Source: L. Katz and Margo (2014).

middle-skilled jobs (clerical and sales) and high-skilled occupations (managers and professionals) grew, by ten and sixteen percentage points respectively. The year 1980 proved to be a turning point in employment patterns. The fall in the share of blue-collar workers intensified. The fortunes of moderately skilled occupations reversed: the proportion of clerical and sales jobs declined by almost three percentage points in the following three decades. By contrast, managerial and professional occupations rose as a share of total employment at a faster rate.

As with the Detroit model of production, the transformation of the labor market has not been exclusive to the United States. European economies have undergone similar employment shifts over the last few decades. Figure 4.2 shows the change in occupational employment shares in low-, middle-, and high-wage occupations in the four largest European economies—France, Germany, Italy, and the United Kingdom—plus one Scandinavian country, Sweden, between 1993 and 2010, and in the United States from 1979 to 2007.[3] The employment share of high-wage occupations rose by an average of four percentage points—with the largest rises

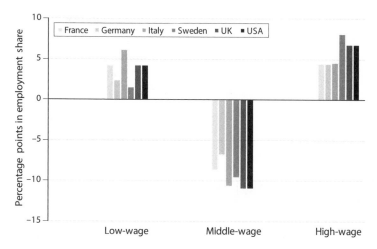

FIGURE 4.2 Change in occupational employment shares in low-, middle-, and high-wage occupations in the five European economies (1993–2010) and in the United States (1979–2007). Sources: Europe, Goos, Manning, and Salomons (2014); United States, Autor (2010).

in Sweden, the United Kingdom, and the United States and the lowest ones in continental Europe. On the opposite side of the labor market, demand for low-skilled jobs, which tend to have a high manual component and are arguably less affected by the computer revolution, grew as well. By contrast, middle-skilled occupations, mainly concentrated in manufacturing production, administrative positions, and sales and technical work, were struck by the process of substitution of computers: their numbers fell everywhere—particularly in Italy, the United Kingdom, and the United States.[4] All in all, the structure of employment gradually polarized—with a shrinking center and growing tails—across the advanced industrial world.

ICTs not only affected employment (and wages) directly, by substituting computers and algorithms for individuals. They also reshaped the volume and nature of foreign investment and trade and, as a result, the existing international division of labor. As multinational corporations offshored and outsourced part of their production to developing nations, a growing fraction of unskilled and semi-skilled labor in the advanced industrial world had to compete openly with workers in the world's periphery. In addition, a strong inflow of migrants intensified the transformation of the labor market in the developed world. I turn to examine these momentous changes in the next section.

Globalization 2.0

After the Allied victory in 1945, Washington and London called for the creation of an open world economy to avoid a repetition of the Great Depression of 1929, the formation of closed and increasingly hostile regional trade blocs, and the spiral of tariff and devaluation wars that preceded and arguably paved the road to World War Two. As President Truman insisted in his address at Baylor University in March 1947, restoring free trade was imperative, because "as each battle of the economic war of the thirties was fought, the inevitable tragic result became more and more apparent. From the tariff policy of Hawley and Smoot, the world went on to Ottawa and the system of imperial preferences, from Ottawa to the kind of elaborate and detailed restrictions adopted by Nazi Germany. Nations strangled normal trade and discriminated against their neighbors, all around the world." Creating an "open trading system," he said, ought to be one of the "cornerstones of our plans for peace" (quoted in Ikenberry 2011, 170–71). And bringing it back and maintaining it, together with a good measure of currency and overall financial stability, would have to be implemented through new sets of rules, such as the General Agreement on Tariffs and Trade (GATT), and underpinned by regional free-trade areas at the continental level—of which the European Common Market would be the most significant example.

In a sharp reversal of the protectionist regime built up during the interwar period, trade barriers fell across the board in a few years. In Europe, the median tariff, which had risen from 9 percent in 1925 to 22.3 percent in 1933, had fallen to 5 percent by 1950. In

America and Oceania, it dropped from 23 percent at the peak of the Great Depression to less than 10 percent in 1950. By 1970, the world median tariff was just 6 percent.[5] After collapsing in the 1930s, world trade was back to its pre–World War One volume by 1948. It then quadrupled over the next twenty years. By 1975, it was six times larger than in 1913. Total exports and imports rose from being less than forty percent of world output to about seventy percent in less than three decades (Rogowski 1989).

Yet, despite that roaring expansion of world trade, the global reach of the new commercial regime remained incomplete. The advanced economies of North America, Western Europe, Japan, and Australasia became deeply integrated with one another over time. In 1980, about seventy percent of all their exports went to other advanced countries (United Nations Conference on Trade and Development [UNCTAD] 1992). Intra-industry trade—that is, exports and imports of the same types of goods belonging to the same industry (such as automobile parts or machinery)—accounted for a very substantial part of those exchanges: over two-thirds of all trade among developed nations by the middle of the 1970s. By contrast, OECD countries stayed disconnected from Eastern Europe, at that time under Soviet control. Only three percent of all their exports ended up going to the Socialist bloc in 1980. Likewise, trade with developing nations remained of secondary importance to advanced countries. In 1980, the sum of all exports from developing to developed nations represented less than twenty percent of all world exports. More crucially, OECD imports from Africa, Asia, and Latin America were highly skewed in content: they were essentially limited to primary goods. Manufacturing products accounted for just five percent of all exports from developing to developed countries in 1955. And they were still a meager fifteen percent of all their exports as late as 1980 (Wood 1994; UNCTAD 2005). In short, the advanced world constituted an "isolated core" or, in the words of British economist Adrian Wood, a "manufacturing autarky" vis-à-vis the rest of the world (Wood 1994, 40).

Within the rich core, which was tightly interconnected through intra-industry trade, workers were relatively homogeneous in their qualifications and earned comparable wages. By contrast, their potential counterparts in the periphery received much lower salaries. In 1975, for example, the hourly compensation cost (that is, wages, benefits, and taxes) of an American or German production worker in manufacturing was twenty times higher than that of a Sri Lankan production worker in the same sector (US Bureau of Labor Statistics 2004, table 1). In principle, that should have lured American, European, and Japanese firms to locate part or all of their production in the poor countries. But a combination of weak property rights and low literacy rates in the developing world and high costs incurred coordinating and monitoring production across continents deterred investment flows from rich to poor countries. In 1980, developing countries only received 13.6 percent of the world's foreign direct investment (UNCTAD 2016). Most of this was circumscribed to the extraction of minerals. Precisely because the output of foreign manufacturing plants in the developing periphery was minimal as a share of world industrial production and trade, the blue-collar working class of the capitalist core was effectively shielded from any competition from the labor force in the "periphery" during most of the Cold War period. As a result, the globalization in place during the postwar era remained relatively innocuous—at least for the average industrial worker in the developed world.

The isolation of the industrial core with respect to the developing periphery started to break down in the 1970s following a sharp fall in transportation and communication costs. The introduction of standardized steel containers in the 1960s multiplied the productivity of dock labor by a factor of seventeen and, by reducing "pilferage, damage and theft that were so common in the age of break-bulk shipping," slashed insurance costs by more than eighty percent in just five years (Bernhofen, El-Sahli, and Kneller 2016, 39). In addition, air shipping rates fell from $3.87 per ton-kilometer in 1955 to less than $1 in 1972, and then more gradually to under $0.30 in 2004 (all in constant US dollars of 2000). Even though air transport was still more expensive than maritime cargo, it had the advantage of delivering goods in a certain and timely fashion, enabling firms to adjust their shipments to the needs of their processing plants and to the fluctuations of consumer markets. The air share of imports into the United States (excluding trade with Canada and Mexico) grew from none in 1950 to 31.5 percent in 2004. The share of US exports (outside North America) shipped by air rose from 0 percent to 52.8 percent over the same period (Hummels 2007). With faster ocean speed and the extensive use of air cargo, average shipping time across the world was cut by almost four in a period of fifty years: from 40 days in 1950 to 10.5 days in 1998—a change equivalent to slashing tariffs from 20 to 5.2 percent (Hummels and Schaur 2013).

In turn, a rapid improvement in telecommunications technologies, the diffusion of the personal computer, and the invention of the Internet reduced the costs of managing all the tasks involved in any production process substantially. When added to the decline in transportation costs, the increasing ability to coordinate any off-site tasks had momentous consequences for the spatial location of factories and the organization of firms. Under the Manchester and Detroit models, the factory was the firm. As examined earlier in this book, modern industry resulted from the combination of three things. First, splitting the process of production into a set of highly specialized tasks to maximize economic efficiency and output. Second, mechanizing as many of those tasks as possible. Last, but not least, clustering them in a relatively small space—the factory plant, Marx's mechanical monster—to effectively monitor the effort and diligence of workers, minimize energy consumption and manufacturing time, and ensure the fabrication of fully standardized goods. As transportation and communication costs tumbled down, however, the need to centralize all of a firm's activities in a single factory or a spatially connected set of processing plants, headquarters, and distribution centers fell accordingly. Companies could locate different steps of their production process in different countries to exploit the comparative advantages of each of them, because the costs of managerial control and production coordination had become much lower.

Two political developments reinforced the process of globalization triggered by the fall in communication and transportation costs. Tariff reductions in the developing world bolstered the decisions of companies to either relocate production or subcontract tasks outside the OECD's "industrial core": the average tariff rate in developing nations, which had peaked at twenty percent in 1978, fell from around eighteen percent in 1986 to ten percent in 1994.[6] In addition, the failure of Maoism and the collapse of the Soviet Union made available vast geographic areas into which Western multinationals could move their industrial operations to minimize production costs.[7]

Given the distribution of skills and wages across the globe, a natural way to unbundle production operations consisted in maintaining high-skilled, highly paid tasks in advanced countries while moving unskilled, low-wage activities to developing economies. More precisely, a company situated in an OECD nation could keep the operations of product development and marketing as well as the control of higher-end sales and distribution in its original headquarters, but relocate the manufacturing stage of production abroad. There, it could either build factories under its direct control or subcontract specialized foreign suppliers. Examples of that unbundling strategy abound. In its 2012 financial report filed with the Securities and Exchange Commission, Nike indicated that "our principal business activity is the design, development, and worldwide marketing and selling of high quality footwear, apparel, equipment, accessories, and services," adding that "virtually all of our footwear is produced by factories we contract with outside of the United States" (quoted in Bayard, Byrne, and Smith 2015, 85). Car companies like Honda and BMW outsourced the fabrication of components to subcontractors in Vietnam and India (Baldwin 2016). After Apple started making Apple II computers in Texas and Ireland in 1980, it kept opening new manufacturing plants in the United States until the middle of the 1990s. However, from 1996 it gradually shifted their fabrication abroad, until it closed its last American factory in 2004 (*ibid.*). Intel prints its circuits on large disks of silicon in Ireland, Israel, the United States, and, more recently, China, while locating its assembly and test sites in China, Costa Rica, Malaysia, and Vietnam (Krugman 2008; Intel [2011]).

What the literature has labeled "factoryless manufacturing" or "factoryless good producing" firms (Bernard and Fort 2015)—that is, those firms that perform all preproduction activities (such as design and engineering) in their headquarters' country while conducting all their production activities abroad (directly or through purchases of contract manufacturing services)—had already emerged in the US apparel sector in the 1950s. However, they spread much more widely into other sectors in the wake of the transportation and information revolution a few decades later: from the consumer goods industry, such as toys, in the 1970s to the production of semiconductors and final goods such as electronics at the turn of the twenty-first century.[8] According to Hanson, Mataloni, and Slaughter (2005), US multinational corporations account for half of all American exports. Within manufacturing, more than ninety percent of their exports to their foreign manufacturing affiliates turn out to be inputs for further processing. Based on the 2012 annual reports of all companies listed in the Standard and Poor (S&P) 500, Bayard, Byrne, and Smith (2015) note that almost half of them engage in some kind of factoryless manufacturing.

The extent of production fragmentation, also referred to as vertical specialization in the literature, varies quite heavily by sector. The share of S&P 500 companies employing factoryless manufacturing is high in the case of toys and games and apparel (one hundred percent), the electronic-components sector (ninety-four percent), computers and communications equipment (eighty-two percent), and pharmaceuticals and medicine (seventy percent), and moderate for food, beverage, and tobacco (fifty-two percent); paper, plastic, and wood products (forty-five percent); nonpharmaceutical chemicals and other final elec-tronics (thirty-seven percent). In Japan, about one-quarter of all firms had offshored production by the middle of the 2000s (Ando and Kimura 2011). In Germany, about one-quarter of all companies and close to sixty percent of large companies (those with five hundred or more employees) had done so too (Kinkel, Lay, and Maloca 2007).[9]

We find the same kind of evidence about the integration of markets at the international level when we look at this process from the perspective of developing economies and the extent to which they rely on the purchase of imported products to pro-duce final goods to be exported. In 2002, China's imported inputs accounted for 35.9 percent of all Chinese exports to the world. Again, the import context of exports varied by sector. China's most vertically specialized industries were in the plastics, steel-processing, communications-equipment, industrial-machinery, metal-products, and electronic-computers sectors—where im-ported intermediate inputs were equivalent to between fifty-two and seventy-six percent of the value of Chinese exports (Dean, Fung, and Wang 2011).

The process of vertical specialization within multinational firms, as well as the expansion of exporting domestic companies exploiting developing countries' comparative advantage in un-skilled labor, resulted in the rise of a hyperglobalized world. World output tripled in real terms between 1970 and 2015. Foreign direct investment and world trade, which had essentially tracked global GDP until the middle of the 1980s, grew at a much faster pace afterward. Foreign direct investment leapt up by a factor of five from US\$290 billion in 1985 to US\$1.56 trillion in 2015—and from 0.5 to 2.5 percent of world GDP. From 1980 to 2011, world mer-chandise exports quadrupled in real terms. Exports of manufac-turing goods multiplied by six (World Trade Organization 2013). With trade rising faster than world output, the value of exports expanded from sixteen percent to thirty percent of world GDP in the same period.

The growth of foreign direct investment was mostly driven by outward capital flow from the industrial core to the developing periphery. Foreign direct investment to developing economies rose from 13.5 percent of total foreign direct investment in 1980 to 44.4 percent of total investment in 2011. The geographic origin of exports changed even more dramatically. Exports from developing countries as a share of all world exports went up from a third to almost half, mostly boosted by East Asian countries. As a fraction of all exports by developing nations, the latter's exports rose from almost 12 percent in 1965 to 55 percent in 2003. Sectorwise, the industrial sector drove the expansion of world trade. Manufactured goods, which represented at most 15 percent of all the exports of developing countries until 1980, accounted for about 50 percent of all their exports in 1989 and over three-quarters by 2003 (Wood 1994; UNCTAD 2005). Advanced nations switched from being pure industrial exporters up to the 1970s to importing manufactures from the South: manufactured goods from developing economies jumped from being less than 4 percent of all OECD imports in 1965 to almost one-quarter in the early 2000s (UNCTAD 2005).

ICTs, Globalization, and the Evolution of Employment. The precise effect of vertical specialization and a rising manufacturing sector in parts of the developing world, especially East Asia, on the employment structure of the old industrial core has been the object of considerable controversy. Estimations about the exact number of jobs lost due to changing trade flows have varied as a function of the methodology employed and the period under observation. The first analyses of the effects of foreign competition from developing countries on employment, which were done in the late 1980s and early 1990s, attributed about ten percent of the overall fall in demand for unskilled labor in advanced countries to trade (Freeman 1995). Later work by British economist Adrian Wood estimated that trade explained about half of all the drop in demand for unskilled labor. Very recent research, which tends to rely on a longer span of time, seems to be settling for

intermediate figures. Rising import competition from China may
have accounted for ten percent of all direct job losses in the American manufacturing sector in the last fifteen years, and for twenty
percent of all indirect job losses (due to its impact on suppliers,
and so on) (Autor, Dorn, and Hanson 2015).

Recent work by Dutch economists Bart Los, Marcel Timmer,
and Gaaitzen De Vries (2014), who rely on detailed information
from the World Input-Output Tables, allows us to examine simultaneously the impacts of direct technological change (i.e. the
substitution of capital for labor) and globalization (through the international reallocation of production) on employment. Table 4.1
reproduces their results for changes in job demand (by skill type)
for the EU15 (the fifteen first members of the European Union),
the United States, and Japan during the period from 1995 to 2008
resulting from three economic forces: first, strict technological
change making labor more efficient and therefore depressing labor
demand; second, changing trade flows as a result of either a change
in the location of production of intermediate goods purchased
by domestic firms to make final goods and services or the relocation of the plants were production was finally completed;[10] third,
changes in the level of consumption (with consumers spending
more or less over time) as well as in the composition of the budgets of consumers (for example, substituting Catalan grenaches
for Belgian beers).

The members of EU15 (essentially, Western Europe) created
over 26 million jobs in net terms from 1995 to 2008 (column
2). That result was the outcome of two opposing forces. On the
one hand, stronger consumer demand (at home and abroad) for
European products led to the generation of 54.4 million jobs
(column 5). On the other hand, strict laborsaving technological
progress reduced the demand for labor by almost 16.8 million
jobs (column 3). Likewise, changes in the location of intermediate and final goods production depressed labor demand in
the EU15 area—by about 11.4 million jobs (column 4). In other
words, locational decisions accounted for about forty percent of

TABLE 4.1. Changes in Overall Labor Demand (in Million Jobs) by Skill Type, 1995–2008

| Skill Type | Net Job Changes | CAUSE OF JOB LOSSES | | |
		Technology	Trade	Consumption
EU15	All	26.3	−16.8	−11.4	54.4
	High	2.6	−8.9	−1.0	12.5
	Medium	14.4	−5.1	−3.9	23.4
	Low	−8.6	−20.7	−6.5	18.5
Japan	All	−3.8	−5.0	−2.5	3.7
	High	4.1	3.5	−0.4	1.0
	Medium	−2.1	−3.9	−0.7	2.6
	Low	−5.9	−4.5	−1.4	0.0
United States	All	17.8	−29.8	−8.0	55.6
	High	13.2	−0.8	−2.0	16.0
	Medium	5.5	−24.2	−4.7	34.4
	Low	−0.9	−4.8	−1.3	5.1

Source: Los, Timmer, and De Vries (2014, table 1).

all job losses. The remaining sixty percent came from the application of laborsaving technologies in plants and offices remaining in the EU15 space.

The evolution of Japan and the United States tells a similar story. In both countries, growing consumption led to more jobs. By contrast, technological change and the relocation of production abroad reduced labor demand. Due to a deflationary economy and a shrinking population, Japanese consumption could not compensate for technology- and trade-induced job losses. As a result, Japan lost 3.8 million jobs in net terms. Demand for American products and services resulted in the creation of 55.6 million new jobs—a figure similar to Europe's. However, the fall in labor demand due to technological change and trade was higher in the United States than in the European Union by almost 10 million jobs—probably owing to the technological leadership and labor-market flexibility of the former. Production relocation accounted for twenty percent of that fall.

It is worth emphasizing that the employment effects of technological change varied with the skill content of jobs. ICTs boosted
the demand for high-skilled occupations in Europe (9 million)
and Japan (3.5 million) and had a minimal negative effect on high-
skilled jobs in the United States, perhaps because most of their
positive impact had run its full course in the ICT leader in previous years. By contrast, they caused a dramatic drop in the demand
for semiskilled and unskilled jobs everywhere—over 25 million
in the EU15, over 8 million in Japan, and more than 29 million in
the United States.

The shift in the geographic location of production reduced the
demand for all kinds of job categories. However, in line with the
new international division of labor, in which developing nations
were now housing low-value-added tasks in the production chain,
most of the decline in labor demand in advanced nations was concentrated in semiskilled and unskilled jobs: ninety-one percent in
Europe, eighty-five percent in Japan, and seventy-four percent in
the United States.

Wage Polarization

As had happened with the transition from the Manchester factory to Ford's assembly line, the new ICTs introduced in the
1970s and 1980s reshaped the existing distribution of earnings in
the advanced world. But the identities of the winners and losers turned out to be radically different. The technological change
brought about by Detroit capitalism had made the central mass of
the labor force—semiskilled blue-collar workers and white-collar
employees—complementary to capital and, as a result, the direct
beneficiaries of the strong economic growth of the twentieth century. By contrast, Silicon Valley, with its progressive substitution
of machines for routinizable jobs and the relocation of jobs to
newly emerging economies, benefited highly educated individuals
while arguably depriving other workers of the productivity gains
of the computer revolution.

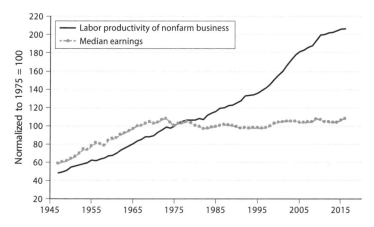

FIGURE 4.3 Evolution of labor productivity and median earnings in the United States, 1947–2016. Source: US Bureau of Labor Statistics, www.bls.gov/data.

Figure 4.3 shows the evolution of labor productivity in non-farming business and weekly earnings for the median US employee (i.e., the employee at the fiftieth percentile in the whole earnings distribution) from 1947 to 2016. Values are normalized to 100 for the year 1975 for comparability reasons. As we already saw in chapter 3, productivity and earnings increased at the same rate during the postwar period—until about the middle of the 1970s. Afterward, however, their evolution diverged starkly. On average, US labor productivity continued to grow at a similar rate as in the postwar period, doubling between 1975 and 2016. Median earnings, now unhinged from productivity growth, remained flat throughout all the period following the oil shocks of the 1970s.

That development was not exclusive to the United States. Figure 4.4 graphs the evolution of both labor productivity in the manufacturing sector and median earnings in France, Japan, and the United Kingdom from 1970 to 2007. Although the period shown is shorter than that for the United States in figure 4.3 owing to data availability constraints, the graphs reveals the same trends. Productivity and income grew in parallel until the late 1970s. Afterward, they moved apart from each other. While labor

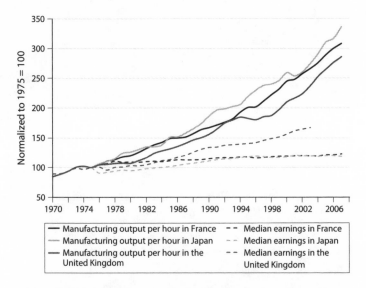

FIGURE 4.4 Evolution of labor productivity and median earnings in France, Japan, and the United Kingdom, 1970–2007. Sources: output, US Bureau of Labor Statistics, www.bls.gov/data; earnings, OECD, https://data.oecd.org.

productivity in manufacturing tripled in three decades, median earnings hardly changed.

We can examine the differential impact of Silicon Valley's technologies on salaries with the aid of figure 4.5, which plots the evolution of weekly earnings of full-time male workers by different levels of education in the United States from 1963 to 2012. Earnings, reported in constant dollars of 2012, are displayed on the vertical axis. The graph draws a horizontal dotted line equivalent to the earnings of a high-school dropout in 1963. Up until the middle of the 1970s, all education groups enjoyed relatively similar levels of wage growth. The average weekly earnings of a high-school dropout rose almost twenty percent in real terms—from $554 in 1963 to $652 in 1979. Earnings for individuals with completed college degrees grew at the exactly same rate. The year 1980 proved, however, to be a dramatic turning point. Salaries of high-school dropouts began to fall in real terms. In 2012 a high-school dropout

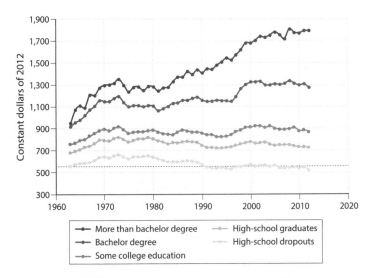

FIGURE 4.5 Real weekly earnings of full-time US male workers by education, 1963–2012. Earnings are reported in constant dollars of 2012. The horizontal dotted line indicates the earnings of a high-school dropout in 1963. Source: Autor (2014).

was making ninety-three percent of what he would have earned half a century earlier. Among individuals with high-school diplomas, labor earnings stagnated—they were only six percent higher in 2012 than in 1963. Earnings growth was only marginally better among men with some college years—their weekly earnings were fourteen percentage points higher at the end of the period.

The replacement of routine tasks with computers pushed a fraction of middle-skilled workers out of their former occupations, forcing them to adjust their wages in response to a shrinking pool of jobs and, not infrequently, to take less well paid routine jobs. That growing labor competition from semiskilled workers then interacted with the final computerization of a considerable number of manufacturing tasks to level out the wages for low-skilled jobs. The forces of globalization also contributed to slowing down salary growth. The development of vertical specialization at the international level, with an increasing number of firms outsourcing their labor-intensive intermediate and final goods production *why?*

to low-wage countries, reinforced the downward pressure on the salaries of both semiskilled and unskilled employees.[11]

Strong migratory flows may have also affected the wages of natives by reshaping the pool of available workers. In the United States alone, the number of foreign-born individuals grew from about 24.5 million in 1995 to 42.3 million in 2014. Estimates of the effect of immigration on wages vary widely—mostly as a result of the theoretical assumptions and methods employed by different economists. Its overall effect on the wages of natives seems to have been small. However, immigration appears to have pushed wages downward for those workers who are closer in nature to and therefore in more direct competition with low-educated immigrants from developing economies: prior immigrants, as well as American-born individuals with a high-school diploma or less. The most pessimistic studies calculate that a 1 percent increase in the labor share of immigrants reduced the wages for native high-school-dropouts by 0.9 percent. Most research, however, puts the effect at a much smaller fraction of that number.[12]

In contrast to the anemic growth of non-college-diploma salaries, the earnings of highly educated men grew smartly over the entire period. Men with bachelor degrees earned forty percent more in real terms in 2012 than in 1963. Men with postgraduate education doubled their average salaries over that fifty-year period. Although not reproduced here, weekly earnings among US full-time female employees evolved in a similar manner.[13] Such change appeared to be directly related to the information and communications technological revolution. Demand for more-skilled workers increased in those industries and companies that invested in ICT more heavily.[14] Salaries did too: using individual-level data for the United States, Cortes (2016) has recently estimated that wages fell by seventeen percent in routine-task-intensive jobs, and grew by twenty-five percent in nonroutine abstract or cognitive occupations between 1976 and 2007.[15]

Higher demand for highly educated employees could have spurred a higher supply of college-degree individuals. That, in turn, would have moderated wage rises for educated employees and spread the benefits of the new ICTs to a larger number of individuals. In a way, that is what happened under the model of Detroit capitalism, where a rising demand for semiskilled workers was followed by rapid growth in the number of high-school graduates. A balanced rise of both labor demand and labor supply then distributed, across a broad swath of the population, the productivity gains generated by the introduction of assembly lines and batch-production machines and the rise of administrative jobs in large corporations.

Unfortunately, things have worked out differently in the last four decades. In the United States, the number of college-educated individuals grew rapidly in the 1960s and 1970s, boosted by the postwar demographic boom and, in part, by men looking to avoid the Vietnam War draft. However, it slowed down considerably afterward. In the wake of the employment effects of the computer revolution, a relatively fixed pool of highly skilled workers entailed a growing wage premium for graduate and postgraduate individuals.

Information on the evolution of earnings by educational level is not as detailed for Europe as for the United States. But we have enough data to examine the evolution of the distribution of wages in both continents during the last few decades. Figure 4.6 shows male gross wages (that is, before taxes and transfers) at the tenth, fiftieth, and ninetieth percentiles of the wage distribution in the economies of France, Japan, Sweden, the United Kingdom, and the United States in both the mid-1970s and early 2000s. The figure reports the wages (adjusted for inflation) as a multiple of the wage of the individual at the tenth percentile of the wage distribution in each country in the year 1975.

The extent of wage inequality varied across countries in the mid-1970s. It was relatively high in France and the United States, and much lower in Japan, Sweden, and the United Kingdom. In 1975 the US median wage (the wage at the fiftieth percentile of the wage distribution) was 1.93 times larger than the wage of a

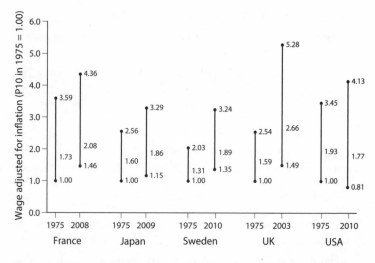

FIGURE 4.6 Male gross wages at the tenth, fiftieth, and ninetieth percentiles of the wage distribution. Wages are adjusted for inflation and shown as a multiple of the wage of an individual at the tenth percentile (P10) of the wage distribution in each country in 1975. Source: OECD Statistics, https://data.oecd.org.

worker at the tenth percentile of the wage distribution. In turn, the wage for a US worker in the ninetieth percentile was 3.45 times the wage of a worker in the tenth percentile. Wage dispersion was even higher in France: a worker in the ninetieth percentile earned 3.59 times more than one in the tenth percentile. By contrast, in Sweden, which, as discussed in chapter 3, was experimenting with extremely equalizing wage agreements at the time, an individual at the ninetieth percentile only made twice as much as one in the tenth percentile.

In the following decades, differences in the wage distribution increased everywhere. In the United States, while the wages earned by individuals in the bottom half of the distribution collapsed, those received by individuals in the ninetieth percentile of the wage distribution grew faster than the rest and ended up being 4.13 times higher in 2010 than the baseline wage (at the tenth percentile) of 1975. Japan, Sweden, and the United Kingdom also experienced considerable wage polarization. Although low and median wages (those at the tenth and fiftieth percentile respectively) did better than in the United States, they rose at a slow pace—by less than one percent annually. By contrast, wages received by individuals in the ninetieth percentile of the wage distribution grew quickly, so that by the early 2000s they were almost 5.3 times higher than the low (tenth percentile) wage in Britain in 1975, 3.3 times higher in Japan, and 3.2 times higher in Sweden. As a result, the absolute distance between the wages in the ninetieth percentile and those in the tenth percentile widened in all those economies between 1975 and the early 2000s—by about forty percent in Japan, eighty percent in Sweden, and over a factor of two in the United Kingdom. Starting from the highest level of wage dispersion, the rise of wage inequality was more subdued in France. Low wages grew at the British and Swedish pace. High wages rose as well, but at a slower pace. The gap between low and high wages only widened by about ten percent.

The Employment-Equality Dilemma

The ICTs of Silicon Valley capitalism (and the related process of hyperglobalization) "shocked" the employment performance and wage structure of all economies. Nonetheless, as we have seen in previous sections, the breadth and depth of that shock differed across countries. Understanding the sources of those differences is valuable in itself. But, it has an additional important advantage: we can draw upon the past and current experiences of different countries to inform our responses to the future challenges imposed by automation and globalization (as I do in chapter 6).

Figure 4.7 offers a stylized graph to understand, in a simple manner, the interaction between domestic conditions—primarily the educational composition of the workforce and the institutions that regulated the labor market in each country—and the changes brought about by Silicon Valley capitalism.[16] Figure 4.7A represents an economy before the Silicon Valley shock. The horizontal axis depicts the level of skills of any given individual, going from

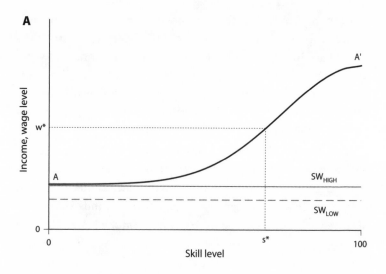

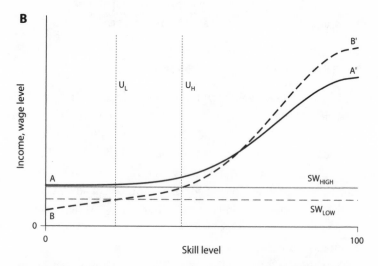

FIGURE 4.7 Wage structure in (A) a pre–Silicon Valley economy, and (B) a Silicon Valley economy. The curve AA' represents the correspondence between skill level and wage: skill level s* corresponds to wage w*. This curve becomes steeper, BB', following a shock to the skills-wage relation due to technological change and globalization. SW_{HIGH}, level of high social wage; SW_{LOW}, level of low social wage; U_H, level of unemployment following a shock to the skills-wage relation in a high-social-wage economy; U_L, the corresponding level in a low-social-wage economy. Sources: Boix (1998) and Adserà and Boix (2000).

none (left-hand side) to high (right-hand side). The vertical axis represents the wage associated with each level of skill (and, more generally, as we will see, individual income).

Figure 4.7A plots two lines: the skill-wage schedule AA' and the social-wage schedule SW. AA' represents the correspondence between a given level of skills and the wage paid to workers: for example, skill level s* corresponds to the wage w*. The relationship is a positive one: a higher skill level makes workers more productive and firms more willing to pay higher wages. The "social-wage" schedule represents a minimum threshold below which no individual income is allowed to fall in that particular economy. The social wage may be thought of as a minimum wage regulated by law. It can be the result of a national wage floor negotiated by trade unions and applying to all workers. Finally, it may also consist of some cash paid or goods and services provided by the state to individuals to make sure no person lives in poverty or under conditions that are deemed socially unacceptable. Unemployment benefits are the standard and most extended form of social wage across advanced democracies: they provide a fixed source of income to make up for a temporary job loss. But the social wage may also include supplementary services, ranging from food stamps to free medical care and subsidized housing, given to some individuals—in the graph, those who are the least advantaged or skilled.

The social wage varies with each country's policies and institutions. For the sake of the discussion, figure 4.7A shows two social wages: a generous one (SW_{HIGH}) and a low one (SW_{LOW}). In both cases, the social wage remains below the wage received by the least-skilled individual. In a situation of full employment (which is the one implicitly drawn here), no person has any incentive to stop working to receive the social wage instead.[17] In that instance, the full spread (on the vertical axis) of the schedule AA' defines the level of (pretax) income inequality (provided there are no rents from capital). In turn, when there is a temporary economic shock that results in some involuntary unemployment, those individuals who lose their jobs now receive the social wage (normally in the form of unemployment benefits). The spread of wages (a crude measure of inequality) remains unchanged in a high-social-wage economy and it increases, marginally, in a low-social-wage economy.

Figure 4.7B shows the effect of a shock to the skills-wage relation that approximates the one that has taken place in the last few decades. The old schedule AA' shifts to a steeper schedule, BB', pulled by the following forces. On the one hand, a process of capital-labor substitution pushes the wages for medium-skilled (routinizable) jobs downward. A growing supply of unskilled labor (due to offshoring or to immigration) may also depress the wages for low-skilled occupations. Workers have the same skills they had before but, competing against machines or, simply, more people, are paid less by firms. On the other hand, the wage premium being paid to high-skilled workers rises with the ICT revolution. Without any social wage in place, those changes would result in a wider (pretax) income distribution. The presence of a social wage, however, moderates the income and inequality impact of the Silicon Valley shock. By how much it does so will depend on the level of social wage. In countries where the social wage is low, the final incomes of low-skilled individuals drop and inequality increases considerably—driven by changes at both the lower and the higher ends of the distribution. That has been the case in the United States, where wages for those at the tenth percentile fell by almost twenty percent in real terms (figure 4.6) while high earnings rose also by about twenty percent. In those countries where the social wage is more generous, low-skilled workers may not see their final incomes fall. Income inequality still rises, but it does mostly owing to higher earnings among very skilled or educated workers.

Curbing inequality is not cost free. In a high-social-wage economy, low-skilled, low-paid jobs are effectively pushed out of the labor market. Firms have few incentives to offer jobs compensated at a rate (determined through a regulated minimum wage or through wage negotiations) above the level set in a competitive market. Workers do not have any incentive either to take jobs that pay less than the social wage (plus the cost of searching for a job). The unemployment rate rises to U_H.[18] By contrast, in an economy with a low social wage, unemployment stabilizes at U_L. In other words, in the wake of the Silicon Valley shock, countries experience an employment-equality trade-off.[19] Allowing economies to adjust to technological change and globalization results in a process of income polarization. Sustaining past levels of inequality leads to unemployment and less economic dynamism.

Advanced economies differed substantially in their respective levels of minimum wages, the nature of wage agreements, and the generosity of their welfare states during the twentieth century. As discussed in chapter 3, before World War Two and mostly throughout the postwar period, the labor markets and wage-bargaining systems of advanced industrial economies gradually sorted out, generally speaking, into two groups: nations like the United States, where wages were set at the individual and company level; and countries, mostly continental European economies, where employers and workers negotiated wages and labor conditions at the industry and national level.

Until the early 1960s, the dispersion of earnings was broadly unrelated to the type of wage-bargaining system—either decentralized or centralized—in place (cf. figure 3.7). In the context of the Detroit model, defined by the assembly line and the multiplication of interchangeable (and similar) tasks and jobs, most of the variation in (a relatively compressed) wage structure responded to the distribution of the level of educational attainment within the labor force. However, starting in the second half of the 1960s, countries with centralized wage institutions moved toward flatter, more equal wage distributions. By 1980, the level of earnings inequality (measured through the earnings inequality ratio introduced in chapter 3) was almost twenty percent lower in centralized economies than in decentralized bargaining systems. That was, arguably, the result of having more combative trade unions in a context of labor demand outstripping labor supply.

The technological and globalization shocks that took place in the following decades simply intensified the differences between wage bargaining systems. In decentralized systems, labor markets were highly flexible and wages grew quickly among the highly educated. By contrast, wage dispersion remained mostly unchanged in economies where labor agreements were made at either the industry or the national level. Just before the Great Recession of 2007, the average level of earnings inequality was twenty-five percent higher in decentralized markets. Those differences were reinforced by the welfare state in economies with nationally coordinated wage systems. In economies with decentralized wage-bargaining systems, public expenditure and social security transfers averaged 41.7 and 11.8 percent of GDP respectively in 1990–99. In countries with semicentralized or centralized wage-bargaining institutions, they averaged 49.6 and 15.6 percent of GDP in the same decade.[20]

Those divergent inequality paths were mirrored by divergent employment paths. In the United States as well as those economies that either had institutions closer to the American model of flexible, individual-level wage negotiations or decided to introduce them, the downward adjustment in the wages of low or semiskilled workers came hand in hand with positive employment growth in the private sector. Between 1980 and 2006, the size of the American workforce employed in the private sector grew by over thirty-five million jobs in net terms (that is, jobs created minus jobs lost)—or an average annual growth rate of 1.5 percent. Private employment expanded at similar rates in Canada and Britain in the same period. By contrast, in "regulated" economies, where low wages sometimes rose at the same rate that high wages did, the flip side of earnings equality was a slowdown in the generation of jobs in the private sector. Private-employment growth ranged between a quarter and a half of the rates in Anglo-American economies.

To capture that employment-equality trade-off, figure 4.8 plots the relative change in private-sector jobs between the late 1970s and the early 2000s on the vertical axis. For example, in the United

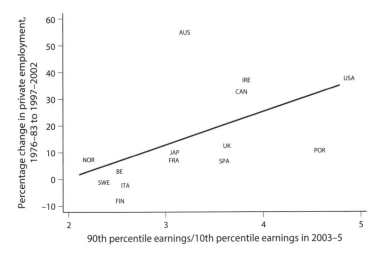

FIGURE 4.8 Earnings dispersion and creation of private employment. AUS, Australia; BE, Belgium; CAN, Canada; FIN, Finland; FRA, France; IRE, Ireland; ITA, Italy; JAP, Japan; NOR, Norway; POR, Portugal; SPA, Spain; SWE, Sweden; UK, United Kingdom; USA, United States. Sources: employment, System of National Accounts, SNA-OECD, https://data.oecd.org, and data kindly shared by Thomas Cusack at the Science Center, Berlin; earnings, chapter 3.

States the total number of jobs in the private sector grew from around 83 to over 115 million jobs during that period of time—that is, a thirty-eight percent increase. In Sweden, they remained practically unchanged at 2.9 million. The horizontal axis displays the ratio between earnings in the ninetieth percentile and in the tenth percentile in the overall earnings distribution just before the Great Recession of 2007, which should give us a good sense of each country's tolerance toward inequality.

The number of observations is not high—data are not available on all OECD countries for such long periods of time—but the pattern is straightforward. With the exception of Australia, which enjoyed an economic boom driven by strong foreign demand for its natural resources, there is a clear-cut correlation between earnings inequality and private-employment creation. Strong job growth, in countries such the United States, Canada, or Ireland, coincided with a wider earnings distribution. By contrast, economies with a more compressed earnings structure experienced negligible employment growth, such as Belgium, or even a decline in jobs in the private sector in net terms, such as Finland or Italy.

Faced with a trade-off between a wider dispersion of earnings and poorer employment performance, the different OECD countries embraced a somewhat diverse set of policy responses. Some governments chose to make labor markets more flexible in one or several dimensions: reducing the costs of hiring and firing borne by firms; dismantling corporatist wage-bargaining institutions in favor of decentralized, company-level negotiations; and, in some instances, directly reducing unemployment benefits and other forms of social spending. Thatcher's reforms in Britain in the 1980s were directly aimed at weakening trade unions, decentralizing the wage-bargaining system, and reinforcing the incentives to work. After defeating the National Union of Miners in 1984, the British government required strikes to be approved in secret ballots, subjected union officers to periodic reelection, abolished the closed-shop system, and empowered individuals to sue their own unions. Unemployment benefits were taxed, firms were exempted from following minimum wages set up in nationwide agreements, and the process of job dismissal was simplified and its costs for employers reduced. In the mid-2000s, Schroeder's red-green coalition passed a set of far-reaching labor-market reforms to adjust German industries to heightened international competition: unemployment benefits were tied to workfare programs; the level of income support for the long-term unemployed, now merged with social-assistance programs, was reduced; and new, more flexible forms of jobs were created.

Other countries prioritized, instead, the preservation of equality. But that entailed implementing a set of measures to offset tepid growth in private-sector jobs. The Netherlands made part-time work fiscally attractive. By the early 2010s, three-quarters of all Dutch women and one-quarter of Dutch men worked less than thirty-six hours a week. In France, successive governments bet on the expansion of different work-sharing schemes: center-right administrations incentivized early retirement with the aim of lowering youth unemployment; socialist cabinets reduced the working week. Scandinavian countries expanded public employment aggressively. Table 4.2 reports the levels of employment, separately, for the manufacturing sector, nonmanufacturing sectors (minus the public sector), the public sector, and the overall economy both in the late 1970s or early 1980s and in 2007—in the months leading up to the last Great Recession.[21] The countries selected are those for which we have long enough time series—but they are representative of the different paths taken across all advanced economies. The upper part of table 4.2 displays employment in each country and year as a percentage of the working-age population—that is, the population aged fifteen to sixty-four. The lower part of table 4.2 shows the levels of employment in absolute terms (in millions of jobs). For both parts of the table, the last four right-hand columns calculate the annual rate of change for each type of employment over the whole period (with respect to the level in the initial year). In the following paragraphs I will mainly discuss the results displayed in the upper part of the table.

In all countries without any exception, employment in the manufacturing sector declined both as a proportion of working-age population and in absolute terms—at an average rate of 1.5 percent every year. In the middle of the 1970s, the manufacturing sector employed almost one in five working-age individuals (except in the United States, where it employed 11.9 percent). That was certainly much lower than in the immediate postwar period, where up to one in three worked in the industry sector. But, thirty years later, only 10 percent or less of the working-age population—with an exceptionally high 15 percent in Germany—did.

By contrast, the trajectories of the nonmanufacturing and public-employment sectors differed considerably across economies. Accordingly, countries have been grouped in each part of the table as a function of their performance in those sectors. In the United States, Britain, and (unified) Germany, the share of

TABLE 4.2. Evolution of Total Employment by Sector, 1975–2007

	MANUFACTURING		NONMANUFACTURING (PRIVATE)		PUBLIC SECTOR		TOTAL EMPLOYMENT		MANUFACTURING	NONMANUFACTURING (PRIVATE)	PUBLIC SECTOR	TOTAL
	1975	2007	1975	2007	1975	2007	1975	2007				
	Employment as Percentage of Working-Age Population								*Yearly Change over Period*			
USA	11.9	8.0	44.3	55.7	10.2	11.0	66.4	74.7	-1.4	1.1	0.3	0.5
UK	21.8	9.3	34.3	49.3	15.1	14.3	71.2	72.9	-1.8	1.4	-0.2	0.1
Germany	20.5	15.4	38.0	46.0	9.1	8.3	67.6	69.7	-1.6	1.3	-0.5	0.2
France	17.6	9.8	36.5	40.7	11.0	14.9	65.1	65.4	-1.4	0.4	1.1	0.0
Denmark	16.3	9.4	39.6	42.2	17.1	23.7	73.0	75.3	-1.2	0.2	1.1	0.1
Norway	16.4	8.9	38.7	45.8	14.0	23.7	69.1	78.4	-1.4	0.6	2.2	0.4
Sweden	21.4	10.9	36.0	43.6	19.9	21.1	77.3	75.6	-1.5	0.7	0.2	-0.1
	Total Employment (in Millions)								*Yearly Change over Period*			
USA	18.5	16.3	68.7	108.9	15.8	22.2	103.0	147.4	-0.5	2.4	1.7	1.8
UK	7.6	3.7	12.1	19.9	5.3	5.6	25.0	29.2	-1.6	2.0	0.2	0.5
Germany	11.3	8.4	21.0	25.1	5.1	4.5	37.4	38.0	-1.6	1.2	-0.7	0.1
France	5.8	4.0	12.0	16.4	3.6	6.0	21.4	26.4	-1.0	1.1	2.1	0.7
Denmark	0.5	0.3	1.3	1.5	0.6	0.9	2.4	2.7	-1.0	0.5	1.6	0.4
Norway	0.4	0.3	1.0	1.4	0.4	0.7	1.7	2.4	-1.0	1.5	3.4	1.3
Sweden	1.1	0.7	1.9	2.6	1.0	1.3	4.1	4.5	-1.3	1.2	0.7	0.4

For data availability reasons, the series starts in 1983 for the United States, and in 1991 for (unified) Germany. It ends in 2010 for Denmark.

nonmanufacturing private employment (over working-age population) grew by more than 1 percent every year. As a fraction of the working-age population, the public employment sector shrank in both Germany and the United Kingdom. In the United States it increased slightly (at an annual rate of 0.3 percent), although the growth rate was still below the annual 0.5 percent increase in total employment over the working population. As a result, the nonmanufacturing private sector rose from one-third to about half of all the working population at the onset of the Great Recession. The relative size of the public sector did not vary with respect to the middle of the 1970s: it still employed about one-tenth of all individuals aged fifteen to sixty-four.

Denmark, Norway, and Sweden, which witnessed much lower increases in wage dispersion, offer a pointed contrast in their employment structure. Nonmanufacturing private employment grew at half the annual rate of the United States and the United Kingdom, or less. Public employment rose, instead, by 1.1 percent in Denmark and 2.2 percent in Norway. By the middle of the 2000s, almost a quarter of all the working-age population (or one in three of those employed) worked for the Danish and Norwegian public sectors. In Sweden, the public sector grew by a paltry 0.2 percent every year. Nevertheless, because it was already large in the 1970s, it employed over one-fifth of the working-age population in 2007. With private employment not expanding fast enough, total employment as a fraction of working-age population fell by 1.7 percentage points between 1975 and 2007.

In France, the share of public employment rose at 1.1 percent every year – a rate similar to Scandinavia's. Such strong growth, combined with some expansion of the share of nonmanufacturing private employment over the working-age population, compensated for the fall in manufacturing jobs. But it did not raise the share of total employment. As in many Mediterranean economies, where labor participation rates are below the OECD average, it remained about ten percentage points below the Anglo-American and Scandinavian total employment shares.

Alternative Explanations

Before exploring the political consequences of Silicon Valley capitalism in the next chapter, I discuss three alternative theories that have been proposed to explain the ongoing transformation of employment and the process of wage polarization: the dynamics of capitalism itself, Reagan and Thatcher's conservative policy turn of the early 1980s, and the policy influence of an increasingly powerful capitalist oligarchy.

The Collapse of Capitalism. A few authors portray today's growing inequality as one of the causes as well as the symptom of the imminent collapse of the capitalist system. In "How Will Capitalism End?" German sociologist Wolfgang Streeck writes that "the crash of 2008 was only the latest in a long sequence of political and economic disorders that began with the end of postwar prosperity in the mid-1970s" and that "have proved to be ever more severe, spreading more widely and rapidly through an increasingly interconnected global economy" (2014, 1). To save contemporary capitalism from its inner or structural contradictions (and also with the more prosaic goal of winning elections), Western governments engaged in the following policy sequence: first, they resorted to more public debt; next, they loosened up financial regulations to encourage the growth of private demand (and private debt); finally, they turned to heavy money printing. Each of those measures, implemented to maintain consumption (and therefore production) and to keep capitalists (and noncapitalists) happy, simply bought time while worsening the financial condition of states and the general public, to a point when the economy will eventually crash.

Although Streeck's theory has, with its preoccupation with the profligacy of contemporary capitalism, a Calvinist undertone to it, one can find similar predictions (albeit different in their internal mechanisms) about a final catastrophic moment for capitalism going back to, at least, Marx. Nevertheless, none of those past forecasts ever came to pass. A similar fate seems to await Streeck's for at least two reasons. On the one hand, employment and wages have changed in ways that cannot be explained by particular financial policies (or the dynamics of electoral competition); once again, they derive, instead, from a process of technological change— either directly (job automation) or indirectly (hyperglobalization induced by a fall in transportation and communication costs). On the other hand, Streeck's mechanism of a ballooning financial crisis (leading to a final crash of capitalism) is at odds with the fact that advanced capitalist countries differ considerably among themselves in terms of their current financial health, productivity, and level of employment.

Neoconservatism. A second explanation attributes the growing economic polarization of the last few decades directly to the explicit dismantlement of the economic policies of the postwar period following the triumph of Reagan and Thatcher in the early 1980s, and the gradual diffusion of the latter's economic measures to most European economies (as well as developing economies). After a turbulent decade defined by both accelerating inflation and high unemployment, voters switched their support to a set of reenergized conservative parties that, breaking free from the Keynesian consensus in place, pursued stringent monetary policies, deregulated labor markets, passed an array of measures to weaken unions, pressed for further trade liberalization, and dropped all restrictions on capital flows. It all amounted, in the words of Adam Przeworski (2017), to an "offensive by the Right ... premeditated, planned, vigorously promoted by all kinds of think-tanks, and coercively spread by the influence of the United States in the international financial institutions, codified as the 'Washington consensus'" (12)—something akin to "an *autogolpe* of the bourgeoisie," to bury the "democratic class compromise" of previous decades (9), defined by cooperation between unions (exercising wage restraint), capital (reinvesting profits and accepting high taxes), and governments (funding a generous welfare state).[22]

This explanation, however, runs into its own set of problems very quickly. The structure of employment shifted everywhere, regardless of the party in power. In the last few decades, middle-wage jobs have shrunk and high-wage jobs have expanded in countries as different as France, Sweden, and the United States (see figure 4.2 above). Likewise, median earnings stalled across all Western economies, again independently of the policies that were pursued (cf. figures 4.3 and 4.4).

That does not mean that politics was irrelevant. It probably mattered—but mostly in shaping the way in which different governments responded to the structural changes that emerged in the 1970s. Constrained by the employment-equality trade-off discussed earlier in the chapter, center-right policy makers (but also some left-wing governments operating in countries or at times defined by an acute jobs-equality trade-off) pursued promarket, deregulatory policies that heightened economic polarization. By contrast, center-left responses (and Christian democratic governments in high-value-added economies with a mild employment-equality trade-off) preferred to preserve equality even if that meant slowing down the generation of (private) employment.

The Top One Percent. A third explanation, which has gained some prominence among Anglo-American scholars and public opinion—particularly after the occupation of New York's Zuccotti Park by hundreds of activists rallying under the slogan "We are the 99%" in the fall of 2011—attributes the outcome of economic polarization to the power and resources of an elite of crony capitalists who, exploiting their privileged access to political power, have twisted policies and regulations to their advantage and, as a result, damaged the middle and working classes (Hacker and Pierson 2010; Reich 2015a).

Throughout the postwar era and until the early 1980s, the richest 1 percent of the US population earned around 8 percent of the national income. By 2010, their share of national income had more than doubled to 17.5 percent—similar to its peak in 1933. Moreover, income within the top 1 percent of the population became concentrated in a thin sliver of hyper-rich individuals. In 2010, the top 0.1 percent of the population earned two-fifths of all the income in the hands of the top 1 percent—equivalent to 7.7 percent of all US income.[23] Britain followed a similar trajectory: the share of national income in the hands of the top 1 percent rose from less than 6 percent in 1978 to 15 percent in 2007; the share of the top 0.1 percent climbed above 5 percent before the Great Recession. By contrast, in countries such as France, Germany, and Japan, the income share in the hands of the superwealthy remained flat or even fell.[24]

The differential performance of Anglo-American top incomes came hand in hand with extraordinary growth of the stock market, which in the United States rose from being equal to 40 percent of GDP in 1980 to 137 percent of GDP in 2015;[25] the formation of large investment corporations, such as pension funds;[26] and a rising demand for individuals needed to develop and manage sophisticated financial products. Average earnings for the top twenty-five hedge-fund managers quadrupled from $134 million in 2002 to $537 million in 2012 (in constant dollars of 2010). The sum of fees for venture-capital and private-equity firms grew from less than $2 billion in the late 1980s to about $34 billion in the late 2000s (Kaplan and Rauh 2013). More generally, value added per person, which can be thought of as a good approximation to the profitability of a given economic sector and, in principle, the compensation of its labor force, grew at a much faster rate in the financial sector than in the economy as a whole—at least in the United States.[27] Whereas value added per capita for the whole US economy increased at an annual rate of 1.2 percent from $72,000 in 1990 to $90,000 in 2008, the value added per person in the financial sector rose at an annual rate of 3.75 percent to $176,386 at the end of the period (Boix 2015). By contrast, in countries with smaller financial sectors, such as France and Germany, the value added per capita in finance expanded at an annual rate of 1 percent at most (Spence and Hlatshwayo 2011; Boix 2015).

The remuneration practices of the financial sector spilled over into the rest of the economy—at least in the United States. Financial products such as stock options, which are treated as wage and salary compensation when they are exercised, became a substantial component of executive pay after shareholders favored the introduction of equity-based pay to incentivize the performance of their companies' top managers, and several federal rules made stock options much more attractive from a taxation point of view. Stock options went from representing one-tenth of the median compensation of a CEO (in the S&P 500 firms) in 1980 to almost half of it in 2001 (Murphy 2013).[28] The median pay of an S&P 500 CEO rose from about $2 million in 1993 to $11 million in 2011 (all in constant dollars of 2010). Average earnings of lawyers at top law firms more than doubled from $0.7 million in 1994 to $1.6 million in 2010 (Kaplan and Rauh 2013).

The surge in executive compensation (partly due to the use of financial instruments) has been attributed to the capture of American regulatory bodies by the very wealthy, and the latter's pressure to loosen up a tight regulatory framework in the wake of the Great Depression. In 1975, the elimination of fixed commissions in the New York Stock Exchange lowered the cost of trading for large financial institutions, giving them a strong advantage vis-à-vis individual investors and boosting the market of derivative products such as stock options, equity swaps, and stock futures. After the US Department of Labor ruled in 1979 that risky investments were acceptable if they were part of a well-diversified portfolio, leading pension funds as well as large endowments started to invest in riskier intermediaries. The volume of those investments exploded from $5 billion in 1980 to $175 billion in 2000 (Rajan and Zingales 2003, 70–74). In the 1990s, Congress removed any restrictions on interstate banking and repealed the Glass-Steagall Act of 1933, which had separated commercial from investment banking. Overall, the percentage of US public equity owned by institutional investors rose from thirty percent in 1980 to sixty percent in 2000. The share of private investors declined proportionally. By 2010, the top US banks held fifty percent of all loans and all deposits—twice their share back in 1980. Arguably, that process of capture took place too in company boards, where increasingly powerful CEOs were able to influence and control their members. As claimed, among others, by Piketty (2014) and Reich (2015a), old informal norms that used to constrain executive pay to socially acceptable levels broke down in the context of an extremely bullish economy, and board directors proceeded to approve high compensation packages both for themselves and for their top management teams. Evidence on capture by the wealthy and by top professionals is, however, mixed. The astronomical growth in the earnings of financial managers and top corporate leaders may have just been the result of mounting intercompetition to attract talented professionals in a booming sector (Gabaix and Landier 2008; Mankiw 2013).[29] At the end of the day, the explosion of financial markets (and their concentration in the hands of large institutional investors) was underpinned and reinforced by the ICT revolution. By speeding up the collection of information and by reducing the costs of computational operations (in tasks such as risk assessment or the evaluation of credit scores of mortgage applicants), the new computer revolution enabled the emergence of new financial services, such as ATMs, debit cards, and online banking, and facilitated the formation of new investment products (Frame and White 2015), making the financial sector more productive overall.

Either way, that is, independently of whether pure competitive forces or the capture of the regulatory system and collusive behavior caused the extraordinary growth of income and wealth at the hands of the superwealthy in Anglo-American economies over the last few decades, the rise of the top one percent cannot explain, on its own, either the changing employment patterns or the entire shift in the wage structure (and, particularly, the stagnation of wages in the lower half of the income distribution) happening in almost all economies—including those where individuals in the top one percent have not benefited as much as they did in the United States or Britain. Once again, the mechanisms generated by the deeper and broader forces of technological change and hyperglobalization fit the empirical evidence much better. They also provide a much better grounding to make sense of the political changes triggered by Silicon Valley capitalism, which are examined in the next chapter.

5

Dire Straits

The technological and economic transformations spurred by Detroit capitalism reshaped—mostly over the span of one or two generations—the nature of politics in the advanced industrial world. The rapid expansion of the economy, a much higher rate of social mobility, and a secular trend toward a more equal distribution of earnings pacified the social and class struggles of the nineteenth century. Roosevelt's New Deal relied on the economic and productivity gains of the previous three decades to overcome the Great Depression and buttress public support for a free-market economy in the United States. Europe's postwar growth miracle put to rest the dramatic confrontations that had erupted in that continent during the interwar period. As affluence and relative equality became the new norm everywhere, Left and Right parties came to see democracy and capitalism as inextricably intertwined, converging in their policy promises and competing at the ballot box on the basis of the professionalism and competence of their leaders.

Likewise, the unfolding of Silicon Valley capitalism has transformed both public discourse and the political arena—albeit in a different, often opposite, direction. As both new ICTs and a much deeper form of globalization disrupted the employment and wage patterns that had prevailed during the twentieth century, the liberal postwar consensus looked increasingly fragile. A generalized pattern of attachment to parties and trade unions and of deference toward political elites gave way to a growing sense of mistrust and political alienation—mostly among the American and European working class. In the 1970s, at least fifty percent of respondents in surveys taken in countries as diverse as Austria, France, Germany, Sweden, and the United States believed that politicians cared about what people thought. Thirty years later, that proportion had plunged to thirty percent or even less (Dalton 2004, 26–30). Political mistrust eventually spilled over into actual political behavior. Electoral participation in Europe, which had peaked at over eighty percent during the Cold War, fell after 1980. By the early 2010s, almost one out of every three Europeans—most of them clustered within low-income strata and young cohorts—abstained in national elections. In due course, new populist parties sprang up, at the right and left tails of the political spectrum, to give voice to that growing number of unsatisfied voters. And, rattling the prevailing system of orderly alternation of mainstream parties in government, they threaten to reconfigure the structure and dynamics of political competition that has been in place since the end of World War Two.

Disaffected Democracies

Well after the effects of computerization and globalization percolated into the economy, hollowing the demand for semiskilled jobs and flattening wages for the bottom half of the income distribution, conservative, Christian democratic, and social democratic parties continued to run on their traditional, middle-of-the-road programs and to govern from the center of the policy space. Electoral politics retained its usual share of moderate ideological conflict and partisan discord. Center-right and center-left candidates still disagreed on the optimal level of taxes, the generosity of welfare spending, the type of macroeconomic policy, and, marginally, the extent of trade and financial integration. But they all ultimately subscribed to the key tenets of the political-economic model that had become ensconced in all advanced democracies: the program of classical liberalism—free markets and free trade—now embedded within a welfare state that minimized the risks of economic downturns and protected citizens from illness and aging, and integrated within an international framework that gave national governments enough autonomy to achieve full employment at home.

A fairly standard practice among social scientists to measure the ideological commitments of political parties consists in looking at their electoral manifestos to identify the issues they address and how they frame and respond to them. Following this strategy, figure 5.1A plots the average position of mainstream political parties in the advanced world in economic policy (excluding trade and migration) since the end of World War Two. Mainstream parties are those political organizations that embraced the economic and institutional architecture of the golden age of democratic capitalism, which political scientist John Ruggie (1982) coined as "embedded liberalism." I group them into four families: social democrats, Christian democrats, liberals, and conservatives. A higher number (reported in logged values) means that, on average, parties within a particular ideological family had a more promarket position, a stronger commitment to orthodox macroeconomic policies, and less sympathy for trade unions and the demands of labor.[1] Throughout the whole period under observation, the full span of partisan positions (i.e., including nonmainstream parties) ranged from −5.6 (the position of Norway's Socialist People's Party in 1990) to 3.89 (the position of Australia's National Country Party in 1981). However, mainstream parties were located within a much narrower band—between −2 and 0. In addition, their differences shrunk over time, particularly after both Christian democrats and social democrats tacked to the center in the late 1960s. By the early 2000s, the (average) economic positions of all mainstream parties were within a one-point range in the economic policy left–right scale.[2]

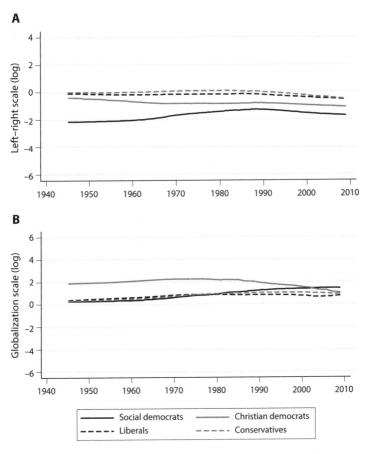

A

B

| Social democrats | Christian democrats |
| Liberals | Conservatives |

FIGURE 5.1 (*A*) Economic policy in party platforms 1945–2010; (*B*) globalization in party platforms 1945–2010. Source: Volkens et al. (2012).

Figure 5.1B plots the average positions on globalization of the same party families. This synthetic index is based on the number and type of references on trade openness, multiculturalism, and the European Union project in their electoral manifestos. A higher positive number implies stronger support for globalization.[3] The full range of party positions turns out to be wider than the previous one for economic policy—from a minimum of −4.76 (the case of France's National Front in 2008) to a maximum of 5.8

(Belgium's Reform Movement in 2010). Yet the differences among mainstream parties on globalization were even smaller than on economic policy. They fluctuated within a two-point band until the 1980s, and became negligible after Christian democratic parties, which had been the strongest supporters of open economies throughout the postwar period, veered toward slightly less pro-globalization policies.[4]

In light of the historical experience of advanced countries, embracing the program of embedded liberalism made economic and political sense. Twentieth-century democratic capitalism had proved to be both successful and resilient: it had delivered high growth, it had allowed governments to fund generous social programs, and it had sent its main political and economic competitor—communism—to the ash heap of history. Its accomplishments may explain also why policy makers (and voters) decided to double down on their support for free markets and open economies in response to the oil shocks of the 1970s and the first signs of structural change as well as a productivity slowdown in the 1980s. To jump-start growth, globalization was deepened through the substitution of the World Trade Organization for GATT, the signing of the North American Free Trade Agreement, the transformation of the European Common Market into the European Union and the latter's territorial expansion, and the introduction of the euro. In addition, labor markets and competition policy were made more flexible—particularly in Anglo-American economies.

Once the economic and social conditions that had led to the postwar consensus started to change, however, that quasi-universal commitment to the program of embedded liberalism proved precarious and, to some extent, politically dangerous. By opening a wedge between mainstream parties and a fraction of their traditional voters, it resulted in a substantial drop in the latter's political support for the former. Popular trust in the Western political establishment had reached record highs during the golden age of democratic capitalism. Figure 5.2 shows the evolution of the percentage of people who agreed with the statement

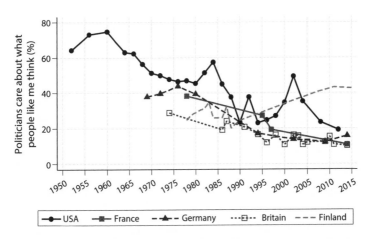

FIGURE 5.2 Political disaffection, 1952–2015. Sources: Finland, *Finnish Voter Barometers 1973–1990* and Finnish National Election Studies (1991, 2003, 2007, 2011, 2015); France, Enquêtes post-électorales françaises (1978, 1988, 1995, 1997) and European Social Survey (2014); Germany, Kaase, Schleth, and Wildenmann (2012) and GESIS-Leibniz-Institut für Sozialwissenschaften (2017); United Kingdom, Barnes and Kaase (2006), and the British Social Attitudes Surveys (1983–2014); United States, American National Election Studies and Stanford University (2015).

that politicians care about what people like them think, from the Cold War period until today. Long-run consistent series (i.e., relying on a statement with the same wording) are only available for a few countries. The question was asked for the first time in the United States in 1952. It was then added to national surveys (in that form or a similar one) in other major democracies in the late 1960s and early 1970s.[5]

Until the mid-1960s, more than sixty percent of Americans thought that politicians cared about their opinions. If anything, their confidence in politicians' responsiveness appears to have risen at the peak of the Cold War—by ten percentage points between 1952 and 1960. Coinciding with the Vietnam War and Watergate, it slid to slightly below fifty percent in the late 1960s. Nonetheless, those critical moments could not account, alone, for the steadily growing disaffection of public opinion toward its representatives. After a brief upturn in the early 1980s, the percentage

of American respondents who thought politicians cared plummeted to about twenty percent. It then remained at those levels,
excluding a short-lived upsurge around 9/11, for the next quarter
of a century. The same downward trend in political trust took place
in France, where the proportion of satisfied citizens dropped from
almost forty percent in 1978 to about ten percent in 2014; in Germany, where it fell from forty-three percent in 1976 to around
twenty percent in the 2010s; and in Britain, where in 2014 only ten
percent of respondents thought parties cared about their opinions.
Although they are not included in figure 5.2, Australia, Canada,
Italy, and Japan exhibit similar negative trends. By contrast, in
small countries the evolution of public opinion has turned out to
be more heterogeneous. Confidence levels declined in Austria and
Sweden but rose in both Finland, which is shown in figure 5.2, and
the Netherlands (Dalton 2004).

Given how generalized those downward trends were, it is difficult to attribute them to some idiosyncratic national characteristic
or singular political event. Moreover, as shown by a growing body
of research, the growth of voters' mistrust toward politicians was
not driven by the presence of a particular party in power or by the
vagaries of the business cycle (Pharr and Putnam 2000; Dalton
2004). Political trust did not pick up during the high-growth period
of the late 1990s and early 2000s. Approval rates toward politicians
were already at dismal levels just before the Great Recession of
2007. The rise of political disaffection coincided with much more
fundamental transformations: a permanent drop in the rate of economic growth and relatively flat median wages since the 1980s.

Political disaffection bred political disengagement. Figure 5.3
plots the proportion of nonvoters as well as the percentage of the
vote for both mainstream parties and extreme parties over the
whole electorate in legislative elections conducted in Western
Europe from 1918 until 2016. Again, mainstream parties include
all parties belonging to the conservative, Christian democratic,
liberal, or social democratic political families. Extreme parties
comprise both far-left organizations (mainly communist parties,

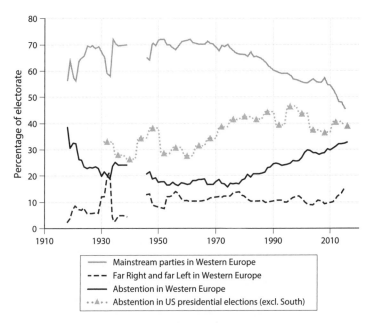

FIGURE 5.3 Vote for mainstream and extreme parties and abstention as a fraction of European electorate, 1918–2016. Countries included are Austria, Belgium, Cyprus, Denmark, Finland, France, Germany, Greece, Ireland, Italy, Luxembourg, the Netherlands, Norway, Portugal, Spain, Sweden, Switzerland, and the United Kingdom. Electoral abstention in the United States shown for comparison. Sources: Europe, data from Simon Hix, London School of Economics; United States, data from Alex Kerchner, Princeton University.

but also, and more recently, parties such as Syriza) and far-right organizations (such as the Nazi Party in Germany, or radical anti-immigration parties today).[6]

After the generalization of universal suffrage following World War One, mainstream parties experienced a steady increase in electoral support—from about fifty-six percent of the whole electorate in 1918 to sixty-nine percent just before the crash of 1929. Most of their growth resulted from a process of electoral mobilization that cut the rate of abstention by half to about twenty percent in the early 1930s. The new voters belonged to low-income strata that had been recently enfranchised and whose participation benefited center-left and left parties. The rise of the Nazi Party in Germany temporarily brought the support of mainstream parties down to its levels of 1918. Everywhere else, however, their vote share remained high. After World War Two, about seventy percent of the whole electorate consistently voted for parties that favored some variant of the political and economic architecture of "embedded liberalism." With abstention at a secular low, the vote for extremist parties represented about ten percent of all the electorate—mostly held by the communist parties of Finland, France, and Italy.

The golden age of middle-of-the-road politics started to erode in the late 1970s. In the aftermath of two oil shocks and in what at first looked like a natural response to a lackluster macroeconomic performance, support for mainstream parties slid gradually. Then, even after unemployment and inflation had been contained, the traditional political forces continued to bleed votes. By 1990, their total vote equaled sixty percent of the electorate. At the onset of the Great Recession, it was fifty-five percent. The economic crisis exacerbated the negative trend. In 2016, only forty-five percent of all those entitled to vote turned out to support them.

The decline of mainstream parties did not benefit their competitors for a long while. Except for a short-lived uptick in the vote for communist parties in the mid- and late 1970s, the share of extreme parties remained unchanged at ten percent until 2010. Most of the loss in support for center-right and center-left forces went into the abstention camp. Electoral turnout started to fall consistently in the early 1980s (Franklin, Lyons, and Marsh 2004; Hooghe and Kern 2017). By 2016, almost one out of every three European adults refrained from voting. Figure 5.3 also displays the nonvoting share of the electorate in the American presidential elections since 1932, for the sake of comparison. It excludes participation in southern states, where blatant discriminatory rules suppressed black turnout until the introduction of the Civil Rights Act.[7] Abstention rates were not particularly different in the American non-South and in Western Europe in the late 1930s.

After World War Two, however, the nonvoting gap between the two continents grew to ten percentage points, perhaps driven the presence of strong socialist and Christian democratic mass parties in Europe, unmatched by American parties in organizational terms. Paralleling the fall in political trust, abstention drifted upward in the United States in the mid- and late 1960s. By the 1970s, the turnout differential across continents had widened to twenty percentage points. It only started to shrink after the European abstention rate grew in the 1980s. By the end of the Great Recession, the turnout gap had been cut to just six percentage points.

With the exception of a few countries (particularly those that retained a system of compulsory voting), turnout collapsed across the advanced world. Between the late 1960s and the mid-2000s, abstention rose by almost seven percentage points in Ireland, Norway, and nonsouthern United States; ten percentage points in the United Kingdom; fifteen percentage points in Japan, Germany, Italy, the Netherlands, and Japan; and almost twenty percentage points in France.

The nature of the electoral system employed in each country, which has always enjoyed a considerable prominence among political scientists as an explanatory variable of turnout, cannot account for such a widespread declining trend. Participation dropped both in countries that abrogated the compulsory vote (the Netherlands in the early 1970s, Italy in the 1990s, a few Swiss cantons) and places that had never compelled their citizens to vote. Nor was the use of different electoral rules to allocate parliamentary seats behind that shift. Abstention rates rose in both majoritarian systems (like France, Japan, or the United Kingdom) and extremely proportional countries (like Austria and the Netherlands).

The fall of turnout seems to be related, instead, to the growth of political disaffection in public opinion. Figure 5.4 displays the percentage of Western European and US respondents who did not vote in their country's latest election (legislative in Europe, presidential in the United States) as a function of two questions: the extent to which respondents believed most people take advantage

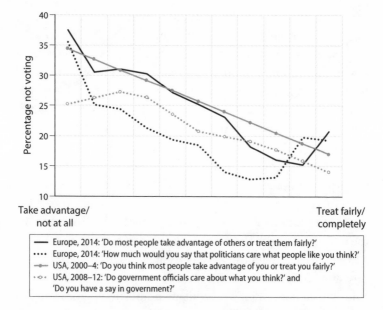

FIGURE 5.4 Political alienation and nonvoting in Western Europe and the United States. Sources: Europe, European Social Survey (2014); United States, American National Election Studies and Stanford University (2015).

of others, and their trust in politicians. The European data are taken from the European Social Survey of 2014. The American data come from the American National Election Studies in the 2000s; the specific date varies, since those questions were not always asked every year. The relationship between political disaffection and political disengagement is remarkably similar in both continents. All the survey instruments show that the level of social and political alienation covaries with the probability of not voting. Abstention climbs to about thirty-five percent among those who feel fully exploited by others, but stays at around twenty percent among those who feel others treat them fairly. The slope is less steep for political alienation, but it shows that abstention is about ten percentage points higher among those who are completely alienated from the political system than those who think that policy makers care about them.[8]

While electoral participation remained high, socioeconomic status was unrelated to the likelihood to vote. After carefully examining the behavior of British voters in the four parliamentary elections that took place between 1966 and 1974, Crewe, Fox, and Alt (1977, 54) concluded that class and education "fail to have any bearings on propensity to vote regularly." In fact, low-income voters turned out to vote at slightly higher rates than high-income individuals—with the effect driven by retirees' slightly higher participation rate with respect to the whole electorate. In Germany, the probability of voting barely differed by any class or occupational characteristics in the early 1980s. The participation rate of college-degree holders was only five points higher than that of unschooled individuals. Skilled blue-collar workers voted at the same rate as professionals. Unskilled workers' turnout rate was only six percentage points lower than the former (Kleinhenz 1998). A similar lack of any relationship between vote and class or income was true for France (Abrial, Cautres, and Mandran 2003), Italy (Tuorto 2010), and Scandinavia (Andersen and Hoff 2001; Martikainen, Martikainen, and Wass 2005). Electoral participation depended, if anything, on the "level of psychological involvement" of citizens—that is, "their attachment to a party, their interest in politics generally and the election in particular, and their degree of exposure to news and discussion about politics in the media or amongst their own circle of relatives and friends" (Crewe, Fox, and Alt 1977, 63–64).

By contrast, the gradual rise of political disengagement has taken on very distinctive sociological contours. Figure 5.5 plots the share of nonvoters in four countries that have witnessed a substantial fall in turnout: Finland, France, the Netherlands, and the United Kingdom. Each graph reports nonvoting shares by income quintile and, within each quintile, three age groups: younger than thirty-five, between thirty-five and fifty-four years of age, and fifty-five or older. The Finnish data refer to the parliamentary elections of 1999 and consist of actual individual-level observations of turnout linked, through Finland's national population register, to the

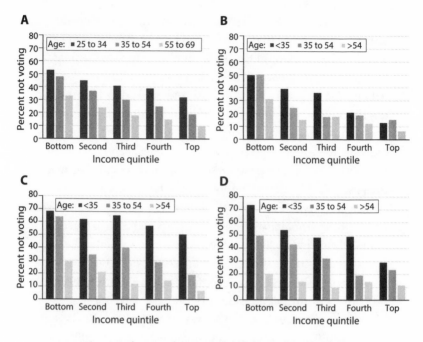

FIGURE 5.5 Nonvoting by age and income in (*A*) Finland, 1999; (*B*) the Netherlands, 2012; (*C*) France, 2013; and (*D*) the United Kingdom, 2010. Sources: Finland, Martikainen, Martikainen, and Wass (2005); France, the Netherlands, and the United Kingdom, European Social Survey (2014).

demographic, social, and economic characteristics of each elector. The data analyzed cover all Finnish electors between twenty-five and sixty-nine years of age—a total of 2,941,834 persons. This unique database, which gives us the true distribution of voters and nonvoters by their social characteristics, avoids two standard problems confronted by any analysis of electoral participation that relies on survey data: first, the possibility that response rates to pollsters differ across individuals and that those differences could be related to the decision not to participate in elections and in politics in general; second, the fact that some respondents tend to overreport their participation at the polls. As a result of those problems, surveys tend to produce much higher voting rates (by around ten percentage points) than the official turnout figures.

The data for France, the Netherlands, and the United Kingdom come from the latest wave of the European Social Survey, a multicountry survey with a vast array of political, economic, demographic, and attitudinal questions administered in over thirty countries. I select these three countries for two reasons. First, they differ substantially in their economic structure and political institutions, therefore providing us with a reasonable coverage of all the variation of advanced democracies. Second, and perhaps more importantly, the deviation between the official turnout data in their latest legislative elections and the aggregate turnout rate uncovered through the survey is relatively small: 1.8 percent in the Netherlands, 2.3 percent in the United Kingdom, and 6.0 percent in France. By contrast, the deviation between survey and official data is much higher in the majority of the remaining countries, reaching 11 percentage points in Germany and 19 percentage points in Switzerland, for example.

Nonvoters amounted to 35.4 percent of all the Finnish electorate in 1999—or twice the rate of thirty years earlier. But the level of abstention differed widely by income and age (figure 5.5A). While 40 percent of all individuals in the bottom quintile of the income distribution did not vote, less than one-fifth of those in the richest quintile did not. Age had its own independent effect on turnout. Within each income quintile, electors whose age was fifty-five or higher were twice as likely to vote as those younger than thirty-five. The differential behavior by age cohort could be the result of either a life-cycle effect or a generational effect (or both). A life-cycle effect takes place when all individuals vary in their probability of voting as a function of age: for example, abstaining when young but then turning out to vote as marriage, parenting, and work concerns, all correlated with age, encourage them to participate more. By contrast, a generational effect occurs when different cohorts behave differently (regardless of their age), generally in response to common historical experiences: for example, individuals who became adults under a situation of war mobilization may be more prone to engage in politics than those who did not. Pulling together electoral surveys for Finland from 1979 through 1999, Wass (2007) shows that the decrease in turnout correlated with age has been mainly driven by a cohort, or generational, effect. New generations have consistently voted at lower rates. Whereas 70.4 percent of those born in 1960 voted when they were nineteen years old (in the 1979 election), only 57.7 percent and 49.6 percent of those who were nineteen in 1987 and 1999 did, respectively. By contrast, there is no discernible life-cycle effect in place: the probability of voting remained stable within each generation—in fact falling slightly with age. For example, among those born in 1960, the average turnout in 1979 fell 1.7 percentage points to 68.7 percent in both 1987 and 1999. Similar generational effects have been found in Canada, where turnout among the generation born in the 1970s has been 25 points lower than amongst pre–baby boomers (Blais, Gidengil, and Nevitte 2004).

Income differences were also strongly correlated with turnout in the Dutch elections of 2012. While only ten percent in the top quintile abstained, about forty percent of those in the bottom quintile did not vote (figure 5.5B). Although age mattered, it did only for the bottom sixty percent of the income distribution, where between forty and fifty percent of those aged thirty-four or younger abstained. Among the two top quintiles, age had a marginal impact on voting behavior.[9]

Age played a larger role in French participation rates of 2013 (figure 5.5C). About two-thirds of all young electors in the three lowest quintiles abstained in the legislative elections of 2013. But even among people younger than thirty-five years in the top quintile of the income distribution the nonvoting share was, at fifty percent, very high. Income was strongly correlated with participation only among electors who were thirty-five years of age or older. While more than sixty percent of middle-aged electors in the bottom quintile abstained, only twenty percent did in the top quintile. Abstention rates were generally lower among senior voters, but income still mattered: seniors in the lowest quintile were three times likelier to abstain than seniors in the top quintile.

The United Kingdom displays an extreme version of the French case (figure 5.5D). With the exception of young individuals in the top quintile, whose abstention is close to the national average, young individuals' nonparticipation rate was uniformly high at around 50 percent—peaking at a dismal 73.4 percent among those thirty-four years or younger in the bottom quintile. In turn, senior electors (those fifty-five or older) continued to vote at the participation rates of previous decades. Income shaped the decision to vote among middle-aged voters: low-income electors abstained at the rates of young individuals; high-income individuals voted almost like senior citizens.

With age and income rising as key correlates of voting, most European democracies converged to the participation patterns that had already been in place in the United States since the 1950s. As detailed by a voluminous literature on turnout in American elections (Lipset 1963; Rosenstone and Hansen 1993; Leighley and Nagler 2013), electoral participation was strongly correlated with socioeconomic status. Throughout the period from 1972 to 2008, about eighty percent of all Americans in the top quintile of the income distribution voted in presidential elections. Only half of those in the bottom quintile did. Likewise, age covaried heavily with vote. Turnout among people younger than twenty-five was twenty to thirty percentage points lower than among electors older than forty-five.

In short, the structure of electoral participation became strongly polarized on both sides of the Atlantic—very much in line with the economic transformations brought about by the decline of industry and by globalization over the last forty years. High-income, well-educated electors, who benefited from the ICT revolution, global trade, and immigration, as well as the oldest cohorts, protected by a robust pension system, remained as politically engaged as previous cohorts with the same social characteristics thirty to forty years ago. By contrast, a disappointing economic performance triggered political disaffection in the rest of the electorate. Voting plummeted among the least affluent social sectors. But abstention rates soared too among young cohorts, particularly in countries where the structural transformations of the last few decades have fallen on post–baby boomers and labor regulations protecting older workers made it hard for young individuals to secure permanent jobs; for instance, about one-quarter of all young individuals in France and over one-third in Italy are regularly unemployed.[10] As a young individual in the constituency of Barking and Dagenham—a thriving part of East London from the time Ford opened its first factory in 1931 until the American car company started winding down all its operations in the 1980s and then closed its last plant in 2002—put it: "The government means nothing to me. If the Queen died tomorrow, the only thing that would change in my life is the head printed on my bank notes. It's everyone out for themselves. As soon as we start getting involved, we get arrested" (reported in Gest 2016, 57). In other words, withdrawal from labor markets and ballot booths seemed to be happening simultaneously.

The Stability of Mainstream Parties

The strong commitment of all mainstream, "Detroit"-style parties to free markets and open borders did not mean that they left unaddressed the disruption brought about by technological innovation and globalization. If anything, the architects of the model of democratic capitalism built over the course of the twentieth century deliberately designed a set of publicly funded mechanisms to protect and compensate those individuals hurt by economic change: unemployment benefits, universal (or quasi-universal) health care, and old-age pensions, since at least the first years of the Cold War, followed, after the 1970s, by the deployment of active industrial policies in response to trade shocks and, as we saw at the end of the chapter 3, the expansion of public-sector jobs (Katzenstein 1985). Seemingly, however, their policy responses did not go far enough to absorb a rising tide of disaffected voters.

In hindsight, softening the blow of structural change had been relatively easy during the golden age of democratic capitalism. But a much lower growth rate and the sharpening equality-employment trade-off examined at the end of chapter 4 made policy makers' choices harder. Making markets more flexible risked widening the distribution of life chances among voters. And vice versa: more generous social policies were seemingly preserving equality at the cost of very tepid employment growth. In addition, directing more public resources to fund those programs appeared to be increasingly out of reach for at least two reasons—both working in tandem. The first one was demographic. The other stemmed from the globalized nature of advanced economies.

The ageing of European, Japanese, and North American populations and a correlated increase in public spending on pensions and health care reduced policy makers' fiscal capacity to address the structural transformations of Silicon Valley. Among the seven largest advanced economies, public expenditure grew by almost ten percentage points of GDP between 1960 and 2007, driven almost entirely by pensions and health programs (Schaechter and Cottarelli 2010). In 2010, public spending on pensions amounted to 8.4 percent of GDP in all advanced countries—or almost two percentage points more than in 1980.[11] Public-health expenditure in European countries belonging to the OECD also trended upward from less than 5 percent of GDP in 1970 to about 8.6 percent of GDP in 2001 (Huber and Orosz 2003). Absent high growth rates (of the kind in place until the 1970s), higher levels of public spending could only be funded either by borrowing from private actors or by raising taxes. Indeed, public debt doubled from about 40 percent of GDP in the mid-1970s to over 80 percent before the Great Recession in advanced industrial economies.[12] Given the considerable size of public expenditure, which generally ranged from 40 to over 50 percent of GDP across the OECD, the available room for substantial tax hikes was rather limited. Moreover, competition from new industrializing countries with much lower taxes and labor costs made it riskier for advanced countries to increase

firms' fiscal burden. In fact, and arguably in response to globalization and constrained by the growth of footloose capital, OECD
governments began in the 1980s to shift the structure of taxation.
Corporate taxation fell sharply—from an average tax rate of 47.7
percent in 1981 to 27.3 percent in 2010. By contrast, personal income taxes and social-security contributions remained roughly
stable over the same period. Value added taxes rose in all OECD
economies by 3 percentage points from the year they were first
introduced in each country (which varied between the late 1960s
and, more frequently, the 1990s) to 2010 (Boix 2011a, tables 1–3).

At the end of the day, however, the reluctance of OECD
governments to recalibrate the existing policy consensus more
drastically derived from straightforward electoral calculations
(greatly shaped by the structure of abstention examined earlier
in this chapter). Figure 5.6 examines the electoral performance
of European mainstream parties from 1918 to 2016—both as a
proportion of the whole electorate (dashed line) and of all votes
(solid line). The graph reports both trends for all mainstream parties together. It displays them too for center-right and center-left
party families separately. As pointed out earlier (in the discussion of figure 5.3), mainstream parties started to lose support
as a fraction of all the electorate after 1980. But, more crucially
for their parliamentary representation and their chances to form
a government, their share of actual votes barely changed up to
2008. Mainstream parties received eighty percent of all ballots
cast in both the late 1970s and, recovering from a brief decline in
the late 1990s, the late 2000s. Hence, despite their loss of support
over the whole electorate, mainstream parties had few electoral
incentives to question the model of embedded liberalism—at least
before the Great Recession.

The political fortunes of mainstream parties were unequally
distributed across party families—in a way that reinforced the
policy status quo (and the disaffection of the least affluent voters).
Center-right parties experienced a strong drop in their share of
support over the whole electorate—from almost fifty percent

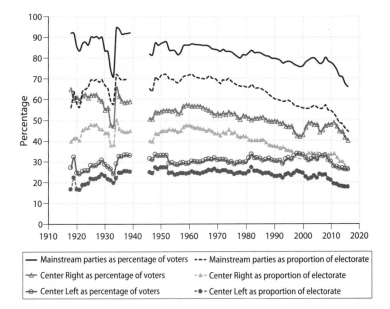

FIGURE 5.6 European mainstream parties as a proportion of voters and of electors, 1918–2016. Countries included are Austria, Belgium, Cyprus, Denmark, Finland, France, Germany, Greece, Ireland, Italy, Luxembourg, the Netherlands, Norway, Portugal, Spain, Sweden, Switzerland, and the United Kingdom. Data from Simon Hix, London School of Economics.

in 1960 to less than thirty percent in 2016—and a softer but still substantial decline in terms of their share of actual votes—from fifty-seven percent in 1960 to about fifty percent in the 1990s and then to slightly over forty percent in 2016. Most losses came from a fall in the Christian democratic vote—an outcome of a process of secularization on the European continent.[13] In contrast to the flagging performance of conservatives and Christian democrats, center-left parties, which at first sight should have been the most damaged by the gradual political alienation of poor and young voters, enjoyed remarkably stable levels of support until 1980—at around thirty percent of all voters. Afterward, their vote share enjoyed a modest upward trend—reaching thirty-three percent of all ballots cast in 2007.

Social democracy's relatively robust electoral performance was rooted in the explicit decision taken by socialist politicians to court middle-class voters, even to the point of sacrificing their historical reliance on blue-collar workers. A secular decline of the manufacturing sector, which fell from comprising a third or more of all employment up to the 1970s to about one-tenth of all jobs in 2010, made it impossible to remain a viable governmental party by appealing only to blue-collar workers. To attract service-sector employees, who represented more than two-thirds of total employment in most countries by the early twenty-first century, socialist parties offered two main policies: a liberal agenda in social issues, and the expansion of public employment. In addition to shoring up their electoral coalition, increasing the number of public employees was defended as a way to ease the employment-equality trade-off faced since the 1980s and to absorb the entry of women into the labor market.

As recently estimated by Silja Häusermann (2017), social democrats mobilized about twice as many working-class voters as middle-class individuals back in 1980. Today, that proportion is roughly the opposite.[14] A great deal of that compositional shift within the center-left electorate was a direct outcome of the growth of nonmanufacturing jobs and the decision of center-left parties to court their holders. But following what electoral sociologists call a "supraclass" strategy (appealing to different social classes instead of relying only on the mobilization of working-class individuals) reinforced the electoral disengagement of part of the traditional base of socialist parties. The proportion of blue-collar workers voting for left-wing candidates fell from about two-thirds in 1980 to less than one-half in 2010.[15] By contrast, the share of middle-class voters voting for Left parties rose from forty to fifty percent on average (with considerable variation across countries) over the same period of time (Gingrich and Häusermann 2015). Fulfilling the social democratic electoral goals behind the expansion of the public sector, public employees were more likely to vote for social democratic parties than were private employees working in the service sector—at least in northern Europe (Häusermann and Kriesi 2015). The new electoral composition of left-wing (and, in fact, all mainstream) parties had important programmatic consequences. It weakened any incentives they may have had to move away from their commitment to globalization (to protect blue-collar workers) because relatively broad swaths of middle-class voters benefited from the importation of cheap manufactures and from the employment of foreign workers in low-paid jobs ranging from restoration to domestic services (Scheve and Slaughter 2001, 2006). In other words, socialists' continuous commitment to the principle of economic openness was reinforced—even if that meant paying a strong price among their old electoral core—by the electoral strategy they developed in response to the transformation of the labor market.[16]

Politics Unhinged

The polarizing effects of a changing employment structure and rising wage inequality took time to become explicit at the ballot box. Figure 5.7 displays the evolution of extreme parties in Europe over the twentieth century—both as a percentage of actual votes (solid line) and as a proportion of the electorate (dashed line). As in figure 5.6, the graph also distinguishes between (in this case, far-) Left parties, marked with circles, and (far-) Right parties, depicted with triangles. Throughout the Cold War, support for extreme parties fluctuated at fifteen percent of total vote (and ten to twelve percent of the whole electorate), with four-fifths of all those ballots going to communist parties. After 1980, the electoral performance of the far Left declined steadily. At the time of the collapse of the Soviet Union, political radicalism seemed close to extinction.

The near death of extreme parties proved short-lived, however. An increasingly anxious and, at points, angry fraction of the electorate switched to a new set of actors promising to tackle, tame, or even block the sources of change: free trade, immigration and,

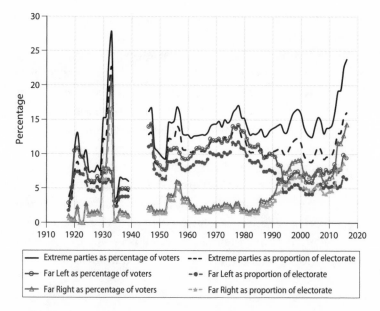

FIGURE 5.7 European extreme parties as a proportion of voters and of electors, 1918–2016. Countries included are Austria, Belgium, Cyprus, Denmark, Finland, France, Germany, Greece, Ireland, Italy, Luxembourg, the Netherlands, Norway, Portugal, Spain, Sweden, Switzerland, and the United Kingdom. Data from Simon Hix, London School of Economics.

much less so, technological innovation. Far-right parties started to grow in the late 1980s, tying at the polls with extreme left-wing parties by the early 1990s. The Great Recession then ratcheted up votes for both extreme right-wing organizations and, mostly in southern Europe, new far-left parties. Still, the aggregate support for all extreme parties over the whole electorate was only marginally above their postwar average. Nevertheless, in the context of very substantial abstention levels, that meant gathering close to one out of every four votes cast by 2015—a number unprecedented since the Great Depression of 1929.

These new alternatives to mainstream politics often emerged employing the colorful language of populism. As Donald Trump proclaimed in his inaugural speech:

We are transferring power from Washington, D.C., and giving it back to you, the people. For too long, a small group in our nation's capital has reaped the rewards of government while the people have borne the cost. Washington flourished, but the people did not share in its wealth. Politicians prospered, but the jobs left. And the factories closed. The establishment protected itself but not the citizens of our country. Their victories have not been your victories. Their triumphs have not been your triumphs. And while they celebrated in our nation's capital, there was little to celebrate for struggling families all across our land. That all changes starting right here and right now. Because this moment is your moment. It belongs to you. (Trump 2017)

A few years earlier, and at the other geographic (and economic) extreme of the Atlantic bloc, George Tsipras, the leader of Syriza, a coalition of radical Left parties, framed the Greek election of 2012 using the same language, and defining it "not [as] a simple confrontation between Syriza and the political establishment of the Memorandum [but] between the Greece of the oligarchy and the Greece of democracy" (quoted in Judis 2016, 116).

Such opposition between the "ordinary people as a noble assemblage not bounded narrowly by class" and "their elite opponents as self-serving and undemocratic" resonated among voters not because it merely triggered emotional and prejudiced responses, as many of the critics of populism claim, but because it blamed directly their fortunes on the "immobilism" of the traditional parties and their unwavering commitment to the "Detroit" consensus (quotations from Michael Kazin's definition of populism, reproduced in *ibid.*, 14). Policy stability in the face of deep structural change could be attributed to the "technocratic," arms-length style of governing of the professional political class, who had become the manager of democratic capitalism without any of the energy or idealism of its founders. For that very reason, it could be rejected in the name of democracy.

At the end of the day, however, "populism" is hardly a meaning-ful term: politicians and the media throw it around to stigmatize and discredit political opponents; and different academics employ it to name different political movements that turn out to have very little in common with one another.[17] Instead, to understand the emergence of American and European "populist" parties, it is more useful to think of most (if not all) of them as the creations of political entrepreneurs intent on transforming the political arena through the introduction of a new policy dimension on which to compete (and succeed) electorally—one that, as a shortcut, we may consider as pitting globalism against nationalism.

To make sense of the new structure of politics (and the irrup-tion of "populist" parties), figure 5.8 graphs a political or electoral space defined by two policy dimensions, locating old and new political actors in it as a function of their most preferred position on each policy issue. The horizontal axis measures the extent to which voters and parties support public compensation mecha-nisms to redress market-induced outcomes; political actors favor-ing higher (lower) taxes and more (less) spending are located to the right (left) of the space. The vertical axis picks up variation in support for economic openness (i.e., trade, immigration, and, more generally, the need to foster or accept economic innova-tion); proglobalization actors are placed at the top of the axis; nationalist ones, at the bottom.

To map the policy preferences of voters, the latter are de-picted, for the sake of simplicity, as one of two types: middle-class and working-class individuals. Middle-class voters comprise a broad set of individuals who range from low clerical workers to company managers—they correspond, roughly speaking, to the relatively educated individuals of figure 4.7. Working-class voters would be mostly blue-collar workers—those semiskilled and unskilled individuals occupying the left half of figure 4.7. Given the constrained nature of globalization before 1980 (with intra-industry trade taking place within the North, hardly any competitive industries in the South, and scant South-to-North

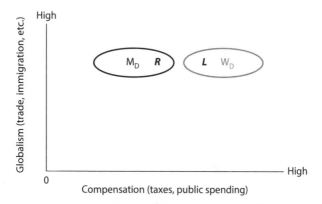

FIGURE 5.8 Electoral politics under Detroit capitalism. The horizontal axis measures support for public-compensation mechanisms to redress market-induced outcomes, with such support increasing to the right. The vertical axis measures support for economic openness, increasing toward the top. M_D, centroid of the area where middle-class voters are located (D denotes preferences under Detroit capitalism); W_D, centroid of the area where working-class voters are located; L and R are the policy platforms of the Left and Right parties, respectively.

migratory flows), voters generally favored the liberal postwar consensus embodied by GATT. Middle-class and working-class voters disagreed, above all, over taxes and the redistributive role of the state. Broadly speaking, working-class voters favored higher taxes and more public spending.[18] Still, preferences within each social group were not completely homogeneous. Within our very broadly defined middle class, individuals in lower-paid clerical occupations may be safely assumed to prefer a more generous welfare state than do top managers and professionals. To capture that diversity of opinions, figure 5.8 draws an elliptical area with a black solid line, within which we assume middle-class individuals are located. The centroid of the area is at M_D, where D denotes preferences under Detroit capitalism. The area is elliptical because the opinions of middle-class voters are not equally heterogenous on both policies: they are more similar on the globalization axis and more diverse on the tax dimension.[19] In turn, working-class voters also exhibit some internal heterogeneity regarding the ideal size of the public sector as a function of their incomes, intensity of their egalitarian commitments, union membership, and so on. Hence, in figure 5.8 they are located within the elliptical structure drawn with a solid gray line with the centroid at W_D.

Mirroring public opinion, center-left -and center-right parties were divided, at least in economic issues, over the appropriate level of taxes and public spending, with left-wing parties typically supporting a more expansive view of the public sector and the welfare state than right-wing parties. By contrast, their disagreements on economic openness were marginal and, in fact, declined in importance over time. Their preferences are reproduced at points L and R respectively, with the Left promising more taxes than the Right but both political parties supporting the same level of economic openness. To construct an electoral majority, both parties espouse more moderate policies than the majority of voters: their ideal points L and R are closer to the midpoint of the horizontal axis than those of the voters that naturally vote for each of them. In the context of this extremely stylized model of electoral politics, in which voters vote for the party that promises the policy closer to their position, blue-collar workers are more likely to vote for the Left. In turn, middle-class voters are likelier to vote for the Right. As shown in chapter 3 (and at the beginning of this chapter), that is indeed what the electoral politics of the postwar period looked like. Mainstream parties, offering similar trade policies and partially different tax-and-spend agendas, commanded the support of most voters. Generally speaking and at least until the 1980s, voters cast their ballots according to income and class—even if the latter's effect declined over time, in line with the powerful equalizing tendencies of Detroit capitalism. In any case, there is no doubt that the structure displayed in figure 5.8 is a very simplified rendition of electoral politics in advanced democracies. Many other factors may drive the vote, such as religion, ethnic identity, beliefs about the efficacy of particular policies (such as favoring low taxation as a precondition to spur growth), and personal judgments about the competence of particular politicians. Whenever they mattered, one would expect a fraction of middle-sector employees to lean leftward and a fraction of blue-collar voters to support center-right parties. That is, for example, what figure 3.13B revealed: in countries with a second strong political cleavage, voting along class lines was more subdued.

Silicon Valley capitalism modified voters' preferences. Particularly in countries where highly educated individuals benefited from a high wage premium, reluctance toward public spending and regulation tended to rise, at least among a fraction of non-working-class voters. That transformation is captured in figure 5.9 by the black dashed ellipsis—larger than the solid-line ellipsis (reproduced following figure 5.8)—to illustrate greater heterogeneity among middle-class voters, and the representative middle-class voter M_{SV} (where SV denotes preferences under Silicon Valley capitalism) moving slightly to the left in the graph. In turn, globalization 2.0 had slightly contradictory effects among the middle class. Among those in routine jobs (and closer to working-class individuals), support for economic openness declined. But among wealthy middle-class voters, proglobalization preferences intensified because the former were its net beneficiaries: immigrants are employed in occupations that are complementary to the jobs of highly educated individuals, and offshoring has mostly jeopardized tasks that require few skills or education (Scheve and Slaughter 2001; Dancygier and Walter 2015). The slightly slanted ellipsis reflects those opposite forces.

Policy preferences among working-class voters changed as well. In response to experiencing flat or negative income growth, they could react in two (not necessarily incompatible) directions. On the one hand, they could attribute (rightly or not) their new economic condition to globalization 2.0—in the form of offshoring and immigration—and, as a result, push back against trade and immigration. On the other hand, they could ask for more compensation (and higher taxes), either because they thought that,

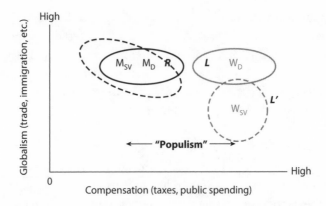

FIGURE 5.9 Electoral politics under Silicon Valley. The axes and graph labels are the same as for figure 5.8. M_{SV}, centroid of the area where middle-class voters are located (where SV denotes preferences under Silicon Valley capitalism); W_{SV}, centroid of the area where working-class voters are located. L' is the policy platform position of a radical(ized) Left candidate.

although globalization was still to blame, more social spending and vocational training could overcome it, or because they attributed their losses to automation rather than economic openness. Figure 5.9 represents the first type of reaction: the antiglobalization turn of working-class voters. (I discuss the second reaction later on.) The location of the representative worker moves from W_D to W_{SV}. The dashed circle around the latter represents—as opposed to the elongated distribution of individuals around W_D—the fact that workers' positions over the extent of openness may have become more diverse.

The antiglobalization shift among working-class voters did not happen automatically in most countries. The story of that transformation went, instead, like this. As long as mainstream parties remained committed to their standard programmatic positions, a new candidate (whom the literature refers to as "populist") appealed to a growing number of voters who felt unrepresented—first, by identifying globalization (in its various forms: trade, migration, political integration at a supranational level) as the main culprit behind economic (and cultural) change affecting voters, and, second, by promising to reject it once in office. In the spatial language of figure 5.9, the new candidate chose to locate herself somewhere on the bottom part of the electoral space.[20]

The "populist" breakthrough amounted, therefore, to the construction of a new electoral coalition in which the "old" working class (but also outsiders in the labor market such as the younger cohorts entering into that market) played a critical role. Already in the French presidential elections of 1995, the leader of the National Front, Jean-Marie Le Pen, referred to his party as "the party of the working class" (quoted in Judis 2016, 103). A few electoral cycles later, his daughter, Marine Le Pen, hired Florian Philippot, a former supporter of Jean-Pierre Chevènement, a leading figure of the left wing of the French Socialist Party, to write a new economic platform for the National Front. In subsequent declarations to a French newspaper, Philippot was adamant in stating that "Jean-Pierre Chevènement's project is carried forward by Marine Le Pen" (quoted in *ibid.*, 145). Across the Atlantic, Donald Trump would defend his presidential bid within the Republican Party, but stating that "five, ten years from now [it will be a] different party. You're going to have a worker's party. A party of people that haven't had a real wage increase in eighteen years, that are angry" (quoted in Gass 2016).

By framing all structural change as a consequence of globalization, protectionism trumped (and quieted) disputes over the size of the welfare state that had played a key role in defining the electoral space in the past. Precisely because antiglobalization parties promised to curb the putative source of economic disruption, economic openness, they could cast aside the idea that public spending should be used as a mechanism to compensate those hurt by trade and the world business cycle. Their ambiguity toward the (size of the) welfare state could help them draw voters from the Left and the Right simultaneously. They could lure left-wing voters with their promise to restore wages and wage growth. They could attract right-wing voters with lower taxes. In short, "populist" parties could build a new coalition that encompassed a fraction of the middle-class voters as well as the old working class.

Using the European Social Survey of 2014, table 5.1 reports the percentage of voters supporting "populist" parties in six European countries: two Nordic countries, Denmark and Finland; two continental cases with high support for nonmainstream parties, France and the Netherlands; Germany; and the United Kingdom. For each country, the table displays the "populist" share in the top, middle, and bottom income quintiles. For each quintile it also shows the share of "populist" parties among individuals working (or having worked) in mining and manufacturing sectors, which are highly exposed to the competition of emerging economies.[21]

Overall, support for nonmainstream parties varies by country. It is low in Germany and the United Kingdom and high elsewhere. Cross-national differences in electoral performance respond to two factors: the structure of the economy and the nature of electoral rules. Globalization 2.0 has mainly hurt workers in industries, such as textiles, toys, and furniture, directly undercut by new emerging economies and the formation of a global value chain. Many of those low-value sectors are (or were) located in the European periphery, but much less so in Mitteleuropa. Hence, nonmainstream parties' poor performance in Germany (or, more precisely, West Germany) may be interpreted as a direct outcome of that country's reliance on high-value-added industries that are still highly competitive in the world economy. As for the United Kingdom, demand for antiglobalist policies is strong in its more deprived regions in terms of education, income, and unemployment—as attested by the outcome of the Brexit referendum (Becker, Fetzer, and Novy 2017). However, the UK Independence Party's lackluster electoral performance is the result of Britain's first-past-the-post electoral system, which kills third parties quite effectively and which gives existing parties time to readjust their programs to preempt the entry of new forces.

Regardless of the average level of electoral support, "populist" parties are consistently stronger among low-income voters—in line

TABLE 5.1. Reported Vote for "Populist" Parties in Selected Countries, mid-2000s

Income Quintile		Denmark	Finland	France	Netherlands	Germany	United Kingdom
				PERCENTAGE OF VOTE			
Top	All	13	13	7	9	8	4
	Manufacturing	13	13	7	9	8	4
Middle	All	22	20	16	24	13	5
	Manufacturing	22	29	17	34	10	10
Bottom	All	25	25	20	30	18	9
	Manufacturing	33	36	28	33	10	11

Source: European Social Survey (2014).

Inclusion in the income quintile is based on a household's total net income (question F41 in the European Social Survey of 2014). Working in the manufacturing sector is derived from recoding question F31. Italy was not included in the survey. Belgium is not reported here because the regional divide makes classifying parties complex. The classification between extreme-left and extreme-right parties is based, following Simon Hix's work, on their membership in the European Parliament. Far-left parties are those included in the European United Left–Nordic Green Left (GUE-NGL) parliamentary group. Far-right parties are part of two European parliamentary groups: Europe of Nations and Freedom and Europe of Freedom and Direct Democracy (known as Europe of Freedom and Democracy until 2014). The True Finns and the Danish People's Party, which were founding members of the Europe of Freedom and Democracy but left it in 2014 to form part of the European Conservatives and Reformists, are also counted as far-right-wing parties.

with the theoretical expectations developed with the help of the model of elections graphed in figure 5.9. Whereas one out of four Danish voters in the bottom quintile supported the People's Party, only one in eight in the top quintile cast a ballot for any populist party. That electoral ratio (or a factor of two poor voters to one rich voter) is similar in Finland (twenty-five to thirteen percent), Germany (eighteen to eight percent) and Britain (nine to four percent). It rises to a factor of three to one in France (twenty to seven percent) and the Netherlands (thirty to nine percent). The share of "populist" voters becomes larger among low-income individuals in tradable sectors in Denmark, Finland, France, and Finland.

The internal composition of the nonmainstream vote varied across countries: a single, strictly antiglobalization party, as in the United Kingdom; a hegemonic left-wing antisystem party, like Germany's Linke (and, then, much later, the Alternative für Deutschland [AfD]); or several populist parties located along the Left–Right electoral dimension, as in France. The particular constellation of populist parties has depended on the electoral system and on the cultural and symbolic repertoire available to them in each country. Majoritarian systems, which impose high entry barriers to new parties, force them to coordinate around one platform and to stress the antiglobalization card while downplaying the compensation dimension. Proportional systems, which make entering parliament much easier than do majoritarian systems, facilitate instead the emergence of separate left-wing and right-wing antiglobalization political forces. Historical memory and the set of programmatic appeals that are acceptable within the existing national discourse may have also mattered. In countries that were not tainted by fascism during World War Two—that is, that did not elect right-wing totalitarian governments or collaborate extensively with Nazi rule—nationalist parties have been able to appeal to national sovereignty as a (or "the") necessary precondition for democracy—the United Kingdom or the United States. In countries like Germany and Italy, haunted by the memory of fascism, antisystem parties have avoided any connection to the idea of nation: to be successful, they have generally stressed technocratic qualities or have run on left-wing appeals. Finally, those countries with a fractured historical experience, such as France, which was painfully split between the Vichy regime and the resistance movement in the 1940s, have developed both nationalist parties on the Right and a postcommunist extreme Left.

The success of new far-right and far-left parties running on antiglobalist programs has relied on their capacity to develop a political narrative linking the structural change of Silicon Valley with globalization.[22] As discussed in chapter 4, skill-biased technological change (as opposed to offshoring and migration) has probably been the main (albeit not the sole) driver of employment change and wage inequality. Yet, in the electoral arena it has played a much more subdued role. The most effective "populist" electoral campaigns have relied on opposing both immigration (and its supposedly deleterious effects on wages, social services, and the homogeneity and quality of old working-class neighborhoods) and deeper financial and trade integration—perhaps because blaming particular social groups or countries may be a more effective strategy to win votes than attacking an impersonal force such as technological innovation.

Nevertheless, the role that political leaders and parties play in structuring and channeling popular discontent means that an antiglobalization program is not the only possible response to the disruptions brought about by Silicon Valley. An alternative political response would consist of explaining the latter as a result of technological innovation rather than globalization, and then promising to follow a more radical compensation strategy—in the form of higher taxes on high-skilled individuals, a universal basic income, and so on.[23] In the political space depicted in figure 5.9, that would be tantamount to locating oneself in a more radical position L'—advocating high levels of taxes and public spending and a pinch of protectionism. In that case, instead of politics being defined by a clash between globalists and nationalists, electoral competition would still take place along the old but now much more polarized Left–Right dimension. Today, this corresponds to Bernie Sanders' critique of the American top one percent as an "oligarchy" that should be taxed and domesticated, and British Labour under Jeremy Corbyn, with its proposal to renationalize railways and some utilities, reestablish rent control, raise taxes on the wealthy, and beef up the minimum wage across the board.

To sum up, the rise of populist-protectionist parties in Europe and the resurgence of radical Left politics constitute different manifestations of the same problem: the wage and employment changes brought about by Silicon Valley capitalism threaten to bury the centripetal politics of the past, replacing it with a level of political polarization and conflict unheard of under the Detroit model. That leads quite naturally to one (or, perhaps, the) key question in our exploration of the possibilities of democratic capitalism: How politically disruptive might all the ongoing technological and economic transformations become, particularly if they persist and accelerate? To what extent can they threaten the combination of democracy and free markets? And, are there any measures that could be taken to sustain democratic capitalism?

I turn to sketch a response to these questions in the concluding chapter. First, I engage in some conceptual brush clearing: I make explicit the set of assumptions behind the great variety of conflicting predictions that are being offered about the nature of automation and its potential economic effects. I then consider the potential long-run political consequences of Silicon Valley capitalism. I finally suggest a set of policy interventions to channel its economic and social effects to the advantage of the majority.

6

Robots vs. Democracy?

For better or for worse, there is little agreement on the future economic and social impact of automation—with forecasts ranging from the most upbeat assessments about the effects of new ICTs to the gloomiest predictions about their consequences on the distribution of wealth and power one or two generations from now.

Technological utopians abound, quite predictably, in today's Silicon Valley. But John M. Keynes was their direct forefather. In his essay "Economic Possibilities for Our Grandchildren," first published in 1930, the British economist wrote that, as machines kept replacing most labor, men would be, in a not too distant future, "only too glad to have small duties and tasks and routines" to perform every day. Any work left to humans would have to be distributed around, "spread[ing] the bread thin on the butter—to make what work there is still to be done to be as widely shared as possible. Three-hour shifts or a fifteen-hour week may put off the problem for a great while. For three hours a day is quite enough to satisfy the old Adam in most of us!" (Keynes 1963, 368–69). Living in a world of plenty, man would finally have to face "his real, his permanent problem—how to use his freedom from pressing

economic cares, how to occupy [his] leisure" (367). And, freed
from the struggle to survive and from the ties of acquisitiveness
and avarice, "we shall once more value ends above means and prefer the good to the useful, ... honour those who can teach us how
to pluck the hour and the day virtuously and well, the delightful
people who are capable of taking direct enjoyment in things, the
lilies of the field who toil not, neither do they spin" (370).[1]

Twenty-first-century post-Keynesian techno-optimists seem
to fancy an even more radical future. They proclaim too that
human labor will soon become obsolete, leading either to a society
of entirely idle people or to a labor market composed, at most, by
an endless variety of yoga and gym teachers (and disciples) trading
new insights on how to become healthy and fit. However, instead
of embracing Keynes's call for a rediscovery of our primeval Adam
and for the cultivation of evangelical virtues, they foresee a breaking or singularity point after which machines will become smarter
than people—a turning point that will result in the gradual blend-
ing of artificial and human intelligence into some kind of cyborg
with the capacity to transcend the biological constraints that have
always defined us (cf. Kurzweil 2005).

On the other side of the aisle, the most extreme dystopian accounts of the change brought about by Silicon Valley capitalism
envision a nasty and brutish world characterized by inequality,
social conflict, and even economic misery. According to our current techno-pessimists, Luddites got it wrong in the nineteenth
century—after all, the labor pains of Manchester, and later Detroit, led to an explosion of new jobs. But today's technological
advances, they claim, are qualitatively different. Machines are
replacing jobs without generating any new significant industries.
And even if new occupations eventually crop up, firms will be able
to rely on the use of powerful algorithms to automatize most, if
not all, of their operations. Somehow revisiting Marx, the future
will be defined by swelling numbers of badly paid or simply unemployable workers and the parallel rise of a narrow stratum of
extremely wealthy owners of superintelligent machines.[2]

Standing somewhere in the middle between techno-optimists and techno-pessimists, techno-skeptics point to the inherent difficulties of automatizing everything by bringing up the so-called Moravec's paradox, according to which high-level reasoning of a logical, informational, and mathematical kind needs little computational power, while low-level sensor and motor skills (of the type learned by an infant and ranging from walking to picking up an object on the floor) require extremely large and hardly understood computational skills (cf. Brynjolfsson and McAffee 2014, 28–29). Accordingly, the rate of technological change may be positive. But it will have a markedly discontinuous nature. In some (perhaps many) tasks, machines will eventually replace all human activity. In the rest, the process of substitution will be negligible.

As it turns out, the accuracy of predictions made about the economic and social effects of technological change has been rather poor so far. In response to a public concerned about the effects of automatization on labor dislocation, President Johnson convened a blue-ribbon commission on "Technology, Automation, and Economic Progress" in 1964. The commission concluded that automation was not threatening employment for the time being, but recommended a guaranteed minimum income for each family and the use of public employment as a last resort. Two years later, several Nobel laureates wrote an open letter claiming that "the traditional link between jobs and income is broken," and that "the economy of abundance can sustain all citizens in comfort . . . whether or not they . . . work" (quoted in Akst 2014). More than two decades ago, in 1995, Jeremy Rifkin predicted, to great acclaim, the end of work and the emergence of massive unemployment in a very near future. Yet, half a century after the Nobel laureates' letter, the American workforce has grown by over seventy-five percent.

In one of the most systematic attempts at assessing the predictive success of existing studies about the coming of artificial intelligence (AI), S. Armstrong and K. Sotala (2015) identified up to ninety-five such forecasts published between 1950 and 2012. The variance in the year predicted is extraordinary—ranging from 1970 to 2107, with most of those studies dating the advent of AI between fifteen and twenty years from the time they saw the light. Strikingly enough, a few of their authors have even suggested different dates in different publications. For instance, Ray Kurzweil, one of the leaders of the singularity movement, predicted that AI's breakthrough would happen both in 2030 and between 2079 and 2099.

Some Guidelines for a Prognosis

The wide variety in opinions about the nature and speed of technological change, reflected in the current flurry of best sellers catering to an increasingly anxious public, derives from the ways in which different authors respond (most of the time, in an implicit manner) to four key questions: What will be the rate and extent of future technological innovation? How successfully will humans adjust to automation? What will be the latter's effects on the use of (and returns to) capital, and therefore on overall inequality? And, last but not least, what will be the nature of the political responses to future technological change? I discuss the first three questions in this section, concluding that, although we can make some educated guesses about the overall trends and effects of technological change, we can neither predict its pace nor depict the society it will give birth to with much precision. That means that any policy response to automation can only proceed in a piecemeal (rather than comprehensive) fashion. It also implies that the overall effects of automation and hyperglobalization will depend on the political reactions and responses to the challenges triggered by those two processes. It is on that understanding that I tackle the fourth question—on the role of politics—in the next section, "Democracy in the West."

The Demand for Labor. All in all, there are few papers or reports attempting to give precise estimates about the pace and range of automation, particularly by economic sector. When they do, their results are anything but watertight. In what has become an extremely influential paper, Oxford researchers Carl Frey and

Michael Osborne disaggregate over seven hundred occupations in terms of the kinds of knowledge, abilities, and skills needed to perform them successfully, and then identify and measure the extent of three types of "bottlenecks," or obstacles to computerization: perception and manipulation (for example, finger dexterity), creative intelligence (such as originality), and social intelligence (including things like persuasive skills). With that information in hand, they proceed to assign to each occupation (and, by aggregation, to economic sectors), a given risk of computerization, from low to high. According to those calculations, forty-seven percent of total US employment falls under the high-risk category, mainly "transportation and logistic occupations, together with the bulk of office and administrative support workers, and labour in production occupations" (Frey and Osborne 2017, 265). By contrast, thirty-three percent of jobs have a low computerization risk, corresponding to "generalist occupations requiring knowledge of human heuristics, and specialist occupations involving the development of novel ideas and artifacts" (266).[3] Offering a plausible classification of all economic sectors according to their technological vulnerability, however, falls short of telling us much about the timing of automation. As Frey and Osborne themselves point out, their analysis simply implies that "[high-risk] occupations are potentially automatable over an *unspecified* number of years, *perhaps* a decade or two" (265; emphasis added). Indeed, there is a simple reason behind their incapacity to date any future technological breakthrough with any precision. By definition, any invention that transforms a field or industry can only be recognized as such at the time it is being invented. Call it the Hegel insight: it is only at the falling of dusk that the owl of Minerva spreads its wings.

The Supply of Labor. Debates about the consequences of automation are even sparser when considering the other side of the equation: the nature of the labor supply—that is, the capacity of human beings to offer the kinds of skills that are complementary to the new tools of production that define Silicon Valley capitalism. To examine this issue and to compare the problems it raises (in relationship to the Manchester and Detroit periods), let us consider a world where the final skills (to be employed in any given occupation) of any person are a function of two things: that person's natural talents and some know-how acquired through education. I define natural talents quite broadly here—encompassing the genetic endowment at birth as well as the intelligence nurtured by a particular family environment. The educational know-how is, instead, the result of an investment made through formal institutions such as schools, vocational training schemes, and so on. Suppose also that, before being subjected to any educational investment, the distribution of natural talents among the population is unequal (at least for a given generation)—that is, that some individuals' talents are higher than others', something that seems well established in the current literature. Assume, finally, that investing in formal education constitutes a key mechanism to reduce the deficiencies in the initial endowment of talents of a fraction of the workforce and therefore the "natural" inequalities in the population—by how much, however, will depend on the investment effort and, naturally, on the effectiveness of that effort.[4]

Now, the economic and welfare effects of these three elements (an unequal distribution of natural talents, human capital formation, and the effectiveness of the latter to compensate for some initial inequality) will vary with the model of production in place. From an economic point of view, the presence of an unequal distribution of natural talents had little importance under Manchester capitalism. Because business mainly hired unskilled individuals, private and public incentives to invest in education were low. As a result, earnings reflected the productivity of individuals according to their natural talents (plus the educational investments made by a narrow segment of the population). All in all, inequality was high but the production system functioned efficiently.

Under Detroit capitalism, firms needed individuals with mid-level skills, capable of reading manuals, making simple mathematical calculations, bookkeeping, and typing. Individuals with medium to high innate abilities benefited directly from the new model of production. In contrast to Manchester, however, those individuals whose natural talents were low could improve their life chances provided they subjected themselves to a schooling system that, by compensating their initial disadvantages, made them productive enough to perform average "Detroit" jobs. Workers were not the only ones who had an incentive to lobby and vote for schools and a comprehensive educational system. As emphasized earlier in this book, businesses did too because having educated workers was indispensable to the satisfactory operation of factories and offices. With the proper educational investment in place, the economy functioned efficiently and, at the same time, growth benefited everyone, narrowing past wage differentials.

Silicon Valley is likely to jeopardize that symbiotic relationship between schooling and technological progress. Imagine, contrary to the opinion of most techno-optimists and techno-pessimists, who believe that work will become scarce, that the process of computerization results in the emergence of new economic sectors and the creation of a great number of jobs. Even under such a (hypothetical) situation of full employment, automation should have very different welfare effects across individuals. According to a recent OECD report that relies on the Survey of Adult Skills, conducted by the Program for the International Assessment of Adult Competencies (PIAAC) in over forty countries, seventy-five percent of adult workers use literacy, numeracy, and problem-solving skills on a daily basis. Among them, four in five employ those skills "with proficiency at a level that computers are close to reproducing" (Elliott 2017, 14). The rest, one in five, "use the PIAAC skills on a daily basis with higher proficiency than computers." Vulnerability to computerization is correlated with the level of skills and wages: as pointed out by Frey and Osborne (2017), whereas "computerisation will mainly substitute for low-skill and low-wage jobs in the near future . . . high-skill and high-wage occupations are the least susceptible to computer capital" (267). Therefore, the capacity of individuals to acquire the relatively high level of abilities demanded by the production model of the future will determine the overall welfare effects of automation. If, compensating for an initially unequal distribution of skills, education investments move individuals upward on the skill ladder, workers will benefit from Silicon Valley. However, if, despite spending heavily in education and training programs, some are unable to acquire those new skills, a fraction of the workforce will remain unemployed, or employed but lowly paid. With labor supply not matching labor demand, inequality will persist over time.[5]

The Evolution of Capital. In principle, automation seems poised to benefit the owners of capital. As the price of using machines (such as robots, software, etc.) falls relative to the wage paid to an employee to make a gadget or give some service, the owners of those laborsaving technologies (or those with access to funds to invest in them) will proceed to robotize plants, factories, and shop floors and to appropriate a correspondingly larger share of the value of the unit or service produced. In the limit—that is, with full automation—only one factor, capital, will be employed and, logically, only its owners—that is, capitalists—will appropriate any returns from production.

Back in 1964, Nobel laureate James E. Meade became one of the first economists to analyze in some detail the impact of automation on the distribution of income. To Meade, even if automation were not to lead, as Marx had predicted, to "an absolute reduction in the real wage rate" to absorb workers made redundant by technological change, it would cause output per head to rise faster than the contribution of labor to output—something that, in a market economy, "would require that an ever-increasing proportion of output accrued to property owners [i.e., the owners of machines]" (Meade 1964, 26). Over time, that dynamic would lead to extreme inequality with "a limited number of exceedingly wealthy property owners," a small "working population required to man the extremely profitable automated industries," and "a large expansion of the production of the labour-intensive goods and services which were in high demand by the few multi-multi-multi-millionaires." In short, "we would be back in a superworld of an immiserized proletariat and of butlers, footmen, kitchen maids, and other hangers-on," which the British economist christened "the Brave New Capitalists' Paradise" (33). That seems to be the world trumpeted by Terry Guo, the CEO of the Taiwanese company FoxConn, in January of 2012, a few months after announcing a plan to deploy over one million robots, when he stated, bluntly, that his firm had "a workforce of over one million worldwide, and as human beings are also animals, to manage one million animals gives me a headache" (quoted in Markoff 2015, 93).

Meade's hypothesis is plausible. Yet, as with most of our theories and predictions, it is built upon very specific assumptions that may or may not be true: in this particular instance, the premise that the number of capital owners is fixed. That derives, in turn, from assuming that there are two barriers to entry high enough to make it impossible for almost everyone to join the existing club of capitalists: substantial costs of innovation, and large fixed costs to produce (in an automatized way) goods and services.

Most innovation is indeed costly. Economic agents cannot invent new technologies easily. They need to have the proper know-how about existing production processes (and, therefore, about the problems faced by current producers and the most likely mechanisms to solve them). That only comes from long-term exposure to the technical and production procedures of a given sector or business. Ford's or Intel's stories—explored at the beginning of chapters 3 and 4 respectively—epitomize this point. The assembly plant took shape in Highland Park through a long trial-and-error process involving quite experienced mechanics and engineers. Fairchild's silicon transistor was designed and manufactured by a team of top physicists and mathematicians embedded in the vibrant research and industrial culture around San Francisco and Stanford.

Even when technological breakthroughs happen outside factories or well-funded labs, innovators and entrepreneurs face a second, crucial hurdle. Setting up most production and distribution processes involves incurring considerable fixed costs. Starting from scratch and without any previous experience in the automobile industry, Tesla is now manufacturing electric cars and Google is striving to produce driverless cars. Both operations have required tapping an unprecedented amount of capital. Tesla had only manufactured a few thousand cars by 2010, after having raised about three-quarters of a billion dollars between 2003 and 2009 (Davis 2010; Kumparak, Burns, and Escher 2015). Securing such levels of funding depends on having a private fortune, substantial collateral, or the right connections. If that is the case, and precisely because automation implies a growing share of capital inputs (as opposed to labor) in the process of production, Meade's predictions should be true: barriers to entry will rise in the future and capital will beget capital over time—feeding, as it were, a Pikettian spiral of inequality.

There are already some signs that capital has grown in relative terms within the economy. Among new firms, the ratio of market value to number of employees has exploded. By mid-2017, Apple, Google, Microsoft, and Facebook had a market capitalization ranging from over $800 billion to close to $500 billion. The number of employees stood at 116,000 for Apple, 61,000 for Google, 74,000 for Microsoft, and 23,000 for Facebook. For the sake of comparison, a Detroit-era firm like General Motors employed a similar number of workers—97,000 in the United States—but its market value, at $51 billion, was ten times smaller than Facebook's. Looking more broadly at the whole American economy, whereas capital income grew at an annual rate of 2.2 percent, labor income barely moved, at a rate of 0.1 percent increase per year, between 2000 and 2014. The US labor share of national income fell from about 64 percent throughout the postwar period to 58 percent from the mid-1980s onward (Elsby, Hobijn, and Sahin 2013). Likewise, Karabarbounis and Neiman (2014) report a fall of five percentage points in the labor share of income in a sample of fifty-nine countries in the period from 1975 to 2013. In the United States, the labor share of income decreased rapidly in economic sectors with high research-and-development intensity—from 80 percent in the mid-1970s to 60 percent in 2011—while remaining flat over the same period of time in less-R&D-intense sectors over the same period (Guellec and Paunov 2017).

And, yet, technological innovation could also have the opposite effect—eventually eroding the position of capital and flattening incomes. ICTs have reportedly raised intercompany competition. With the introduction of digital technologies, the costs of advertising and distributing have declined for any product. Opening a webpage on a digital platform reduces the large upfront investment in branding and related activities. For purely digital products, transportation costs are now zero, therefore reducing part of the high barriers to entry that producers of physical goods traditionally confronted. According to the World Bank, "price comparator websites enhance transparency in prices and result in lower and less dispersed prices for consumers" (2016, 67). In a global survey conducted in 2015, more than two-thirds of firms in the nondigital economy stated that they were experiencing higher levels of competition as a result of digital innovations. Perhaps reflecting all those effects, companies—particularly those with a high digital content—are now facing higher risks in the market: the volatility of stock-market valuations of traded US companies has risen since the late 1980s. That trend has intensified in more-innovation-intensive sectors such as the biotechnology, computer, and electrical-equipment industries (Guellec and Paunov 2017).

More importantly, technological change may end up lowering the costs of producing machines (i.e., of capital investment) directly—to the point of enabling anybody to set up some kind of fully or at least heavily automatized or robotized shop. In other words, future technological innovation could wipe out the traditionally high fixed costs of production and distribution and, with them, the barriers to becoming a capitalist. Thanks to the computer revolution, the cost of executing a set of standard computational tasks (defined as one million computations per second) has

dropped from $500 (in 2006 prices) at the end of World War Two
to less than one-billionth of a cent now. Personal computers and
cell phones have become widely available to almost everyone—
with clear-cut consequences for our economic and social relations. Mobile phones have allowed African farmers to improve
their access to prices, weather conditions, and state-of-the-art
agricultural techniques. Digital platforms have maximized the efficient use of time of independent truck drivers. Craft shops and
local tour operators in developing countries can contract directly
with customers in advanced economies. Further technological
progress—such as the diffusion of 3D printers—could result in
tools easily available to anyone with the skills and creative talents
needed to operate them.

A sharp fall in the prices of machines could then interact with
another fundamental transformation examined in chapter 3 (cf.
the section "Globalization 2.0"). By lowering the costs of monitoring production across tasks, the new technologies of information and communication have reduced the need to integrate all
jobs in a single plant or under a single corporation. Companies
have responded by unbundling their operations across different
cities, countries, or even continents, to tap the comparative advantages of each location—intensifying, as a result, globalization.
In a similar fashion, the fall in monitoring costs could spark a
process of hyperspecialization at the worker level, leading to an
economy where self-employed individuals would engage in very
specific or narrowly defined tasks and would then transact with
one another in the marketplace rather than within an integrated
corporation (as in the past). Topcoder has been showcased as a
paradigmatic case of this atomized production system. It is an
outsourcing company that, once its clients divide their custom design and development projects into tiny parts, offers the latter to a
worldwide community of freelance programmers, engineers, and
developers to design those projects. The number of Topcoder's
designers exceeds, as of today, one million people.[6] Likewise,
the digital platform Airbnb lets homeowners or small companies

offer accommodation online to customers—bypassing the fixed costs incurred by hotel chains and traditional travel agencies. Extended to other sectors of the economy, the combination of cheap capital and low monitoring costs would multiply the number of capital owners (particularly if they had skills complementary to that capital) while tying them through some kind of digital platform or network. In the limit, that could result in the formation of something akin to the highly fragmented production system of craftsmen that prevailed in the past. If that came to pass, Meade would be wrong after all.

Democracy in the West

As in the debate about the economic effects of future technologies, techno-optimists' and techno-pessimists' predictions about the political challenges triggered by automation stand at squarely opposite sides. Among technological optimists, politics is either absent or will evolve, at most, along a rather benevolent path. In their (admittedly sketchy) accounts, techno-optimists assume that the "good society" of the future will follow from technological change in an almost *deus ex machina* fashion. As automation progresses, work hours will shrink and job sharing will take place in a relatively painless manner. At the same time, personal incomes will not drop. Capital and labor will share all productivity gains in a fair manner. If they do not voluntarily, voters and governments will step in to transfer money to the unproductive and to the permanently jobless, compelled by a combination of other-regarding and self-interested reasons. The prevalence of strong ethical commitments (or, perhaps, a strong sense of national solidarity) among the general public will persuade the latter to care for the growing portion of unemployed and badly employed. Moreover, as technological change mounts to the point of threatening a majority of the population, the presence of democratic institutions and elections will enable voters to impose a high-tax high-transfer regime on the minority (of capitalists and highly skilled individuals) that stands to gain from Silicon Valley capitalism. That may even be reinforced by the willingness of winners themselves to pay taxes to minimize social resentment and conflict. In short, democracy will act quite efficiently as a balancing force against the potentially destructive side of automation.

Dystopian renditions of the future stress, by contrast, the conflictual nature of politics and the power of money to reshape governments and institutions. In those accounts, as economic polarization grows, political differences between social sectors will intensify. The losers of automation will oscillate between alienation and anger. Its winners, awash with money and plugged into the right political networks, will maneuver to control the wheels of power. Finally, any meaningful form of democracy will disappear, replaced by some form of oligarchical government that will control the masses through a modern, Huxleyan version of the old Roman system of *panem et circenses*. In other words, political inequality will follow from economic inequality.

As explored earlier in this book, the economic growth and equalization of life chances brought about by Detroit shored up the civil peace and democratic stability of the second half of the twentieth century. Conversely, the high level of both economic inequality and social conflict under Manchester capitalism (as well as most preindustrial economies) was behind the opposition of the nineteenth-century European economic and political establishment to universal suffrage and fully democratic institutions. The increasing economic polarization of the last decades does not mean, however, that capitalism and democracy should be necessarily at odds with each other in the future. Equating Silicon Valley capitalism with Manchester capitalism in a mechanical way, as many techno-pessimists and a new wave of reconstructed Marxists now do, is a mistake because the two periods differ in at least two crucial ways. First, per capita income is fifteen to twenty times higher today than it was 150 years ago in all advanced economies. Second, democratic institutions have been in full operation for at least 100 years in most of today's advanced societies—arguably giving us some tools to manage the economic and social challenges arising today.

The Crisis of Democracy. The possibility of a breakdown of democracy under (an extreme version of) Silicon Valley capitalism appears to be a farfetched proposition. From a large body of empirical research that relies on the history of all sovereign countries during the last two hundred years, we know that the likelihood of having democratic institutions is strongly correlated with the level of per capita income. At the beginning of the twentieth-first century, less than one in five countries with a GDP per capita below $2,000 (in constant dollars of 1996) holds free and competitive elections, while over ninety percent of the countries with a per capita income above $10,000 are democratic. Most of the wealthy countries governed by authoritarian regimes correspond to oil-producing countries, where a political elite excludes the rest of the population from government to avoid sharing the rents that flow from the control and exploitation of oil. We also know that, once established, democracy has never died in wealthy countries. Between 1800 and 2007, there were sixty-nine instances of democratic breakdown—that is, transitions from democracy to dictatorship—such as Germany in 1933 or Chile in 1973. The highest income per capita at which the fall of democracy ever took place was $9,623 in Argentina in 1976. But that is an outlier in the universe of democratic crisis. Half of the democratic breakdowns occurred in countries with a per capita income below $2,500, and one-third in the range $2,500 to $5,000. Just for the sake of comparison, in the early 2000s per capita income was close to $25,000 in Germany and Japan, and above $33,000 in the United States.[7] Employing existing empirical research that explores the relationship between democratic breakdown and income, political scientist Daniel Treisman has estimated, for example, that the probability of the United States turning authoritarian today is less than one in a thousand (Treisman 2018).

Because the Detroit model of industrial capitalism brought about both those very high levels of affluence and a more equal distribution of income (cf. figures 1.1 and 1.2), one could argue that it was the latter that led to the blooming of democratic institutions in the West. If so, one could then conclude that an acceleration of today's growing inequality (due to an intensification of technological change) should lead, regardless of whether a country enjoys a relatively high per capita income or not, to the collapse of democracy. As with the economic effects of technological innovation, we cannot know the correct answer for sure. Still, that interpretation seems debatable, at least in its crudest form, for two reasons.

In the first place, poverty, which was rampant in societies of the past, has been mostly eradicated in advanced economies—a development that has, in turn, eliminated what used to be one of the sources, if not the main source, of riots, revolutions, civil wars, and authoritarian coups.[8] In 1850, about half of the Western European population had a per capita income similar (in real terms) to today's poorest countries in Africa. Back then, Germans at the ninetieth percentile of Germany's income distribution had a per capita income equivalent to the income of today's Argentinians at the twentieth percentile of the income distribution. That situation has been reversed today. Over ninety percent of the population in Europe and North America enjoy an income equal to or higher than the income of an individual in the ninety-fifth percentile of the income distribution in those same continents during the first half of the nineteenth century.[9] Moreover, those figures do not include all the services directly provided by the state today, ranging from free education to a public health system and pensions, which tend to most benefit the poorest strata of society.

In the second place, growing inequality does not need to trigger social anger and a political backlash—particularly if it happens in affluent societies. It is true that numerous surveys across many countries reveal considerable public concern for current (and rising) levels of inequality, as well as relatively strong preferences for a more equal distribution of income. In addition, laboratory experiments conducted with small numbers of people have repeatedly shown that participants tend to distribute resources among themselves on exactly equal shares. Yet, existing surveys also show that, when asked about the optimal distribution of income for their country, respondents prefer having a certain degree of inequality over an outcome of complete equality. Norton and Ariely (2011) found that a majority of Americans consider as their ideal society one in which the sum of the income of individuals in the top quintile of the income distribution is three times larger than all the income of individuals in the bottom quintile. Using survey data from forty countries, Kiatpongsan and Norton (2014) reported that the median respondent considered the ideal ratio between the salary of a CEO and the wage of an unskilled worker to be one in which the former would earn 4.6 times the latter's income. Although that is much less than current pay ratios, it is certainly far from an endorsement of a strictly egalitarian position.[10] Moreover, the ideal ratio appears to be a function of how researchers frame survey questions about the respondent's preferred income distribution. When Americans are asked what should be the average household wealth in each quintile of the distribution (instead of what should be the share of wealth controlled by each quintile, as in Norton and Ariely [2011]), the ideal ratio between the top and the bottom quintile jumps to fifty to one (Eriksson and Simpson 2012). Such tolerance for inequality seems to be conditional on the effective operation of some principle of fairness and moral desert. Individuals appear willing to accept an unequal society if they judge the system of wealth allocation to be equitable or fair. In a set of laboratory experiments that asked participants to evaluate and reward individuals engaged in different levels of effort, the former had no qualms about distributing awards unequally among the latter.[11] Likewise, participants in those experiments judged unequal outcomes arrived at through impartial procedures such as lotteries to be fair (Starmans, Sheskin, and Bloom 2017).

In preindustrial societies, economic inequality had clear-cut political origins. Very much as in the case of contemporary oil economies, the very rich owed a great deal of their wealth, such as land, trade monopolies, etc., to their political connections. Capturing and controlling the state was instrumental both to appropriating as many assets as possible and to maintaining barriers to prevent the entry of other individuals into political institutions, as well as the development of any economic activities that could threaten the privileged position of "ancien régime" elites. In those closed societies, where the final allocation of assets and income did not follow from any principle of fairness and where poverty was the norm, social resentment toward the rich and politically influential had to be rampant, and democracy, blocked precisely by those who profited from controlling the state, was impossible.

The world of modern capitalism replaced, even if very imperfectly, the use of personal ties and the coercion of the state to assign income and reward individuals with a different set of criteria: personal effort and intellectual ingenuity, as valued by market demand. Inequality did not disappear (although it certainly declined over the twentieth century) but its sources were (at least in part) different: it resulted from the profits accrued by entrepreneurs and industrialists from the invention and application of new technologies—from the batch-production machine to new drugs or digital platforms. Most citizens tolerated inequality to the extent that it took place in an open society—that is, in a society roughly based on the principle of merit. Openness implied that there was some degree of social mobility and some turnover among (and of) elites. The latter depended, in turn, on some rate of innovation and, to use Schumpeter's well-known terms, a process of "creative destruction" by which new products replaced current products and, as a result, new producers displaced incumbent producers. Closing the circle, sustained economic growth validated the idea of an open society as the best organizational structure at hand to enhance the welfare of nonelites.[12]

An Open Society? The potential Achilles' heel of Silicon Valley capitalism lies precisely there—in its capacity to sustain a sufficiently open economy to persuade public opinion to accept the possibility of inequality (tempered by the level of educational investment and social protection in place throughout the second half of the twentieth century). Now, maintaining an open economy (that is, one with low barriers to entry and, therefore, with social mobility and some elite turnover) will depend on the final effects of technology (on labor and capital) as described in the section "Some Guidelines for a Prognosis" earlier in this chapter. But it will hinge too on our capacity to preempt any particular individuals or economic sectors from capturing the state, through campaign contributions, political lobbies, and personal connections, to regulate the economy, to block the entry of any potential rivals, and to lock in their initial economic advantage.

The growing concentration of wealth that has taken place in the last few decades does not bode well in that regard for the immediate future. During the last decades, campaign contributions in US federal elections have gradually become concentrated among the superwealthy. The top 0.01 percent of households (in the income distribution) donated between ten and fifteen percent of all campaign contributions until the early 1990s. In 2012, they gave forty percent. Eighty percent of all board members and CEOs from Fortune 500 firms and ninety-seven percent of all the members of the Forbes 400 made political donations in 2012. Millionaires, who now contribute to Republicans and Democrats alike, have displaced other groups such as organized labor as the main source of revenue for political parties. In the 1980s and early 1990s, donations from the top 0.01 percent and from trade unions were roughly similar. In 2012, contributions from the top 0.01 percent were four times greater than labor's. Besides direct contributions, large corporations and industry associations have ramped up lobbying efforts and spending (Bonica et al. 2013). At least in the United States, money appears to be shaping policy makers' preferences and votes. According to Larry Bartels, the views of members of Congress are closer to those of their wealthy constituents than to low-income voters' (Bartels 2008). Martin Gilens, at UCLA, identified close to 1,800 instances between 1981 and 2002 in which a US survey asked respondents information on their income and on whether they favored or opposed specific policy changes. After coding whether

Congress approved that policy, he examined whether that legislative vote reflected the preferences of respondents at the tenth, fiftieth, and ninetieth percentile of the income distribution. As it turns out, whenever the policy preferences of rich and poor diverged, Congress's decisions were skewed toward the former. A particular piece of legislation had a fifty-percent chance of passing if four out of five respondents with an income in the ninetieth percentile supported it. But it only had a thirty-two-percent chance if four in five individuals in the tenth percentile favored it (Gilens 2012). Because Gilens treated all potential policy changes equally and did not differentiate among them according to the magnitude of their impact (budgetary or otherwise), it is hard to know how biased the American policy-making system is in favor of the wealthy. But a growing literature shows that a low participation rate among low-income voters results in lower taxes and less generous social services.[13] Worryingly, as we have seen earlier in the book, electoral turnout, in particular among the most disadvantaged, is not particularly high in the United States, and is declining quickly in most European countries.

The rising power of money may be compounded by a change in the organization of labor. At the peak of twentieth-century capitalism, a substantial number of individuals worked in large corporations, sharing the same physical space (either assembly lines or a maze of office cubicles on vast floors), under similar work rules and conditions. Their organization and mobilization to secure higher wages and more favorable labor conditions were relatively easy to achieve or, at a minimum, to sustain. Just after World War Two, about one-third of the American workforce was unionized. Membership rates were much higher in small European countries—encompassing more than two-thirds of labor. The breakdown of the Detroit factory system—often reinforced by policies adopted in response to the inequality-employment trade-off examined in chapter 4—eroded those political and social organizations. Unionization rates fluctuate now around ten percent in France and the United States, less than one-fifth in Germany, and around one-quarter in the United Kingdom. With much weaker trade unions in place, checking the influence of big corporate donors is harder, although certainly not impossible, to achieve. Putting all these considerations together, democratic elections are not likely at risk any time soon. But democratic accountability could be in the immediate future. To avoid that possibility and to strengthen, instead, the representation of the common voter, a few things would probably help: capping campaign donations by corporations; democratizing the distribution of electoral funds along the lines of the reform proposed by Bruce Ackerman and Ian Ayres (2008) and approved in places such as Seattle;[14] disclosing the (ownership and marketing) relations between media and large firms; and, crucially, bolstering the level of electoral participation. Nonetheless, checking the cronyism tendencies of the capitalism of the future may be possible only in a particular type of country: radically decentralized or, more precisely, small sovereign polities (approximately the size of small European countries).

Size and Democracy. One of the central problems in today's representative democracies is the large territorial scale of politics. Electoral competitiveness, and political accountability with it, tends to decline with the size of the polity. In countries of a continental scale, like the United States, or in midsized nations like France, the sheer magnitude of the electorate makes the costs of entry into an electoral campaign extremely high.[15] In such a mass market, candidates need to mobilize an extraordinary volume of resources to achieve a sufficiently high level of public recognition and be seen as a viable political alternative by voters.

In the past (coinciding, perhaps not by chance, with the period of Detroit capitalism), parties relied on a vast, tightly woven network of militants to shape the information and political ideas of potential voters and to rally them to the polls. In the 1960s, over a fifth of the population belonged to a political party in countries such as Austria, Sweden, and Denmark. Around one-tenth did in Italy, the Netherlands, and the United Kingdom (R. Katz et al. 1992, table 3). Those mass parties were also aided by the presence of large social organizations such as trade unions or religious associations. Today, those labor-intensive systems employed to harvest votes have collapsed almost everywhere. By the late 2000s, party membership had fallen to 5 percent or less of the population everywhere except for Austria—with numbers as low as 1.2 percent in the United Kingdom (Van Biezen, Mair, and Poguntke 2012, table 1).

As a result, politicians and party cliques now need to rely more heavily on money to access the media, reach out to voters, and mobilize potential supporters. Due to the size of their electoral markets, in large countries big money has a clear edge over everyone else in funding electoral campaigns. In addition, the decline of the old mass parties, the pivotal role of national media, and the intensive use of modern marketing strategies have made electoral politics increasingly "vertical." Campaigns have become personalized around a few names. Successful politicians, directly connected to their audiences via television and new social media, "own" the organizational apparatus they have set up to run for office. That, in turn, gives them strong staying power and bolsters their capacity to name their successors. Aided by the standard dynamics of branding in mass markets, those developments may boost dynastic politics (with more relatives of previous incumbents running for office) or may result, at the very least, in the creation of tight cliques of highly professionalized politicians. If, as has happened so far under Silicon Valley capitalism, wealth and income inequality keep rising, all the pathologies of a large electoral market should only increase in the future—generating a coterie of incumbents, both wedded to their main donors and detached from the mass of voters who will be unable to hold them accountable with much precision.[16]

Both continental and midsized countries are large enough to develop all the traits described above: high barriers to entry; politics influenced by money; a great number of policies and conflicts that make it hard for citizens to assign clear-cut responsibilities based on results. Nonetheless, a continent-sized democracy has a key advantage over a medium-sized nation: because of its demographic size, the former generates or accommodates a higher number of separate (often regionally based) elites in competition with one another.[17] As the number of those elites rises, collusion among them is less likely to happen. As a result, elite turnover ought to be higher. Disagreements over policy will be more intense. And a certain pluralism in opinions and ideas will be easier to defend and maintain: dissenters will always be able to tap the support of a sufficiently large number of private media and institutions to resist the power of the state when they are in the opposition. In midsized nation-states, instead, political and economic elites are fewer and have, therefore, a stronger tendency to be in cahoots with one another. Banks and large corporations, concentrated in the nation's capital, enjoy quick access to power and to a favorable regulatory framework. In exchange, they fund the main political forces and offer retired politicians lucrative positions on their company boards and foundations. Some variant of this type of state, which feeds a system of crony capitalism, is already in place in midsized economies like France, Italy, and Spain, generally with deleterious consequences for institutional transparency and economic growth.

In small democracies, where the number of relevant political actors may not exceed several dozen individuals, the latter's degrees of separation from one another are minimal. Cooperation among them should be, in principle, easier to achieve—to the point of developing, with some probability, something akin to an oligopoly or, to employ terms widely used in Europe, political corporatism. However, the deficiencies associated with the scale of large electoral markets are much attenuated (and often overcompensated) by two things. First, the costs of entering politics, launching an electoral campaign, and developing some popular following are low. Additionally, political representatives live in relative proximity to voters, which should make political accountability stronger than in large countries. In the United States, there is one federal member of the House of Representatives for almost 750,000 people and one federal senator for 3.2 million individuals, on average. In Norway, there is one member of the national parliament for around 30,000 people. Second, the political and economic gains politicians may obtain from interacting with (and pleasing) the corporate world are modest in relative terms: the average firm is smaller than in big nations, and the largest corporations are fully internationalized companies that have a weak incentive to capture the national regulator. In short, smaller countries are much better equipped than large polities to combat the declining political accountability that (some forms of) automation may generate in the future, as well the economic inefficiencies brought about by a state captured by a small set of actors.[18]

Labor Polarization and Migration. The polarization of the labor market in advanced countries is taking place in conjunction with low natural rates of population growth (i.e., autochthonous populations are having fewer children than necessary to replace natural deaths) and rising immigration from other continents. The geographic origin and skill level of immigrants varies across countries, in part as a function of the migration policy in place—some countries incentivize the entry of well-educated and/or linguistically closer migrants more than others. Generally speaking, however, most immigrants work in low-skilled jobs in Europe and North America, directly competing with the native working class.

Native-migrant job competition is, to some degree, unavoidable in any society that receives external population inflows. Yet, it is (and will be) exacerbated by the impact of automation and, particularly, by the hollowing out of semiskilled occupations. In an economy where all social groups enjoy economic growth and where social mobility is high, the integration of immigrants happens rather smoothly in the medium run. The United States became a successful melting pot during the late nineteenth and first half of the twentieth century. France effectively absorbed numerous contingents of Polish workers in the interwar period and Italian and Spanish immigrants after World War Two. By contrast, in a polarized labor market, where the costs of jumping to highly skilled jobs and climbing the economic ladder are high, reconciling the expectations and demands of old and new populations becomes much harder. In that context, autochthonous workers may develop strong anti-immigrant attitudes, asking for direct policies to restrict foreign labor and, eventually, for the introduction of educational and welfare policies that give priority to "whites" or, more often, to groups defined by a particular religious heritage.[19] In such a political environment, defined by conflict between natives and newcomers, highly educated individuals are not likely to play a neutral role either. On the one hand, they may encourage the entry of immigrant workers because they benefit from their services. Yet, on the other hand, they may feel less compelled to treat immigrants as equal citizens for two reasons: immigrants are not part of the old national community based on linguistic, ethnic, or historical ties; and perhaps more importantly, the generally liberal values of highly educated individuals may clash with the socially conservative practices of most migrants (Dancygier 2017).

The combination of those two forces—the opposition of low-skilled native workers and the indifference of high-skilled voters—may push advanced democratic countries toward a racially or ethnically divided political system. Elections may pivot around ethnicity-based voting blocs—a situation in which a nativist coalition could be organized to discriminate against "foreigners" in the labor and housing markets, as well as in the educational and political systems. Welfare states could lose their current universal, equalizing nature, replaced by policies that reinforce ethnic divisions and do little to reduce sharp economic inequalities. European countries, whose relative racial homogeneity was only perturbed in the past by religious divisions that have become increasingly tenuous in the last few decades, may become more similar to the highly racialized democracies prevalent in several Latin American countries and in parts of the American South: unequal, polarized, clientelistic, and inefficient. Democratic institutions would then lose much of their efficacy to curb the potential negative effects of automation.

Democracy in the Rest

Wages reflect, above all, the productivity of workers: in well-functioning markets, employees are paid according to the value of their contribution to the production of goods and services. But their earnings and, more generally, the total cost of labor depend also on the institutional and policy environment in which employers invest and hire workers. As put by Harvard economist Dani Rodrik, democracies "pay" higher wages than authoritarian regimes. On average, democracies are better at protecting the rights of association and unionization, and at providing workers with arbitration and judicial mechanisms to challenge businesses' decisions. They are also more likely to impose restrictions on layoffs, require proper working conditions, and set up a minimum wage. That regulatory regime strengthens the bargaining power of employees, leading to higher salaries. The wage of unionized workers, as well as workers covered by collective bargaining agreements, has been shown to be ten to twenty percent higher than the wage earned by nonunionized and uncovered workers in middle-income and low-income countries (Aidt and Tzannatos 2002). Even after taking into account differences in average productivity, wages have been estimated to rise by more than thirty percent in a country switching from authoritarianism to fully representative institutions (Rodrik 1999). In middle-income countries (those with per capita income above $3,000 of 1996), the share of national income in the hands of labor is six percentage points higher in democracies than in dictatorships (Przeworski et al. 2000). In addition, the public sector is larger and social spending is higher in democratic regimes. In middle-income countries, public revenue as a share of GDP is four percentage points higher in a democratic country. In a wealthy country, the difference rises to six percentage points of GDP. Among East Asian economies, where a great deal of the new manufacturing industry is concentrated, the difference between democracies and dictatorships is even larger (Boix 2003, 2004).

Accordingly, the integration of authoritarian countries, such as China and Vietnam, into the world economy, has amplified the effects of globalization 2.0—an expansion of the supply of labor and strong wage competition—on the workers in the West. More precisely, their labor-repressive institutions have given a competitive advantage to those economic sectors that have a level of productivity comparable to firms or industries in advanced countries—generally, low-value-added sectors employing unskilled workers. Output per worker may be similar across countries, but labor costs (and final prices) are lower for firms located in authoritarian regimes. In other words, unskilled and semiskilled workers in the northern core suffer from a pay wedge (between them and workers in the emerging periphery) that is driven by political factors.

The persistence of that pay gap will depend on how the institutions of newly industrialized countries respond to the latter's process of economic development. If democracy follows from growth—that is, if countries become democratic as their populations become wealthier—that politically induced erosion of advanced countries' competitiveness will just be a temporary phenomenon. Once poor countries develop (partly owing to foreign corporations locating their production there to take advantage of the labor-repressive conditions of authoritarian regimes) over a certain income threshold and then democratize, they will introduce labor-friendly institutions and policies and raise both taxes and social spending. The North-South politically generated pay wedge should disappear. There will be an "industrial core"—with similarly productive workers receiving similar salaries—once more. But that core will now be larger, encompassing a much higher proportion of the world's population. Trade is likely to be based on the kind of intra-industry flows—that is, exports and imports of the same kinds of goods belonging to the same industry— that characterized the manufacturing world before 1980.

However, if, as has happened in Singapore, a higher per capita income does not lead to more democratic institutions, there is a distinct possibility that China and similarly situated economies may not democratize as they develop. In that instance, the pay wedge between the West and the rest may remain in place, and the political tensions described in chapter 5 will not go away.

Those tensions may even intensify if newly developed economies start competing in mid- and high-value economic sectors to the point of eroding the salaries of semiskilled and skilled American and European employees. In short, in the absence of true political and institutional convergence between the old industrial core and the emerging economies, "populist" anger in the North will only increase. To survive, mainstream parties will have to choose one of the two policy strategies discussed at the end of the previous chapter: imposing barriers to the entry of persons and goods and products from the (nondemocratic) South; or, alternatively, increasing compensatory measures for those hurt by globalization.[20]

Responding to Automation

As emphasized before, a high degree of uncertainty over both the pace and the effects of automation makes it impossible to develop *ex ante* any comprehensive plan to deal with it. Future policy interventions will have to be deployed in a piecemeal and almost reactive (*ex post*) fashion. Still, we may consider a set of potential measures, which I will present from the more moderate to the more radical, to respond to technological change.

Human Capital Formation. There is a growing, perhaps universal, consensus that policy makers should facilitate the adjustment to the new economy by spending heavily on human capital formation. The expectation is that, in the same way as happened under Detroit capitalism, the benefits of technological change will spread out to everyone as the supply of the right type of workers matches the labor needs of firms. However, it is worth remembering that such a strategy will only work if, first, all individuals can acquire the kind of high skills demanded by ICTs, and, second, the creation of new jobs offsets those tasks that have become automatized. If educational investments cannot overcome initial deficiencies in natural talents or if automation replaces most jobs (including new ones), policy makers will have to consider more

direct methods of compensation and redistribution toward the
losers of Silicon Valley capitalism, such as a universal basic income, more public employment, and the socialization of assets.
Direct Compensation. One possible compensatory strategy
would consist in the provision of a universal basic income—that
is, a regular income paid by public authorities to all individuals
regardless of their income or need, and independently of whether
they work. The universal basic income (or UBI), which has been
the object of exhaustive debate, and the effects of which have
started to be examined through experimental work, can take a
variety of forms. At one extreme there is a negative income tax,
according to which people with earnings below a certain threshold receive supplemental pay in the form of a "reverse tax": the
state transfers an amount proportional to the difference between
their market earnings and an income level set by the government.
At the opposite extreme, some propose a lump-sum payment to
everyone, funded with highly progressive taxes, to the point of
equalizing final incomes across the board.

Many of the supporters of a UBI envision its introduction as
part of a work environment in which job sharing will become increasingly widespread. That process could happen in two ways.
As a UBI is extended to everyone, a growing proportion of the
population, who value either leisure or certain types of nonremu-
nerated jobs more than their current paid occupation, will decide
to work part time. That, in turn, will free working hours to employ
(also part-time) people who would otherwise be unemployed.
Alternatively, the government might limit the number of salaried
hours, supplementing the potential loss of income with a lump-
sum transfer. Either way, the shift can only be funded from growing productivity and, therefore, from taxing capital rents (which
are arguably growing owing to the capital-labor substitution process driven by automation).

Although it has received little attention in the literature, one
of the crucial problems of job sharing is that the "divisibility" of
highly qualified jobs, which are precisely those for which demand

will grow, is low. The acquisition of the skills needed to perform them well requires a substantial investment in resources and time before working. Moreover, acquiring and perfecting those skills continues over a long period of time—in fact, while they are practiced in the workplace. In (low-skilled and midskilled) routinary occupations, most learning takes place up front—that is, in the first months at the job. In highly skilled positions, know-how and productivity increase with experience—surgeons, lawyers, and researchers become highly proficient in their professions as they accumulate hours at the operating table, filing appeals before courts, or pondering over the right way to frame and conduct experiments. Because splitting highly professionalized jobs is inefficient from an economic point of view, job sharing will only make financial sense for unskilled and semiskilled jobs—precisely the kind of employment in decline.

In any case, the UBI has two important advantages. First, it may free individuals from routine, repetitive tasks, allowing them to engage in more creative and inventive professional paths. Second, it should reduce poverty and, arguably, equalize conditions. The extent to which it could equalize the income distribution will be a function of the form the UBI adopts and how far it will complement or replace the existing welfare state. For some of its supporters, the UBI should be paid in addition to the existing welfare spending (from education to unemployment benefits and health care). Given the substantial size of the current public sector, that means that the UBI will remain small (unless the income share of capital grows quickly and is taxed accordingly) and targeted to individuals in most need (through, for example, a negative income tax). As a result, its equalizing impact will be small.

For others, the UBI should replace all current social spending. Eliminating all welfare-state programs (universal health care, pensions, and so on), policy makers would channel all that spending into a fixed direct transfer to each individual. Citizens would still pay taxes on income, property, and so on, but instead of receiving their services from the public sector, they would contract them with private (or public) agencies. Such a scheme would bring an important advantage: it would increase everyone's freedom to choose how to allocate their income. But it would have a far-reaching downside. Welfare states act as risk-pooling mechanisms, distributing more to those who suffer from negative shocks to their incomes (due to sickness, unemployment, or age). By contrast, a UBI would generally be a fixed sum of money, which would not be tailored to the different (permanent or temporary) needs of each one of us. Finally, the equalizing potential of a UBI that replaced the welfare state would depend on its volume. Consider the following back-of-the-envelope calculations for a country with a per capita income of about $50,000 (Germany today) and public spending (excluding police and defense) equivalent to about forty percent of GDP. Transforming all that spending into a UBI would amount to an annual direct transfer of about $20,000 per person. A family of four would receive an annual income of $80,000— not far from the median household income (in Germany). Such a proposal would have radical consequences: it would lead to a very sharp compression of the income distribution. Anything significantly below that amount, such as the proposals made by the conservative sociologist Charles Murray, would reproduce or even exacerbate current levels of inequality.[21]

The introduction of a UBI is not cost free. It generates its own set of rather substantive problems. First, according to results from pretrials of the UBI in Canada and the United States, it tends to distort the incentives people have to work (Sage and Diamond 2017). In those occupational segments for which jobs are still available but where pay is not much different from receiving some income support, many may prefer to sacrifice a few dollars to enjoy more leisure. Second, the UBI may simply be a mechanism to keep the pre-existing structure of inequality unchanged and to subsidize the wages paid by firms, which, knowing that some basic necessities are met by a publicly paid income, can offer lower wages. Third, the lack of real jobs (for those individuals who cannot be moved up in the skill distribution or, in the case where automation becomes pervasive, for almost everyone) may erode an important part of the inner motivations of individuals to school themselves and to go through the normal processes of character formation and development of internal discipline that we often associate with preparing for and having a job. Fourth, voters support the existence of mechanisms such as unemployment benefits or universal health services to protect the unemployed and the sick in the short and medium run. However, they also value having jobs and a full employment economy over receiving a permanent stream of subsidies from the state—at least in those countries with a strong work ethic. Working confers a dignity that the reception of a public handout does not. A fixed universal income may not meet the true preferences of an electorate about how to organize the economy and the welfare state.

Last, but not least, setting up a UBI may break the ideational justifications of the current welfare state and, as a result, the existing social consensus that underpins it. The forefathers of the welfare state did not design it to substitute income transfers for jobs. In the middle of the twentieth century, even the most redistributive governments pursued two main goals: making their economies more productive (something they tried to achieve by ramping up the public provision of education and of basic infrastructure) and creating jobs for everyone. The welfare state was, as it were, "secondary" in importance: it was intended to remedy and neutralize those situations that threatened to impoverish citizens and that were beyond the control of any single individual, such as economic downturns, sickness, and aging. As such, the welfare state was largely conceived (and justified) as an insurance mechanism: a system in which voters had agreed to pool their resources to take care of those among them who, owing to bad luck or some fundamental injustice, risked remaining or becoming poor. Therefore, to the extent that the UBI breaks the link between personal effort and individual earnings, it could pit its beneficiaries against those voters unhappy with the idea of paying for a growing fraction of "undeserving" poor. That may, in turn, jeopardize the existing universal support for the welfare state as a structure protecting everyone, and therefore could endanger its current level of funding and, with it, the very goal of reducing poverty and inequality. At the end of the day, the political success of the UBI will be a function of the extent of automation. At low or sectorally circumscribed levels of capital-labor substitution, the majority of voters will reject its introduction. In a situation of complete or very widespread automation, where jobs have become very scarce and individual effort is not enough to earn one's living for the vast majority of the population, the UBI should gather strong public support.

The Socialization of Capital Ownership. A more radical solution than a UBI would entail socializing the ownership of capital and splitting it up among all citizens. That would be particularly relevant if and when labor disappeared as a relevant production input (to the point that individuals received, on average, a meager or no salary) and, making Meade's hypothesis true, capital became highly concentrated in the hands of a few owners. Under a socialization strategy, individuals would not receive a public transfer or salary from the state but rather a set of company shares that would allow them to live off their rents as capitalists. Dividing the ownership of machines and robots would curb the political power of a capitalist oligarchy (if the latter indeed emerged). It would be also preferable to transferring all property to the state and having a *nomenklatura* controlling, Soviet style, all the wealth and then managing its distribution among the population.

Two key problems posed by the socialization of capital should make us rather skeptical about it. First, innovation and technological change would probably wane under that system, especially if the returns generated by new patents and industries were to be allocated equally—in accordance with the initial idea of treating everyone as a citizen (and not as an owner). Second, it is unclear whether, even in the absence of differential technological change and productivity growth across sectors and firms, redistributing property in equal lots at some point in time would result in the maintenance of an equal society in the long run. Existing evidence about the evolution of the structure of companies' ownership in former socialist economies that privatized (parts of) their business sector and attempted to distribute it equally among their citizens, such as the Czech Republic and Poland, seems to show that the property of capital became rather concentrated rather quickly. For example, by 1999 the largest shareholder in Czech companies privatized through a voucher system held fifty-two percent of capital on average. In only seven percent of those companies did the largest shareholder control less than a fifth of their shares (Grosfeld and Hashi 2007).

Whatever the solutions that end up being taken, from human capital investment to the equal sharing in property, what seems to be crucial to their success is that they should be adopted through fully democratic procedures. That would give everyone an incentive, even if imperfect, to treat everyone else fairly and to think of those measures as ways to minimize the individual (and collective) risks generated by automation.

A Reversal of Fortunes?

So far, most of the debates among policy experts and policy makers on the impact of automation have turned around its employment and wage effects in advanced industrial (or postindustrial) economies. This has been, in fact, the main focus of this book. Nonetheless, the consequences of automation are likely to become geographically much wider in the future: they should shape the location of industry across the world and, as a result, the chances of economic and political development beyond the West. Accordingly, I turn now to discuss the potential effects of automation in the rest of the world.

As pointed out earlier, the information and computational revolution starting in the 1970s sparked the reconfiguration of the international economy in the following decades. As communication and transportation costs declined, firms unbundled their production structure to exploit the specific comparative advantages of each country across the world—mostly maintaining operations based on highly qualified employees in the northern core while moving (or subcontracting) tasks performed by less-skilled labor to the developing periphery. As a result, a few regions of the world—particularly East Asia—began to converge in economic terms with the advanced word. In 1960, Korea's per capita income was, at around $1,600 (in constant dollars of 2011), a tenth of the US per capita income. In 2015, it had increased twentyfold and was seventy percent of the American one. In turn, China's GDP per capita rose from about $1,000 in 1960 to around $10,000 in 2015.

The future intensification of automation may freeze or even undo that process of economic catch-up. That possibility will depend on the evolution of two economic parameters: the extent of automation, which could be partial (leaving high-skilled jobs untouched and, in fact, making them even more complementary to machines) or complete (with robots replacing all kinds of labor);[22] and the costs of both innovation and capital investment, which I discussed at the end of the section "Some Guidelines for a Prognosis" at the beginning of this chapter.

Consider, first, the scenario of quasi-automation, where machines make unskilled and semiskilled labor superfluous but high-skilled workers are still needed to produce goods and services. With sufficiently cheap machines, subcontracting or moving low-skilled tasks to emerging economies would become pointless, and the process of offshoring would reverse itself. Companies in OECD countries would continue to keep all preproduction activities (product development, marketing, control of sales) in their original headquarters. Yet, with no comparative advantage to be drawn from placing fully robotized plants in periphery economies, whose main attraction is having cheap labor, multinationals could open their factories anywhere in the world. In fact, production activities, now fully automatized, would be probably moved back, or "re-shored," to the old core—or, more precisely, closer to consumer markets—to minimize distribution and transportation costs.

The direct beneficiaries of quasi-automation would be capital and highly skilled labor. Semiskilled and unskilled labor in old industrialized countries would not suffer from competition from abroad; but they would not get back any jobs either. The political consequences would be straightforward. Trade competition would stop being an electorally divisive issue. The impact of globalization would be solely debated in terms of the effects of immigration. Policy making would turn around how to deal with the effects of technological progress through the potential introduction of mechanisms, from formal training to direct compensation, to protect (and transform) that fraction of the population who, owing to their poor skills, would become unemployed or badly paid.

Unlike postindustrial economies, whose pre-existing technological basis and wealth enable them to generate and fund the process of capital-labor substitution, the impact of quasi-automation on emerging economies would be strongly mediated by the costs of innovation (to move up the production ladder from low-value-added to high-value-added activities) and of investing in new technologies. If those costs were to become too high, their catching up with Europe, Japan, and the United States would never materialize. Emerging economies would remain, at most, middle-income countries. As a matter of fact, their economies, now shut out from trade with the old core, could even experience some economic backsliding, owing to the process of "re-shoring" (i.e., moving production back to OECD countries). By contrast, with low barriers to capital investment or innovation, they could still make progress on the production ladder (introducing high-value-added industries). Nevertheless, the overall effects of that progression on the welfare of their populations would be a function of their political institutions. Middle-income countries with democratic institutions would have an incentive to adopt policy strategies similar to the ones prescribed for advanced countries: human capital formation or direct compensation in favor of unskilled and semiskilled labor. By contrast, when governed by authoritarian institutions, capital owners (and high-skilled workers) would probably block the sharing of their technology-driven gains with the rest of the population. The result would be a high concentration of capital ownership, a sharply polarized labor market, and significant levels of political and economic inequality.

Finally, without either capital or know-how to jump start their economies beyond their traditional sectors, low-income countries would remain stagnant. Lacking any industrial manufacturing basis, which has historically been the stepping stone toward development, it would be close to impossible for their very unskilled labor force to acquire enough skills and technical capacities to become complementary to the technologies of the future. They would therefore remain the periphery of the periphery—providing primary products to the rest of the world, and services such as tourism.

Would the same predictions apply under the more radical (and highly implausible) scenario of full automation? With much exaggeration, one could think of it as an economy having only one type of machine, the "iEverything," to use the term proposed by former US secretary of labor Robert Reich, which would produce everything without human intervention—"a small box ... capable of producing everything you could possibly desire, a modern day Aladdin's lamp" (Reich 2015b). There, no labor would be employed at all at any stage of production. As with quasi-automation (automation except for high-skilled work), firms would relocate their production centers close to their consumers. The old industrial core would experience a process of "reindustrialization" (even though it would not imply the creation of any new jobs) to serve its wealthy populations. As for middle-income and poor countries, their economic and political fate would depend on the cost of capital even more strongly than in the quasi-automation scenario. If innovation and capital investment remained expensive, then the process of economic modernization of middle-income countries would stop, and reverse itself. The economic takeoff of poor countries would be completely out of the question. In that case—that is, with regional inequalities intensifying—labor migration to the

North would become the main way for people in the South to escape poverty: it would probably become the only redistributive tool in our hands to equalize life chances across the world. If, however, technological innovation resulted in the invention of cheap "iEverythings" (in a way following what has happened to the cost of cell phones and laptops), even poor countries, like poor individuals in wealthy countries, could have a chance to manufacture most kinds of widgets and render most types of services. Economic development would then unfold everywhere—bringing with it a process of political liberalization.

———

In exploring, throughout the book, the evolution of contemporary capitalism, we have learned that, because they operate according to very different principles, democracy and the market are in tension with each other. In the democratic sphere, individuals participate as equal citizens and the decisions of the majority bind everyone. In the sphere of the market, instead, we bring our different talents and (almost always) unequally distributed assets to the table, engaging in innumerable bilateral and multilateral exchanges and negotiations that tie only the parties involved in them. Markets can generate and sustain differences and inequalities that may jeopardize the principle of one person one vote. In turn, the principle of equality that underpins democracy has the potential to distort the freedom of the market: a majority of the population may vote to erase any existing inequalities and to overturn any private contracts it may dislike, sometimes provoking a backlash from those threatened by elections.

We have also learned, however, that the intensity of those tensions has varied over time—as a function of the type of capitalism in place. Modern capitalism and full democracy were at loggerheads throughout the nineteenth century. By contrast, the story of the twentieth century, particularly in the advanced world, was the story of the triumph of democratic capitalism—that is, the conciliation of democratic politics and free markets—to a great extent because the technologies of production employed at that time benefited broad swaths of society. Today, technological innovation appears, be it in the old industrial core or in the developing periphery, as a sharp double-edged sword of uncertain effects. It could end up benefiting the majority directly, as it did in the past. But it may not. For that reason, the role of politics has grown in importance to make sure it does. At the national level, that requires sustaining democratic institutions, blocking the formation of closed elites, maintaining well-functioning markets, and compensating losers. At the global level, it calls for a coordinated response to manage the geographically heterogeneous impact of technological progress and to foster mechanisms (especially migration to the most prosperous economies) that ensure the gains of automation reach everyone.

NOTES

Chapter 1: Introduction

1. Sources for the US data: for the nineteenth century, Lindert and Williamson (2016); for 1913–63, Plotnick et al. (1998, fig. 2); after 1963, Milanovic (2016). Sources for the United Kingdom: up to 1913, Lindert and Williamson (1983); after 1960, Milanovic (2016). Sources for Japan: before World War Two, Minami (2008); after World War Two, United Nations University-WIDER (2015).

2. Cohn-Bendit Brothers, *Obsolete Communism: The Left-Wing Alternative* (New York: McGraw-Hill, 1968), cited in Przeworski and Meseguer (2006, 184).

3. Data on manufacturing employment come from US Bureau of Labor Statistics (2018). Data on industrial output are taken from the Bureau of Economic Analysis (2018).

4. This paragraph relies on accounts from Cassidy (2014) and Kasparov (2018).

Chapter 2: Prelude: Manchester

1. The data come from Kanefsky (1979).

2. For a review of different and to some extent opposed interpretations about the pace and depth of the industrial revolution, see, e.g., Temin (1997).

3. For a summary of these debates, see Feinstein (1998) and Mokyr (2009, ch. 18).

4. The evolution of wages in the first half of the nineteenth century did not result from a decline in the number of hours worked—indeed, workers could have decided to work less in response to hourly productivity gains. The number of working hours per day dropped from about twelve in the late eighteenth century to about ten by the middle of the nineteenth century, but that trend was offset by a fall in the observance of old holy days and of Saint Monday (the tradition of absenteeism on a Monday) owing to the disappearance of an independent artisanal class as well as the regimentation of workers in factories.

5. Komlos (2017) reports a similar downward trend in height among American workers in the United States before the Civil War.

6. The difference between labor and capital income shares is accounted for by the (declining) share of income in the hands of landowners.

7. Low-income individuals tended to develop later and so heights converged to some extent. Still, for individuals in their mid-twenties, professionals were more than 6 cm taller than laborers in 1883 (Anthropometric Committee 1883).

8. Engels's work followed many others, such as James Kay-Shuttleworth's *The Moral and Physical Condition of the Working Classes Employed in the Cotton Manufacture in Manchester* (1832), Peter Gaskell's *The Manufacturing Population in England* (1833), and William Alison's *Observations on the Management of the Poor in Scotland* (1840), as well as several parliamentary reports.

9. Antitechnological protests were not exclusive to Britain. As far back as the early seventeenth century, the States General of Holland restricted the use of a ribbon-loom machine, and the German emperor banned it in response to widespread popular revolts.

Chapter 3: The Golden Age: Detroit

1. The quote comes from the magazine *Nation* and is reproduced in Hounshell (1984, 218).

2. Again, those very high growth rates were, in part, the result of rebuilding all the capital destroyed during World War Two and moving back to their pre-1939 economic levels.

3. Output per hour worked is derived from table 3.1 through linear interpolation. The data on earnings are taken from Mitchell (2013) for the period until 1937 and from Kopczuk, Saez, and Song (2010) for the period afterward. All data have been normalized to a base index that equals 100 in 1937.

4. The data on output per hour worked for Germany and the United Kingdom are for the whole economy and come from Broadberry (2006). The data on earnings are also for the whole economy, and come from Mitchell (2013). The French data on both labor productivity and earnings are for the industry sector and are taken from Boyer (1978). All data have been normalized to a base index that equals 100 in 1937.

5. At the industry level, for which we also have data for Germany and the United Kingdom, German productivity behaved in a way similar to that in France: it grew by 305%. In Britain it rose more slowly, by 244%.

6. The World Top Incomes Database, which compiles the work of a wide number of scholars led by Tony Atkinson, Thomas Piketty, and Emmanuel Saez, is available at http://wid.world/.

7. The data come from eleven countries (Australia, Canada, France, Germany, Japan, the Netherlands, New Zealand, Sweden, Switzerland, the United Kingdom, and the United States) and the period 1979–95. The correlation index is 0.82.

8. The income share in the hands of the top percentile fell in a relatively correlated and synchronized manner among both war participants and war nonparticipants.

9. For a forceful defense of this thesis in the context of the American economy, see Goldin and Katz (2008).

10. Fig. 3.9 also graphs the 95% confidence interval (drawn with dashed lines) of the estimated relationship—that is, the area for which we can be certain about the relationship. In this specific case, the confidence area indicates that, if we repeated the procedure to estimate the functional form (represented as the solid line), we would get all the estimates within that area 95% of the time. The confidence area in fig. 3.9 is quite narrow, meaning that the relationship between inequality and education is very unlikely to be random.

11. Because the proportion of people with primary and secondary education may affect the democratic chances of a given country, it is difficult to disentangle whether democracy caused education or vice versa. Notice, however, that the divergence takes place in enrollment rates (as opposed to educational attainment or human capital stock) and that it happened early in the twentieth century (as more countries became democracies).

12. The full testimony was published in the *Bulletin of the Taylor Society* 11 (June–August 1926): 95–196.

13. For an analysis of the growth and decline of American socialism, see Marks (1989, ch. 6).

14. The number of workers involved in strikes comes from Ross and Hartman (1960) for the United States and from Mitchell (2013) for Britain and Germany. The number of workers by economic sector comes from Mitchell (2013).

15. Data from Tomka (2013, ch. 6).

16. See Bell (1988, "Afterword, 1988").

17. The Alford index constitutes one of the possible measures to estimate class voting. Notice that very different levels of support for the Left may result in the same Alford index. Suppose, for example, that all manual workers and half of all nonmanual workers vote for the Left. The Alford index would be 50. But it would also be 50 if only half of all manual workers and no nonmanual workers supported the Left. Thus, the Alford index should be taken as a measure of relative class support or, more precisely, of the role played by class across social groups in relative terms. The Alford index was developed at a time and in a context (defined by the presence of a large manufacturing sector) in which the manual-nonmanual distinction was highly relevant to describe employment and arguably class configurations. Over time, the proportion of manual workers has shrunk substantially and sociologists have developed alternative classifications of class structure. That has been followed by an important debate over whether the patterns measured through the Alford index have much value at all (or at least currently). In a comprehensive test of the Alford index as well as other indexes of class-based voting, based on data for 20 countries during the period 1945–90, Nieuwbeerta and De Graaf (1999, 47) conclude that "the various measures of class voting yielded the same conclusions with respect to the class-voting ranking of countries," and that they "could not detect major differences between measures in the rate of decline of class voting."

18. The Alford index was 48 in districts with a majority of Protestant voters, but close to 0 in Catholic districts. In the latter, the Catholic party Zentrum was preferred by blue-collar workers to either the socialists or the communists. In other words, Protestant Germany was closer to the countries represented in fig. 3.13A, at least during the interwar period (Boix 2012).

Chapter 4: Transformation: Silicon Valley

1. The details of Shockley's story come from Brock (2012, 2013).

2. Of that fall in routine manual jobs, 94% was concentrated in male high-school dropouts of all ages and male high-school graduates under the age of fifty. In turn,

about two-thirds of the decline in routine cognitive jobs took place among young and prime-aged women with either high-school diplomas or some college education (Cortes, Jaimovisch, and Siu 2017).

3. For Europe, high-paying occupations are corporate managers; physical, mathematical, and engineering professionals; life-sciences and health professionals; other professionals; managers of small enterprises; physical, mathematical, and engineering associate professionals; other associate professionals; life-sciences and health associate professionals. Middle-paying occupations are stationary-plant and related operators; metal, machinery, and related trade work; drivers and mobile-plant operators; office clerks; precision, handicraft, craft-printing, and related trade workers; extraction and building-trades workers; customer-service clerks; machine operators and assemblers; and other craft and related trade workers. Low-paying occupations are laborers in mining, construction, manufacturing, and transport; personal- and protective-service workers; models, salespersons, and demonstrators; and sales and service elementary occupations. For the United States, the high-skilled jobs encompass managerial, professional, and technical positions. Medium-skilled jobs include sales, office and administrative positions, production and craft tasks, operators, fabricators, and laborers. Low-skilled occupations comprise protective services, food preparation, janitorial and cleaning jobs, and personal-care and personal-service jobs.

4. Using industry-level data for eleven countries, Michaels, Natraj, and Van Reenen (2014) also corroborate that "industries that experienced the fastest growth in ICT also experienced the fastest growth in the demand for the most educated workers and the fastest fall in demand for workers with intermediate levels of education" (74). There is also an abundant literature finding similar patterns at the country level: see Autor, Dorn, and Hanson (2015) for the United States; Dustmann, Ludsteck, and Schönberg (2009) for Germany; and Goos and Manning (2007) for the United Kingdom.

5. Tariffs are measured as the value of import duties over the value of total imports. Data for the period from 1865 to 1950 encompass thirty-five nations. Data for the United States and Australasia have been generously provided by Jeffrey Williamson (Clemens and Williamson 2001). Data for Europe come from Mitchell (2013). The data for the period 1970–99 come from the World Bank Development Indicators.

6. The reduction in tariffs arguably resulted from the decision of developing nations to respond directly to the fall in transportation and communication costs that had been taking place over the previous two decades: in a context of growing competition for investment, it would have become too costly not to liberalize their economies to attract readily available capital. Still, we cannot discard the possibility that developing economies opened their borders influenced by the failure of communism and import-substitution industrial strategies.

7. An alternative explanation, according to which the process of production unbundling was caused by an improvement of domestic institutions in developing economies, is unconvincing. The average levels of expropriation risk, corruption, rule of law, and bureaucratic quality in the developing world or in Asia (based on the IRIS Dataset constructed by Steve Knack and Philip Keefer, drawing from the *International Country Risk Guide* [Knack and Keefer 1995]) did not experience any

significant (discrete or continuous) improvement in their trend from the early 1980s to the mid-1990s.

8. The literature on production unbundling and the emergence of factoryless manufacturing is quite large now. See Feenstra (2007) and Baldwin (2016) for an accessible discussion, and Ando and Kimura (2005); Los, Timmer, and De Vries (2014); and Bayard, Byrne, and Smith (2015) for more specialized analyses.

9. Most cross-border production fragmentation happened within distinct world regions. In North America, manufacturers set up "twin plants" on both sides of the US-Mexican border. Japanese, Korean, and Taiwanese firms offshored their most labor-intensive tasks first to China and later to Vietnam and other Southeast Asian countries. In 2006, among all the Japanese firms that had affiliates abroad, 87% had at least one affiliate in other East Asian countries (Ando and Kimura 2011). By the early 2000s, half of the German manufacturing companies that had chosen to send part of their operations abroad had placed them in Eastern European countries joining the European Union (Kinkel, Lay, and Maloca 2007).

10. Notice, in any case, that the trade component measures the effect of a shift in the location of production without telling us anything about the causes of that shift. As examined at the beginning of this section, firms' locational decisions were in part due to changes in the technologies of transportation and communication.

11. For a review of the literature on the effects of trade on inequality, see Harrison, McLaren, and McMillan (2011).

12. For an up-to-date discussion on the wage effects of immigration, see National Academies of Sciences, Engineering, and Medicine (2016).

13. Initially growing at the same rate across educational levels, by 1985 female weekly earnings were 20% higher than in 1963 regardless of skills. From the late 1980s onward, however, salary trends diverged by educational level. Less educated women did poorly—at least in relative terms. Female high-school dropouts experienced a small increase in real terms of eighteen percentage points—higher than male dropouts but far below the mean among women. By contrast, women who had completed a bachelor degree earned 54% more on average. By 2012, postgraduate women had almost doubled their 1963 earnings. The data come from Autor (2014).

14. See Doms, Dunne, and Troske (1997) and Goldin and Katz (2008) for the United States, and Goos and Manning (2007) for Europe.

15. Wage stagnation had a clear generational component. According to recent work by Guvenen et al. (2017), the median lifetime income of men entering in the job market in the 2000s fell by 10% to 19% with respect to the median lifetime income of men who got their first job in the late 1960s. The share of young individuals earning more than their parents did at age thirty fell from 90% for those born in the 1940s to barely half for those born in the 1980s (Chetty et al. 2017).

16. This figure and its discussion draw from Boix (1998) and Adserà and Boix (2000).

17. More precisely, no person has any incentive to stop working provided that the utility derived from his or her wage minus the costs of working is higher than the utility of drawing a social wage.

18. Fig. 4.7A assumes full employment or, at most, temporary unemployment due to transient economic shocks.

19. They do for an unchanged distribution of skills. But this should not be the case if skills rise. I consider this possibility in more detail in ch. 6, in the context of a discussion about how to respond to further robotization.

20. The author's own calculations based on data from Armingeon et al. (2015) and the index of wage-bargaining institutions used in ch. 3.

21. For data availability reasons, the series starts in 1983 for the United States, and in 1991 for (unified) Germany. It ends in 2010 for Denmark.

22. A variant of this explanation stresses the competitive pressure of communist countries (and their eventual breakdown) to explain the emergence of the model of "embedded liberalism" (and the latter's supposed dismissal). According to that story, Western elites would have agreed to the deal of democratic capitalism to dissuade the working class from embracing the Soviet model and voting for communist parties. Those same elites would have then turned their backs on that political deal as soon as the Soviet system collapsed. This explanation looks fragile, however, for two reasons. First, the model of embedded liberalism was adopted in different places at different times, even though the threat of communism was constant for all countries. Second, the employment and wage changes identified in this chapter preceded the fall of the Soviet Union and the program of economic liberalization of China.

23. Wealth became even more unequally distributed. By 2010, the top 1% owned 42% of all assets in the United States. The hyperwealthy in the top 0.1% controlled 22% of all US national wealth—three times their share back in 1978 (Saez and Zucman 2014).

24. Data on the income share of the top 0.1% come from Atkinson, Piketty, and Saez (2010, table 13.2).

25. Data from World Bank (2017).

26. Leading pension funds and large endowments grew from $5 billion in 1980 to $175 billion twenty years later (Rajan and Zingales 2003, 70–74).

27. Value added per capita is the difference between the value of inputs used to produce a given good or service and the market value of that good or service, adjusted per person employed.

28. The "stock option explosion" was not exclusively driven, however, by CEOs' compensation. About 95% of the option grants went to lower-level executives and employees.

29. Still, the empirical support for this view is inconclusive. Pay levels and general stock prices moved together until 2002, but not afterward.

Chapter 5: Dire Straits

1. Party positions are derived from the data collected in the "Party Manifesto Project" (Volkens et al. 2012) as follows. The position of party i in the left–right (economic policy) scale is calculated as the log odds ratio $\theta_i = (\log R_i + 0.5) - (\log L_i + 0.5)$, where R_i is the sum of references to right-wing themes in party i's manifesto (categories 401, 402, 414, 505, and 702 in the Party Manifesto Project), and L_i is the sum of

references to left-wing themes in party i's manifesto (categories 403, 404, 413, 504, 506, and 701). For a description of the log odds-ratio scaling method, see W. Lowe et al. (2011). The countries included are all Western European countries with continuous democratic elections since 1948, plus Australia, Canada, Japan, New Zealand, and the United States.

2. A separate examination for each country of the evolution of party positions shows the same pattern. Mainstream parties converged everywhere in the economic policy dimension.

3. The position of party i in the globalization scale is calculated as the log odds ratio $\theta i = (\log O_i + 0.5) - (\log C_i + 0.5)$, where O is the sum of references to proglobalization themes in party i's manifesto (categories 108, 407, and 607 in the Party Manifesto Project) and C is the sum of references to antiglobalization themes in party i's manifesto (categories 110, 406, and 608).

4. A separate examination for each country of the evolution of party positions on the globalization dimension also shows a process of generalized convergence—except for Austria, Switzerland, the United Kingdom, and, moderately, Denmark, in the 2000s.

5. The exact question and the sources of the data are as follows. For the United States, "I don't think public officials care much what people like me think," from American National Election Studies and Stanford University (2015). For France, "A votre avis, est-ce que les hommes politiques, en général, se préoccupent beaucoup, assez, peu ou pas du tout de ce que pensent les gens comme vous?" in Enquêtes postélectorales françaises (1978, 1988, 1995, 1997) and European Social Survey (2014). For Germany, "I do not think public officials care much for what people like me think," from Kaase, Schleth, and Wildenmann (2012) and GESIS-Leibniz-Institut für Sozialwissenschaften (2017). The question in Finland and the United Kingdom is different. In Finland, it is "Political parties are only interested in people's votes, not in their opinions," taken from Finnish Voter Barometers 1973–1990 (2017) and the Finnish National Election Studies for 1991, 2003, 2007, 2011, and 2015. In Britain the series reports the percentage of respondents who disagreed with the statement "Parties are only interested in votes, not opinions." The sources for Britain are Barnes and Kaase (2006), and the British Social Attitudes Surveys (1983–2014).

6. The data have been generously shared by Simon Hix at the London School of Economics.

7. The data have been shared by Alex Kerchner at Princeton University. In the US South, turnout fluctuated around 25% in the 1930s and 1940s.

8. Numerous studies show that respondents overreport their true electoral participation in surveys. Overreporting does not seem to be biased in terms of income or satisfaction with the political system, at least positively—that is, richer and more satisfied individuals do not lie more about voting. If anything, the opposite may be true. Less-satisfied citizens seem to hide their abstention more frequently. Therefore, the slope in fig. 5.4 may be steeper in the real world.

9. Notice that whereas the young cohort in the Finnish data only includes those between twenty-five and thirty-four, it encompasses those between eighteen and

thirty-four in the other three countries. Because very young voters tend to participate less, this may explain higher abstention rates in our data for the Netherlands and,
particularly, in France and the United Kingdom.

10. The effects of age and income on turnout are also present for all the other
Western European countries, also surveyed in the European Social Survey but not
plotted in fig. 5.5.

11. This includes all Western European countries (except for Iceland), Australia,
Canada, Japan, New Zealand, and the United States. Figures are based on the OECD
Social Expenditure Database (SOCX), available at http://www.oecd.org/social
/expenditure.htm.

12. The figure comes from Cecchetti, Mohanty, and Zampolli (2010). The countries included are Australia, Austria, Belgium, Canada, Denmark, France, Finland,
Germany, Greece, Ireland, Italy, Japan, the Netherlands, New Zealand, Norway, Portugal, Spain, Sweden, Switzerland, the United Kingdom, and the United States.

13. By contrast, the electoral fortunes of liberal parties hardly changed after
World War Two: they were supported by 10.7% of the electorate (12.9% of all voters)
in 1950, 8.5% of all the electorate (and 10.4% of votes cast) in 1970, and 7.6% of the
electorate (and 10.6% of all votes) in 2007.

14. For additional research on the electoral transformation of social democratic
parties, see Cronin, Ross, and Shoch (2011), Keating and McCrone (2013), Kitschelt
and Rehm (2015), and Rennwald and Evans (2014).

15. The incapacity of social democratic parties to retain blue-collar workers was
arguably due to a gradual decline of trade unions and to a growing divergence of policy preferences between the old working class and the new middle class. I explore the
latter below, with the aid of figs. 5.8 and 5.9.

16. In fact, many European social democratic parties ended up reinforcing some
of the macroeconomic policies (most fundamentally, the adoption of the euro with its
quasi-gold-standard quality) that "narrowed" their room for maneuver in monetary
and regulatory policies even more.

17. For a systematic review of populism and its multiple meanings, see, e.g., Gidron and Bonikowski (2013).

18. See, among a vast literature on voters' preferences toward public policy,
Hibbs (1977, 1987).

19. A more precise representation would consist of graphing the location of each
individual voter as a dot or point in fig. 5.8. Here, the elliptical figure simply indicates
that all middle-class voters are contained within it (and distributed inside with equal
probability). Notice also that the ellipses do not represent, as is standard in spatial
models of elections, the structure of the utility function of one voter (a representative
agent of the middle class, for example) with respect to his or her ideal or bliss point.
Once again, they represent the location of all the ideal points of voters.

20. Notice that a simple move from the Left toward middle-class positions in
response to a reduction in the number of blue-collar workers would not have in itself changed the structure of electoral competition, which would have been still

dominated by the compensation axis. The electoral space only changed—adding a new dimension—when some fraction of the electorate started to challenge globalization.

21. Inclusion in the income quintile is based on a household's total net income (question F41 in the European Social Survey of 2014). Working in a tradable sector is derived from recoding question F31. Italy was not included in the survey. Belgium is not reported here because the regional divide makes classifying parties complex. The classification between extreme-left and extreme-right parties is based, following Simon Hix's work, on their membership in the European Parliament. Far-left parties are those included in the European United Left–Nordic Green Left (GUE-NGL) parliamentary group. Far-right parties are part of two European parliamentary groups: Europe of Nations and Freedom, and Europe of Freedom and Direct Democracy (known as Europe of Freedom and Democracy until 2014). The True Finns and the Danish People's Party, which were founding members of Europe of Freedom and Democracy but left it in 2014 to form part of the European Conservatives and Reformists, are also counted as far-right-wing parties.

22. Once again, it also relies on an "unresponsive" political establishment. Populist parties pointed to the latter's "bank-friendly" response to the financial meltdown of 2007–8 to "demonstrate" a growing disconnection between mainstream parties and the true concerns of voters.

23. An even more radical (Luddite) policy program would offer to block technological change altogether. However, that seems less plausible given a generalized faith in technological progress in Western societies and the fact that, after being banned or heavily taxed, technological innovation would continue to happen in a different political jurisdiction. Still, there have been recent protests against technologically driven change, such as the introduction of Uber or similar platforms in regulated taxi markets.

Chapter 6: Robots vs. Democracy?

1. For a very recent restatement of Keynes's positions, see Brynjolfsson and McAfee (2014).

2. See, for example, M. Ford (2015).

3. According to the World Development Report of 2016, two-thirds of jobs in developing countries and between 50% and 60% in Europe and the United States could be automated over the coming decades (World Bank 2016, 126). Employing different criteria may lead, however, to sharply different results—Arntz, Gregory, and Zierahn (2016) estimate that only 9% of jobs in OECD countries are highly automatable.

4. Two things are worth emphasizing here. First, I have made, for the sake of simplicity, a strong (and debatable) separation between genetic and environmental determinants of natural talents. Research on the sources of intelligence (understood as general cognitive ability) has shown that its inherited part changes in interaction with the parental and social context in which children are raised. See, for example, Plomin and Spinath (2004). Second, I say little about the relative weight of "genetic"

as opposed to "environmental" factors in determining "natural talents." In a way, that is irrelevant for the purposes of the problem of labor supply I am discussing. In any case, recent work seems to show that the impact of genes on IQ and cognitive abilities is low—around 10% and certainly not more than 20% (Rothwell 2018, ch. 6).

5. For the sake of simplicity, I refer to the acquisition and development of skills for a strongly automatized society as moving upward on the skill ladder. It is possible (and already the object of debate in the educational community) that the new skills needed in the future will not just be about having "more" knowledge, but rather about enjoying the kind of soft, noncognitive skills that make each individual able to interact with the fully developed ICTs.

6. See Malone, Laubacher, and Johns (2011). Information from https://www.topcoder.com/, as of November 3, 2017.

7. Data from Boix, Miller, and Rosato (2013). For a discussion of the (extremely large) literature on democratization and democratic stability, see Geddes (2007) and Boix (2011b).

8. See, for example, Londregan and Poole (1990) and Miguel, Satyanath, and Sergenti (2004).

9. Author's own calculation, based on data from Bourguignon and Morrisson (2002).

10. Ideal pay ratios varied substantially across countries, from two in Denmark to twenty in Taiwan. The ideal ratio in the United States was seven.

11. For evidence that the level of toleration for inequality varies with national political culture, see Almås, Tungodden, and Cappelen (2018).

12. All this generalized consensus around the legitimacy of some inequality did not exclude social contestation about the particular level of inequality (low versus high) considered to be acceptable and about the actual definition of fairness. For some, the latter meant rewarding pure effort. For others, it required public intervention to correct strong initial differences in natural talents.

13. For the United States, see McCarty, Poole, and Rosenthal (2006). For non-US cases, see Boix (2003) and, exploiting a quasi-experimental condition, Ferwerda (2015).

14. Ackerman and Ayres's system consists in giving to each citizen a fixed number of dollars to be spent in the electoral campaign in the way (that is, on the candidate) that citizen prefers. That proposal is complemented by the decision to establish a blind trust in which all private donations are put—to be transferred to the candidates or parties chosen by the donors. As with the secret ballot, the secrecy of donations should reduce the lobbying by well-identified donors.

15. Employing data reported in Nassmacher (2009, 85–120) on the cost of electoral campaigns, in the late 1990s average spending (by all candidates and parties) per legislative seat (in national elections) was $1.7 million in the United States, $1.3 million in Japan, over $0.6 million in Germany, and between $0.3 and $0.5 million in France and the United Kingdom. In small countries like the Netherlands and Denmark, spending fluctuated around $100,000 per seat. In Ireland, it was $30,000. All the figures are in (purchasing-power-parity-adjusted) dollars of 2002.

16. The constraining effects of size are compounded by the fact that large countries tend to use majoritarian electoral systems, which, in contrast to proportional-representation rules, impose high barriers to entry to new candidates. Among other reasons, large nations use majoritarian rules to avoid an excessive fragmentation of parties and interests in parliaments, and its corresponding political volatility and governmental instability.

17. The reference group here is democracies with well-functioning market economies: the United States and, on those occasions in which it does not function as an alliance between the political elites of national states, the European Union. Therefore, it does not include those continent-sized countries that have a system of state capitalism with a central elite in control of the state and key corporations—mainly China and Russia.

18. Reducing the impact of money on large polities could certainly be done by engaging in some process of radical decentralization without breaking countries into smaller units. Notice, however, that, even in those (federalized) countries where some policies are in the hands of subnational units (in the form of states, regions, or local governments), control of the national government is of paramount importance. Central governments appoint all regulatory bodies (that govern the structure of markets), determine overall taxes and spending, and act as the potential gatekeepers of all the international forces behind many of the structural transformations of Silicon Valley. If anything, their role has grown over time. Hence, radical decentralization (without sovereignty fragmentation) could work. But it would probably require making sure that each subnational unit bore the full cost of its policies. On this last point, see Rodden (2006).

19. The latter is somewhat paradoxical, given the fact that actual religious practice has become close to zero among precisely those who demand some kind of preferential treatment against "outsiders."

20. A third strategy could consist in investing more effort in changing (democratizing) the political regimes of the South and Far East.

21. For a review of UBI structures, see Van Parijs (2004). In his proposal, Murray (2016) calculates a much lower UBI—at $13,000. The difference comes from the exclusion of several programs (such as education) and the smaller size of the American welfare state (compared with the European one). Social benefits are about ten percentage points of GDP lower in the United States than in Europe.

22. For the sake of simplicity, I here exclude the fact that very-hard-to-automatize manual jobs (such as gardeners, etc.) will remain in place. I have considered them earlier in several places in this book. In interaction with globalization, I did so in the subsection "Labor Polarization and Migration" at the end of the section "Democracy in the West" in this chapter.

REFERENCES

Abrial, Stephanie, Bruno Cautres, and Nadine Mandran. 2003. "Turnout and Abstention at Multi-level Elections in France." Fifth Framework Research Programme (1998–2002): Democratic Participation and Political Communication in Systems of Multi-level Governance. Working paper, Centre d'Informatisation des Donnés Socio-Politiques, Centre National de la Recherche Scientifique, Grenoble.

Ackerman, Bruce, and Ian Ayres. 2008. *Voting with Dollars: A New Paradigm for Campaign Finance.* New Haven, CT: Yale University Press.

Adserà, Alícia, and Carles Boix. 2000. "Must We Choose? European Unemployment, American Inequality and the Impact of Education and Labor Market Institutions." *European Journal of Political Economy* 16 (November): 611–38.

Aidt, Toke S., and Peter S. Jensen. 2013. "Democratization and the Size of Government: Evidence from the Long 19th Century." *Public Choice* 157 (3–4): 511–42.

Aidt, Toke S., and Zafiris Tzannatos. 2002. *Unions and Collective Bargaining: Economic Effects in a Global Environment.* Washington, DC: World Bank.

Aitkin, Don. 1982. *Stability and Change in Australian Politics.* Canberra: Australian National University Press.

Akst, Daniel. 2014. "What Can We Learn from Past Anxiety over Automation?" *Wilson Quarterly* 2014 (summer).

Alford, Robert R. 1962. "A Suggested Index of the Association of Social Class and Voting." *Public Opinion Quarterly* 26 (3): 417–25.

———. 1963. "The Role of Social Class in American Voting Behavior." *Western Political Quarterly* 16 (1): 180–94.

Allen, Robert C. 2001. "The Great Divergence in European Wages and Prices from the Middle Ages to the First World War." *Explorations in Economic History* 38 (4): 411–47.

———. 2009. "Engels' Pause: Technical Change, Capital Accumulation, and Inequality in the British Industrial Revolution." *Explorations in Economic History* 46 (4): 418–35.

Almås, Ingvild, Bertil Tungodden, and Alexander W. Cappelen. 2018. "Cutthroat Capitalism versus Cuddly Socialism: Are Americans More Meritocratic and Efficiency-Seeking than Scandinavians?" Working paper, Norwegian School of Economics.

American National Election Studies and Stanford University. 2015. *ANES Time Series Cumulative Data File (1948–2012).* Ann Arbor, MI: Inter-university Consortium for Political and Social Research. https://doi.org/10.3886/ICPSR08475.v15.

Andersen, Jørgen G. 1984. "Decline of Class Voting or Change in Class Voting?: Social Classes and Party Choice in Denmark in the 1970s." *European Journal of Political Research* 12 (3): 243–59.

Andersen, Jørgen G., and Jens Hoff. 2001. "Electoral Participation." In *Democracy and Citizenship in Scandinavia*, edited by Andersen and Hoff, 31–46. London: Palgrave.

Ando, Mitsuyo, and Fukunari Kimura. 2005. "The Formation of International Production and Distribution Networks in East Asia." In *International Trade in East Asia, NBER-East Asia Seminar on Economics*, vol. 14, edited by Takatoshi Ito and Andrew Rose, 177–216. Chicago: University of Chicago Press.

Ando, Mitsuyo, and Fukunari Kimura. 2011. *Globalizing Corporate Activities in East Asia and Impact on Domestic Operations: Further Evidence from Japanese Manufacturing Firms*. Research Institute of Economy, Trade and Industry (RIETI), Discussion Paper 11-E-034. Tokyo: RIETI.

Ansell, Ben W. 2010. *From the Ballot to the Blackboard: The Redistributive Political Economy of Education*. New York: Cambridge University Press.

Anthropometric Committee. 1883. "Final Report of the Anthropometric Committee." Facsimile available online at Galton.org. http://galton.org/essays/1880 -1889/galton-1883-rba-anthro-report-final.pdf.

Armingeon, Klaus, Christian Isler, Laura Knöpfel, David Weisstanner, and Sarah Engler. 2015. *Comparative Political Data Set 1960–2013*. Bern: Institute of Political Science, University of Berne.

Armstrong, Stuart, and Kaj Sotala. 2015. "How We're Predicting AI—Or Failing To." In *Beyond Artificial Intelligence: The Disappearing Human-Machine Divide*, edited by Jan Romportl, Eva Zackova, and Josez Kelemen, 11–29. Cham, Switzerland: Springer.

Arntz, Melanie, Terry Gregory, and Ulrich Zierahn. 2016. *The Risk of Automation for Jobs in OECD Countries: A Comparative Analysis*. OECD Social, Employment and Migration Working Papers, no. 189. Paris: OECD.

Aron, Raymond. 1957. *The Opium of Intellectuals*. New York: Doubleday.

Atkinson, Anthony B., Thomas Piketty, and Emmanuel Saez. 2010. "Top Incomes in the Long Run of History." In *Top Incomes: A Global Perspective*, edited by Atkinson and Piketty, ch. 13. New York: Oxford University Press.

Autor, David H. 2010. *The Polarization of Job Opportunities in the US Labor Market: Implications for Employment and Earnings*. Washington, DC: Center for American Progress and The Hamilton Project.

———. 2014. "Skills, Education, and the Rise of Earnings Inequality among the 'Other 99 Percent.'" *Science* 344 (6186): 843–51.

———. 2015. "Why Are There Still So Many Jobs?: The History and Future of Workplace Automation." *Journal of Economic Perspectives* 29 (3): 3–30.

Autor, David H., David Dorn, and Gordon H. Hanson. 2015. "Untangling Trade and Technology: Evidence from Local Labour Markets," *Economic Journal* 125: 621–46.

Autor, David H., Lawrence F. Katz, and Alan B. Krueger. 1998. "Computing Inequality: Have Computers Changed the Labor Market?" *Quarterly Journal of Economics* 113 (4): 1169–213.

Baldwin, Richard. 2016. *The Great Convergence: Information Technology and the New Globalization.* Cambridge, MA: Belknap Press.

Barnes, Samuel H., and Max Kaase. 2006. *Political Action: An Eight Nation Study, 1973–1976.* Ann Arbor, MI: Inter-university Consortium for Political and Social Research. https://doi.org/10.3886/ICPSR07777.v1.

Barro, Robert J., and Jong-Wha Lee. 2015. *Education Matters. Global Schooling Gains from the 19th to the 21st Century.* New York: Oxford University Press.

Bartels, Larry M. 2008. *Unequal Democracy: The Political Economy of the New Gilded Age.* Princeton, NJ: Princeton University Press.

Bayard, Kimberly, David Byrne, and Dominic Smith. 2015. "The Scope of US Factoryless Manufacturing." In *Measuring Globalization: Better Trade Statistics for Better Policy,* vol. 2, *Factoryless Manufacturing, Global Supply Chains, and Trade in Intangibles and Data,* edited by Susan N. Houseman and Michael Mandel, 81–120. Kalamazoo, MI: W. E. Upjohn Institute for Employment Research.

Becker, Sascha O., Thiemo Fetzer, and Dennis Novy. 2017. "Who Voted for Brexit?: A Comprehensive District-Level Analysis." *Economic Policy* 32 (92): 601–50.

Bell, Daniel. 1988. *The End of Ideology.* 2nd ed. Cambridge, MA: Harvard University Press.

Beramendi, Pablo, and David Rueda. 2014. "Inequality and Institutions: The Case of Economic Coordination." *Annual Review of Political Science* 17: 251–71.

Bernard, Andrew B., and Teresa C. Fort. 2015. "Factoryless Goods Producing Firms." *American Economic Review* 105 (5): 518–23.

Bernhofen, Daniel M., Zouheir El-Sahli, and Richard Kneller. 2016. "Estimating the Effects of the Container Revolution on World Trade." *Journal of International Economics* 98: 36–50.

Blais, André, Elisabeth Gidengil, and Neil Nevitte. 2004. "Where Does Turnout Decline Come From?" *European Journal of Political Research* 43 (3): 221–36.

Boix, Carles. 1998. *Political Parties, Growth and Equality: Conservative and Social Democratic Economic Strategies in the World Economy.* New York: Cambridge University Press.

———. 2003. *Democracy and Redistribution.* New York: Cambridge University Press.

———. 2004. "The Public Sector in Asia." In *Global Change and East Asian Policy Initiatives,* edited by Shahid Yusuf, M. Anjum Alraf and Kaoru Nabeshima, ch. 6. Washington, DC: World Bank and Oxford University Press.

———. 2011a. "Redistribution Policies in a Globalized World." In *Making Globalization Socially Sustainable,* edited by Marion Jansen and Marc Bachetta, ch. 8. Geneva: World Trade Organization and International Labour Organization.

———. 2011b. "Democracy, Development, and the International System." *American Political Science Review* 105 (4): 809–28.

———. 2012. "El auge de la socialdemocracia." In *Democracia y socialdemocracia: Homenaje a José María Maravall,* edited by Adam Przeworski and Ignacio Sánchez-Cuenca, 195–240. Madrid: Centro de Estudios Políticos y Constitucionales.

———. 2015. "Prosperity and the Evolving Structure of Advanced Economies." In *The Politics of Advanced Capitalism,* edited by Pablo Beramendi, Silja Hausermann,

Herbert Kitschelt, and Hans- Peter Kriesi, ch. 2. New York: Cambridge University Press.

Boix, Carles, Michael Miller, and Sebastian Rosato. 2013. "A Complete Data Set of Political Regimes, 1800–2007." *Comparative Political Studies* 46 (12): 1523–54.

Bolt, Jutta, and Jan Luiten van Zanden. 2014. "The Maddison Project: Collaborative Research on Historical National Accounts." Maddison Project Database, version 2013. *Economic History Review* 67 (3): 627–51.

Bonica, Adam, Nolan McCarty, Keith T. Poole, and Howard Rosenthal. 2013. "Why Hasn't Democracy Slowed Rising Inequality?" *Journal of Economic Perspectives* 27 (3): 103–23.

Bourguignon, François, and Christian Morrisson. 2002. "Inequality among World Citizens: 1820–1992." *American Economic Review* 92 (4): 727–44.

Boyer, Robert. 1978. "Les salaires en longue période." *Economie et Statistique* 103 (September): 27–57.

Bresnahan, Timothy F. 1999. "Computerisation and Wage Dispersion: An Analytical Reinterpretation." *Economic Journal* 109 (June): F390–415.

British Social Attitudes Surveys. 1983–2014. National Centre for Social Research. Yearly. http://www.bsa.natcen.ac.uk.

Broadberry, Stephen. 2006. *Market Services and the Productivity Race, 1850–2000: British Performance in International Perspective*. New York: Cambridge University Press.

Brock, David C. 2012. "From Automation to Silicon Valley: The Automation Movement of the 1950s, Arnold Beckman, and William Shockley." *History and Technology* 28 (4): 375–401.

———. 2013. "Shockley's Robot Dream." *IEEE Spectrum* 50 (12): 40–55.

Brynjolfsson, Erik, and Andrew McAffee. 2014. *The Second Machine Age: Work, Progress, and Prosperity in a Time of Brilliant Technologies*. New York: W. W. Norton.

Cassidy, Mike. 2014. "Centaur Chess Brings Out the Best in Humans and Machines." Bloomreach. December 15. https://www.bloomreach.com/en/blog/2014/12/centaur-chess-brings-best-humans-machines.html.

Cecchetti, Stephen G., Madhusudan S. Mohanty, and Fabrizio Zampolli. 2010. "The Future of Public Debt: Prospects and Implications." Bank for International Settlements Working Paper no. 300. Available at SSRN: https://ssrn.com/abstract=1599421.

Chandler, Alfred D. 1977. *The Visible Hand: The American Revolution in American Business*. Cambridge, MA: Belknap.

———. 1997. "The Computer Industry: The First Half-Century." In *Competing in the Age of Digital Convergence*, edited by David B. Yoffie, 37–122. Boston, MA: Harvard Business School Press.

Charlton, John. 1997. *The Chartists: The First National Workers' Movement*. London: Pluto.

Chetty, Raj, David Grusky, Maximilian Hell, Nathaniel Hendren, Robert Manduca, and Jimmy Narang. 2017. "The Fading American Dream: Trends in Absolute Income Mobility since 1940." *Science* 356 (6336): 398–406.

Clemens, Michael A., and Jeffrey G. Williamson. 2001. "A Tariff-Growth Paradox? Protection's Impact the World Around 1875–1997." National Bureau of Economic Research (NBER) Working Paper no. 8459.

Cortes, Guido M. 2016. "Where Have the Middle-Wage Workers Gone? A Study of Polarization Using Panel Data." *Journal of Labor Economics* 34 (1): 63–105.

Cortes, Guido M., Nir Jaimovisch, and Henry E. Siu. 2017. "Disappearing Routine Jobs: Who, How, and Why?" *Journal of Monetary Economics* 91 (November): 69–87.

Crewe, Ivor, Anthony Fox, and James Alt. 1977. "Non-voting in British General Elections 1966–October 1974." In *British Political Sociology Yearbook*, vol. 3, edited by Colin Crouch, 38–109. London: Croom Helm.

Cronin, James E., George W. Ross, and James Shoch, eds. 2011. *What's Left of the Left: Democrats and Social Democrats in Challenging Times.* Durham, NC: Duke University Press.

Dalton, Russell J. 1988. *Citizen Politics in Western Democracies: Public Opinion and Political Parties in the United States, Great Britain, West Germany, and France.* London: Chatham House.

———. 2004. *Democratic Challenges, Democratic Choices: The Erosion of Political Support in Advanced Industrial Democracies.* New York: Oxford University Press.

Dancygier, Rafaela M. 2017. *Dilemmas of Inclusion: Muslims in European Politics.* Princeton, NJ: Princeton University Press.

Dancygier, Rafaela M., and Stefanie Walter. 2015. "Globalization, Labor Market Risks, and Class Cleavages." In *The Politics of Advanced Capitalism*, edited by Pablo Beramendi, Silja Häusermann, Herbert Kitschelt, and Hanspeter Kriesi, 133–56. New York: Cambridge University Press.

Davis, Joshua. 2010. "How Elon Musk Turned Tesla into the Car Company of the Future." *Wired.* September 27. https://www.wired.com/2010/09/ff_tesla/.

Dean, Judith M., Kwok-Chiu Fung, and Zhi Wang. 2011. "Measuring Vertical Specialization: The Case of China." *Review of International Economics* 19 (4): 609–25.

Deaton, Angus. 2013. *The Great Escape: Health, Wealth, and the Origins of Inequality.* Princeton, NJ: Princeton University Press.

De Pleijt, Alexandra M., and Jacob L. Weisdorf. 2017. "Human Capital Formation from Occupations: The 'Deskilling Hypothesis' Revisited." *Cliometrica*, 11 (1): 1–30.

Dickinson, Edward B. 1896. *Official Proceedings of the Democratic National Convention.* Logansport, IN: Wilson, Humphreys.

Doms, Mark, Timothy Dunne, and Kenneth R. Troske. 1997. "Workers, Wages, and Technology." *Quarterly Journal of Economics* 112 (1): 253–90.

Dustmann, Christian, Johannes Ludsteck, and Uta Schönberg. 2009. "Revisiting the German Wage Structure." *Quarterly Journal of Economics* 124 (2): 843–81.

Elliott, Stuart W. 2017. *Computers and the Future of Skill Demand.* Paris: OECD.

Elsby, Michael W. L., Bart Hobijn, and Ayşegül Şahin. 2013. "The Decline of the US Labor Share." *Brookings Papers on Economic Activity* 2013 (2): 1–63.

Enquête post-électorale française. 1978. Paris: Centre d'Étude de la Vie Politique Française. http://bdq.quetelet.progedo.fr/fr/Details_d_une_enquete/517.

Enquête post-électorale française. 1988. Paris: Centre d'Étude de la Vie Politique Française. http://bdq.quetelet.progedo.fr/fr/Details_d_une_enquete/518.

Enquête post-électorale française. 1995. Paris: Centre d'Étude de la Vie Politique Française. http://bdq.quetelet.progedo.fr/fr/Details_d_une_enquete/460.

Enquête post-électorale française. 1997. Paris: Centre d'Étude de la Vie Politique Française. http://bdq.quetelet.progedo.fr/fr/Details_d_une_enquete/519.

Eriksson, Kimmo, and Brent Simpson. 2012. "What Do Americans Know about Inequality?: It Depends on How You Ask Them." *Judgment and Decision Making* 7 (6): 741–45.

Erixon, Lennard. 2010. "The Rehn-Meidner Model in Sweden: Its Rise, Challenges and Survival." *Journal of Economic Issues* 44: 677–715.

European Social Survey (ESS). 2014. European Social Survey Round 7 Data. Data file edition 2.1. NSD (Norwegian Centre for Research Data) Data Archive and distributor of ESS data for ESS ERIC.

Feenstra, Robert C. 2007. "Globalization and Its Impact on Labour." Vienna Institute for International Economic Studies (WIIW) Working Paper no. 44. July.

Feinstein, Charles H. 1998. "Pessimism Perpetuated: Real Wages and the Standard of Living in Britain during and after the Industrial Revolution." *Journal of Economic History* 58 (3): 625–58.

Ferwerda, Jeremy. 2015. "The Politics of Proximity: Local Redistribution in Developed Democracies." Unpublished PhD dissertation, MIT.

Finnish Voter Barometers 1973–1990: Combined Data. Codebook. 2017. Finnish Social Science Data Archive.

Finnish National Election Study 1991. Codebook. 2015. Tampere, Finland: Finnish Social Science Data Archive, University of Tampere.

Finnish National Election Study 2003. Codebook. 2017. Tampere, Finland: Finnish Social Science Data Archive, University of Tampere.

Finnish National Election Study 2007. Codebook. 2017. Tampere, Finland: Finnish Social Science Data Archive, University of Tampere.

Finnish National Election Study 2011. Codebook. 2017. Tampere, Finland: Finnish Social Science Data Archive, University of Tampere.

Finnish National Election Study 2015. Codebook. 2017. Tampere, Finland: Finnish Social Science Data Archive, University of Tampere.

Flora, Peter, and Arnold Joseph Heidenheimer, eds. 1981. *The Development of Welfare States in Europe and America.* Piscataway, NJ: Transaction.

Floud, Roderick, Kenneth Wachter, and Annabel Gregory. 1990. *Height, Health and History: Nutritional Status in the United Kingdom, 1750–1980.* New York: Cambridge University Press.

Ford, Martin. 2015. *Rise of the Robots: Technology and the Threat of a Jobless Future.* New York: Basic Books.

Ford, Robert, and Matthew J. Goodwin. 2014. *Revolt on the Right: Explaining Support for the Radical Right in Britain.* London: Routledge.

Frame, W. Scott, and Lawrence J. White. 2015. "Technological Change, Financial Innovation, and Diffusion in Banking." In *The Oxford Handbook of Banking,* 2nd ed., edited by Allen N. Berger, Philip Molyneux, and John O. S. Wilson, 486–507. New York: Oxford University Press.

Franklin, Mark N., Patrick Lyons, and Michael Marsh. 2004. "Generational Basis of Turnout Decline in Established Democracies." *Acta Politica* 39 (2): 115–51.

Freeman, Richard B. 1995. "Are Your Wages Set in Beijing?" *Journal of Economic Perspectives* 9 (3): 15–32.

Frey, Carl Benedikt, and Michael A. Osborne. 2017. "The Future of Employment: How Susceptible Are Jobs to Computerisation?" *Technological Forecasting and Social Change* 114 (January): 254–80.

Gabaix, Xavier, and Augustin Landier. 2008. "Why Has CEO Pay Increased So Much?" *Quarterly Journal of Economics* 123 (1): 49–100.

Gallup, George H., ed. 1976. *The Gallup International Public Opinion Polls, Great Britain, 1937–1975*. New York: Random House.

Gass, Nick. 2016. "Trump: GOP Will Become 'Worker's Party' under Me." *Politico.* May 26. https://www.politico.com/story/2016/05/trump-gop-workers-party -223598.

Gazeley, Ian. 2014. "Income and Living Standards, 1870–2010". In *The Cambridge Economic History of Modern Britain*, vol. 2, *Economic Maturity, 1860–1939*, edited by Roderick Floud and Paul Johnson, 151–80. New York: Cambridge University Press.

Geddes, Barbara. 2007. "What Causes Democratization." In *The Oxford Handbook of Comparative Politics*, edited by Carles Boix and Susan C. Stokes, ch. 14. New York: Oxford University Press.

GESIS-Leibniz-Institut für Sozialwissenschaften. 2017. Politbarometer Partielle Kumulation 1977–2015 (Partial cumulation of politbarometers 1977–2016). GESIS Data Archive, Cologne. April 19, 2017. ZA2391 data file version 7.0.0. doi:10.4232/1.12733.

Gest, Justin. 2016. *The New Minority: White Working Class Politics in an Age of Immigration and Inequality*. New York: Oxford University Press.

Gidron, Noam, and Bart Bonikowski. 2013. "Varieties of Populism: Literature Review and Research Agenda." Harvard University, Weatherhead Working Paper Series, no. 13-0004.

Gilens, Martin. 2012. *Affluence and Influence: Economic Inequality and Political Power in America*. Princeton, NJ: Princeton University Press.

Gingrich, Jane, and Silja Häusermann. 2015. "The Decline of the Working Class Vote, the Reconfiguration of the Welfare Support Coalition and Consequences for the Welfare State." *Journal of European Social Policy* 25 (1): 50–75.

Goldin, Claudia, and Lawrence F. Katz. 1996. "The Origins of Technology-Skill Complementarity." NBER Working Paper no. 5657.

———. 2008. *The Race between Education and Technology*. Cambridge, MA: Harvard University Press.

Goldin, Claudia, and Robert A. Margo. 1992. "The Great Compression: The Wage Structure in the United States at Mid-Century." *Quarterly Journal of Economics* 107 (1): 1–34.

Goos, Maarten, and Alan Manning. 2007. "Lousy and Lovely Jobs: The Rising Polarization of Work in Britain." *Review of Economics and Statistics* 89 (1): 118–33.

Goos, Maarten, Alan Manning, and Anna Salomons. 2014. "Explaining Job Polarization: Routine-Biased Technological Change and Offshoring." *American Economic Review* 104 (8): 2509–26.

Gordon, Robert J. 2004. "Two Centuries of Economic Growth: Europe Chasing the American Frontier." NBER Working Paper no. 10662.

———. 2014. "The Demise of US Economic Growth: Restatement, Rebuttal, and Reflections." NBER Working Paper no. 19895.

———. 2016. *The Rise and Fall of American Growth: The US Standard of Living since the Civil War*. Princeton, NJ: Princeton University Press.

Grosfeld, Irena, and Iraj Hashi. 2007. "Changes in Ownership Concentration in Mass Privatised Firms: Evidence from Poland and the Czech Republic." *Corporate Governance: An International Review* 15 (4): 520–34.

Guellec, Dominique, and Carolina Paunov. 2017. "Digital Innovation and the Distribution of Income." NBER Working Paper no. 23987.

Guvenen, Fatih, Greg Kaplan, Jae Song, and Justin Weidner. 2017. "Lifetime Incomes in the United States over Six Decades." NBER Working Paper no. 23371.

Hacker, Jacob S., and Paul Pierson. 2010. *Winner-Take-All Politics*. New York: Simon and Schuster.

Hanson, Gordon H., Raymond J. Mataloni Jr., and Matthew J. Slaughter. 2005. "Vertical Production Networks in Multinational Firms." *Review of Economics and Statistics* 87 (4): 664–78.

Harrison, Ann E., John McLaren, and Margaret McMillan. 2011. "Recent Perspectives on Trade and Inequality." *Annual Review of Economics* 3 (1): 261–89.

Hatton, Timothy J., and Jeffrey G. Williamson. 1998. *The Age of Mass Migration: Causes and Economic Impact*. New York: Oxford University Press.

Häusermann, Silja. 2017. "Electoral Realignment and Social Policy Positions of Social Democratic Parties." Working paper, University of Zurich.

Häusermann, Silja, and Peter Kriesi. 2015. "What Do Voters Want?: Dimensions and Configurations in Individual-Level Preferences and Party Choice." In *The Politics of Advanced Capitalism*, edited by Pablo Beramendi, Silja Häusermann, Herbert Kitschelt, and Hanspeter Kriesi, 202–30. New York: Cambridge University Press.

Hibbs, Douglas A. 1977. "Political Parties and Macroeconomic Policy." *American Political Science Review* 71 (4): 1467–87.

———. 1987. *The Political Economy of Industrial Democracies*. Cambridge, MA: Harvard University Press.

Hooghe, Marc, and Anna Kern. 2017. "The Tipping Point between Stability and Decline: Trends in Voter Turnout, 1950–1980–2012." *European Political Science* 16: 535–52.

Hounshell, David. 1984. *From the American System to Mass Production, 1800–1932: The Development of Manufacturing Technology in the United States*. Baltimore, MD: Johns Hopkins University Press.

Huber, Manfred, and Eva Orosz. 2003. "Health Expenditure Trends in OECD Countries, 1990–2001." *Health Care Financing Review* 25 (1): 1–22.

Huck, Paul. 1995. "Infant Mortality and Living Standards of English Workers during the Industrial Revolution." *Journal of Economic History* 55 (3): 528–50.

Hummels, David L. 2007. "Transportation Costs and International Trade in the Second Era of Globalization." *Journal of Economic Perspectives* 21 (3): 131–54.

Hummels, David L., and Georg Schaur. 2013. "Time as a Trade Barrier." *American Economic Review* 103 (7): 2935–59.

Ikenberry, John. 2011. *Liberal Leviathan*. Princeton, NJ: Princeton University Press.

Intel. [2011]. "Intel Global Manufacturing Facts." Factsheet. http://download.intel.com/newsroom/kits/22nm/pdfs/Global-Intel-Manufacturing_FactSheet.pdf.

Jerome, Harry. 1934. *Mechanization in Industry*. New York: NBER.

Judis, John B. 2016. *The Populist Explosion: How the Great Recession Transformed American and European Politics*. New York: Columbia Global Reports.

Kaase, Max, Uwe Schleth, and Rudolf Wildenmann. 2012. Politics in the Federal Republic (August 1969). GESIS Data Archive, Cologne. ZA0525 data file version 3.0.0. doi:10.4232/1.11457.

Kahan, Alan. 2003. *Liberalism in Nineteenth Century Europe: The Political Culture of Limited Suffrage*. New York: Palgrave Macmillan.

Kanefsky, John W. 1979. "The Diffusion of Power Technology in British Industry, 1760–1870." Unpublished PhD dissertation, University of Exeter.

Kaplan, Steven, and Joshua Rauh. 2013. "It's the Market: The Broad-Based Rise in the Return to Top Talent." *Journal of Economic Perspectives* 27 (3): 35–56.

Karabarbounis, Loukas, and Brent Neiman. 2014. "The Global Decline of the Labor Share." *Quarterly Journal of Economics* 129 (1): 61–103.

Kasparov, Garry. 2018. *Deep Thinking: Where Machine Intelligence Ends and Human Creativity Begins*. New York: PublicAffairs.

Katz, Lawrence F., and Robert A. Margo. 2014. "Technical Change and the Relative Demand for Skilled Labor: The United States in Historical Perspective." In *Human Capital in History: The American Record*, edited by Leah Platt Boustan, Carola Frydman, and Robert A. Margo, 15–57. Chicago: University of Chicago Press.

Katz, Richard S., Peter Mair, Luciano Bardi, Lars Bille, Kris Deschouwer, David Farrell, Ruud Koole, et al. 1992. "The Membership of Political Parties in European Democracies, 1960–1990." *European Journal of Political Research* 22 (3): 329–45.

Katzenstein, Peter J. 1985. *Small States in World Markets: Industrial Policy in Europe*. Ithaca, NY: Cornell University Press.

Keating, Michael, and David McCrone, eds. 2013. *The Crisis of European Social Democracy*. Edinburgh: Edinburgh University Press.

Kennedy, John F. 1962. "Remarks of President John F. Kennedy, Commencement Exercises, Yale University, New Haven, Connecticut, June 11, 1962." Press copy. National Archives Catalog, collection JFK-3, series Speech Files, 1961–63, identifier 193922. https://catalog.archives.gov/id/193922?&sp=%7B%22q%22%3A%22*%3A*%22%2C%22f.parentNaId%22%3A%22193921%22%2C%22f.level%22%3A%22item%22%2C%22sort%22%3A%22naIdSort%20asc%22%7D&sr=0.

Keynes, John M. 1963. *Essays in Persuasion*. New York: Norton.

Keyssar, Alexander. 2000. *The Right to Vote: The Contested History of Democracy in the United States*. New York: Basic Books.

Kiatpongsan, Sorapop, and Michael I. Norton. 2014. "How Much (More) Should CEOs Make? A Universal Desire for More Equal Pay." *Perspectives on Psychological Science* 9 (6): 587–93.

Kinder, Hermann, and Werner Hilgemann. 2003. *The Penguin Atlas of World History: From the French Revolution to the Present.* Vol. 2. New York: Penguin Group USA.

Kinkel, Steffen, Gunter Lay, and Spomenka Maloca. 2007. "Development, Motives and Employment Effects of Manufacturing Offshoring of German SMEs." *International Journal of Entrepreneurship and Small Business* 4 (3): 256–76.

Kirchheimer, Otto. 1966. "The Transformation of the Western European Party Systems." In *Political Parties and Political Development,* edited by Joseph La Palombara and Myron Weiner, 177–200. Princeton, NJ: Princeton University Press.

Kitschelt, Herbert, and Philipp Rehm. 2015. "Party Alignments: Change and Continuity." In *The Politics of Advanced Capitalism,* edited by Pablo Beramendi, Silja Häusermann, Herbert Kitschelt, and Hanspeter Kriesi, 179–201. New York: Cambridge University Press.

Kleinhenz, Thomas. 1998. "A New Type of Nonvoter? Turnout Decline in German Elections, 1980–94." In *Stability and Change in German Elections: How Electorates Merge, Converge, or Collide,* edited by Christopher J. Anderson and Carsten Zelle, 173–98. Westport, CT: Praeger.

Kleppner, Paul. 1982. *Who Voted? The Dynamics of Electoral Turnout, 1870–1980.* New York: Praeger.

———. 1987. *Continuity and Change in Electoral Politics, 1893–1928.* New York: Greenwood.

Knack, Stephen, and Philip Keefer. 1995. "Institutions and Economic Performance: Cross-Country Tests Using Alternative Institutional Measures." *Economics and Politics,* 7 (3): 207–27.

Komlos, John. 1989. *Nutrition and Economic Development in the Eighteenth-Century Habsburg Monarchy: An Anthropometric History.* Princeton, NJ: Princeton University Press.

———. 1998. "Shrinking in a Growing Economy?: The Mystery of Physical Stature during the Industrial Revolution." *Journal of Economic History* 58 (3): 779–802.

———. 2017. "Hidden Negative Aspects of Industrialization at the Onset of Modern Economic Growth in the US." *Structural Change and Economic Dynamics* 41 (June): 43–52.

Kopczuk, Wojciech, Emmanuel Saez, and Jae Song. 2010. "Earnings Inequality and Mobility in the United States: Evidence from Social Security Data since 1937." *Quarterly Journal of Economics* 125 (1): 91–128.

Kumparak, Greg, Matt Burns, and Anna Escher. 2015. "A Brief History of Tesla." *TechCrunch.* July 28, 2015. https://techcrunch.com/gallery/a-brief-history-of-tesla/.

Kurzweil, Ray. 2005. "Human Life: The Next Generation." *New Scientist* 24: 32–37.

Landes, David. 1969. *The Unbound Prometheus: Technological Change and Industrial Development in Western Europe from 1750 to the Present.* New York: Cambridge University Press.

Leighley, Jan E., and Jonathan Nagler. 2013. *Who Votes Now? Demographics, Issues, Inequality, and Turnout in the United States*. Princeton, NJ: Princeton University Press.

Lindert, Peter H. 2004. *Growing Public*. Vol. 1, *The Story: Social Spending and Economic Growth since the Eighteenth Century*. New York: Cambridge University Press.

Lindert, Peter H., and Jeffrey G. Williamson. 1983. "Reinterpreting Britain's Social Tables, 1688–1913." *Explorations in Economic History* 20 (1): 94–109.

———. 2016. "Unequal Gains: American Growth and Inequality since 1700." *Juncture* 22 (4): 276–83.

Lipset, Seymour M. 1963. *The First New Nation: The United States in Comparative and Historical Perspective*. New York: Basic Books.

———. 1964. "The Changing Class Structure and Contemporary European Politics." *Daedalus* 93 (1): 271–303.

Londregan, John B., and Keith T. Poole. 1990. "Poverty, the Coup Trap, and the Seizure of Executive Power." *World Politics* 42 (2): 151–83.

Los, Bart, Marcel Timmer, and Gaaitzen De Vries. 2014. "The Demand for Skills 1995–2008: A Global Supply Chain Perspective." OECD Economics Department Working Paper No. 1141. Paris: OECD.

Lowe, Robert. 1867. "Speech before the House of Commons." *Hansard Parliamentary Debates*, 3d series, vol. 188, cols. 1540–43.

Lowe, Will, Kenneth Benoit, Slava Mikhaylov, and Michael Laver. 2011. "Scaling Policy Preferences from Coded Political Texts." *Legislative Studies Quarterly* 36 (1): 123–55.

Macaulay, Thomas. 1842. "Speech before the House of Commons." *Hansard Parliamentary Debates*, 3d series, vol. 63, cols. 45–49.

Maddison, Angus. 2001. *The World Economy: A Millennial Perspective*. Paris: OECD.

Maier, Charles S. 1987. *In Search of Stability: Explorations in Historical Political Economy*. New York: Cambridge University Press.

Maier, Charles S. 1988. *Recasting Bourgeois Europe: Stabilization in France, Germany, and Italy in the Decade after World War I*. Princeton, NJ: Princeton University Press.

Malone, Thomas W., Robert J. Laubacher, and Tammy Johns. 2011. "The Age of Hyperspecialization." *Harvard Business Review* 89 (7/8): 56–65.

Mankiw, N. Gregory. 2013. "Defending the One Percent." *Journal of Economic Perspectives* 27 (3): 21–34.

Marglin, Stephen A., and Juliet B. Schor, eds. 1990. *The Golden Age of Capitalism: Reinterpreting the Postwar Experience*. New York: Oxford University Press.

Markoff, John. 2015. *Machines of Loving Grace: Between Humans and Robots*. New York: HarperCollins.

Marks, Gary W. 1989. *Unions in Politics: Britain, Germany, and the United States in the Nineteenth and Early Twentieth Centuries*. Princeton, NJ: Princeton University Press.

Martikainen, Pekka, Tuomo Martikainen, and Hanna Wass. 2005. "The Effect of Socioeconomic Factors on Voter Turnout in Finland: A Register-Based Study of 2.9 Million Voters." *European Journal of Political Research* 44 (5): 645–69.

Marx, Karl. (1867) 1906. *Capital: A Critique of Political Economy*. Edited by F. Engels. Chicago: Charles H. Kerr.

————. 1934. *The Class Struggles in France, 1848 to 1850*. New York: International Publishers.

McCarty, Nolan, Keith T. Poole, and Howard Rosenthal. 2006. *Polarized America: The Dance of Ideology and Unequal Riches*. Cambridge, MA: MIT Press.

Meade, James E. 1964. *Efficiency, Equality and the Ownership of Property*. London: Allen and Unwin.

Meredith, David, and Deborah Oxley. 2014. "Nutrition and Health, 1700–1870." In *The Cambridge Economic History of Modern Britain*, vol. 1, *Industrialization, 1700–1870*, edited by Roderick Floud and Paul Johnson, 118–48. New York: Cambridge University Press.

Merritt, Anna J., and Richard L. Merritt, eds. 1970. *Public Opinion in Occupied Germany: The OMGUS Surveys, 1945–1949*. Urbana, IL: University of Illinois Press.

Michaels, Guy, Ashwini Natraj, and John Van Reenen. 2014. "Has ICT Polarized Skill Demand?: Evidence from Eleven Countries over Twenty-Five Years." *Review of Economics and Statistics* 96 (1): 60–77.

Miguel, Edward, Shanker Satyanath, and Ernest Sergenti. 2004. "Economic shocks and civil conflict: An instrumental variables approach." *Journal of Political Economy* 112 (4): 725–753.

Milanovic, Branko. 2016. *Global Inequality: A New Approach for the Age of Globalization*. Cambridge, MA: Harvard University Press.

Minami, Ryoshin. 2008. "Income Distribution of Japan: Historical Perspective and Its Implications." *Japan Labor Review* 5 (4): 5–20.

Mitchell, Brian R. 2013. *International Historical Statistics, 1750–2010*. Basingstoke, UK: Palgrave Macmillan.

Mokyr, Joel, ed. 2009. *The British Industrial Revolution: An Economic Perspective*. New York: Routledge.

Murphy, K. J. 2013. "Executive Compensation: Where We Are, and How We Got There." In *Handbook of the Economics of Finance*, edited by George M. Constantinides, Milton Harris, and Rene M. Stulz, 211–356. Amsterdam: Elsevier.

Murray, Charles. 2016. *In Our Hands. A Plan to Replace the Welfare State*. Washington, DC: American Enterprise Institute.

Nassmacher, Karl-Heinz. 2009. *The Funding of Party Competition: Political Finance in 25 Democracies*. Baden-Baden: Nomos Verlagsgesellschaft.

National Academies of Sciences, Engineering, and Medicine. 2016. *The Economic and Fiscal Consequences of Immigration*. Washington, DC: National Academies Press.

Nieuwbeerta, Paul, and Nan Dirk De Graaf. 1999. "Traditional Class Voting in Twenty Postwar Societies." In *The End of Class Politics: Class Voting in Comparative Perspective*, edited by Geoffrey Evans, 23–56. New York: Oxford University Press.

Nordhaus, William D. 2007. "Two Centuries of Productivity Growth in Computing." *Journal of Economic History* 67 (1): 128–59.

Norton, Michael. I., and Dan Ariely. 2011. "Building a Better America: One Wealth Quintile at a Time." *Perspectives on Psychological Science* 6 (1): 9–12.

Nye, David. 2000. *America's Assembly Line*. Cambridge, MA: MIT Press.

Ober, Harry. 1948. "Occupational Wage Differentials, 1907–1947." *Monthly Labor Review* 67: 127.

O'Rourke, Kevin H., and Jeffrey G. Williamson. 2001. *Globalization and History: The Evolution of a Nineteenth-Century Atlantic Economy*. Cambridge, MA: MIT Press.

Oscarsson, Henrik, and Sören Holmberg. 2015. *Swedish Voting Behavior*. Gothenburg: University of Gothenburg, Swedish National Election Studies Program. https://valforskning.pol.gu.se/digitalAssets/1548/1548537_swedish-voting-behavior.pdf.

Piketty, Thomas. 2014. *Capital in the Twenty-First Century*. Cambridge, MA: Belknap.

Piore, Michael J., and Charles F. Sabel. 1984. *The Second Industrial Divide: Possibilities for Prosperity*. New York: Basic Books.

Piven, Frances Fox, and Richard A. Cloward. 1988. *Why Americans Don't Vote*. New York: Pantheon Books.

Plomin, Robert, and Frank M. Spinath. 2004. "Intelligence: Genetics, Genes, and Genomics." *Journal of Personality and Social Psychology* 86 (1): 112–29.

Plotnick, Robert D., Eugene Smolensky, Eirik Evenhouse, and Siobhan Reilly. 1998. "The Twentieth Century Record of Inequality and Poverty in the United States." University of Wisconsin-Madison, Institute for Research on Poverty. Discussion paper no. 1166-98.

Pollard, Sidney. 1978. "Labour in Great Britain." In *The Cambridge Economic History of Europe*, vol. 7, *The Industrial Economies: Capital, Labour and Enterprise*, pt. 1: *Britain, France, Germany and Scandinavia*, edited by Peter Mathias and Michael Moïssey Postan, 97–179. New York: Cambridge University Press.

Pontusson, Jonas. 1992. "At the End of the Third Road: Swedish Social Democracy in Crisis." *Politics and Society* 20 (3): 305–32.

———. 2005. *Inequality and Prosperity: Social Europe vs. Liberal America*. Ithaca, NY: Cornell University Press.

Przeworski, Adam. 2017. "What's Happening?" Unpublished manuscript, New York University.

Przeworski, Adam, Michael E. Alvarez, Jose Antonio Cheibub, and Fernando Limongi. 2000. *Democracy and Development: Political Institutions and Well-Being in the World, 1950–1990*. New York: Cambridge University Press.

Przeworski, Adam, and Covadonga Meseguer. 2006. "Globalization and Democracy." In *Globalization and Egalitarian Redistribution*, edited by Pranab Bardhan, Samuel Bowles, and Michael Wallerstein, ch. 7. Princeton, NJ: Princeton University and Russell Sage Foundation.

Rajan, Raghuram, and Luigi Zingales. 2003. *Saving Capitalism from the Capitalists*. New York: Crown Business.

Reich, Robert B. 2015a. *Saving Capitalism: For the Many, Not the Few*. New York: Alfred A. Knopf.

Reich, Robert B. 2015b. "The 'iEverything' and the Redistributional Imperative." RobertReich.org. March 16, 2015. http://robertreich.org/post/113801138315.

Rennwald, Line, and Geoffrey Evans. 2014. "When Supply Creates Demand: Social Democratic Party Strategies and the Evolution of Class Voting." *West European Politics* 37 (5): 1108–35.

Rodden, Jonathan. 2006. *Hamilton's Paradox: The Promise and Peril of Fiscal Federalism*. New York: Cambridge University Press.

Rodrik, Dani. 1999. "Democracies Pay Higher Wages." *Quarterly Journal of Economics* 114 (3): 707–38.

———. 2017. "Premature Deindustrialisation in the Developing World." *Frontiers of Economics in China* 12 (1): 1–6.

Rogowski, Ronald. 1989. *Commerce and Coalitions: How Trade Affects Domestic Political Alignments*. Princeton, NJ: Princeton University Press.

Rosenstone, Steven J., and John Hansen. 1993. *Mobilization, Participation, and Democracy in America*. New York: Macmillan.

Ross, Arthur M., and Paul T. Hartman. 1960. *Changing Patterns of Industrial Conflict*. New York: Wiley.

Rothwell, Jonathan. 2018. "A Republic of Equals: How to Create a Just Society." Unpublished MS. Washington, DC.

Rudé, George. 1981. *The Crowd in History: A Study of Popular Disturbances in France and England, 1730–1848*. London: Lawrence and Wishart.

Ruggie, John. 1982. "International Regimes, Transactions, and Change: Embedded Liberalism in the Postwar Economic Order." *International Organization* 36 (2): 379–415.

Saez, Emmanuel, and Gabriel Zucman. 2014. "Wealth Inequality in the United States since 1913: Evidence from Capitalized Income Tax Data." NBER Working Paper no. 20625.

Sage, Daniel, and Patrick Diamond. 2017. "Europe's New Social Reality: The Case against Universal Basic Income." Policy Network paper. February.

Schaechter, Andrea, and Carlo Cottarelli. 2010. *Long-Term Trends in Public Finances in the G-7 Economies*. Issues 2010–2013 of International Monetary Fund (IMF) Staff Position Notes. Washington, DC: IMF.

Scheve, Kenneth F., and Matthew J. Slaughter. 2001. "Labor Market Competition and Individual Preferences over Immigration Policy." *Review of Economics and Statistics* 83 (1): 133–45.

———. 2006. "Public Opinion, International Economic Integration, and the Welfare State." In *Globalization and Self-Determination: Is the Nation-State under Siege?* edited by David R. Cameron, Gustav Ranis, and Annalisa Zinn, 51–94. London: Routledge.

Scheve, Kenneth F., and David Stasavage. 2009. "Institutions, Partisanship, and Inequality in the Long Run." *World Politics* 61 (2): 215–53.

———. 2016. *Taxing the Rich: A History of Fiscal Fairness in the United States and Europe*. Princeton, NJ: Princeton University Press.

Schickler, Eric, and Devin Caughey. 2011. "Public Opinion, Organized Labor, and the Limits of New Deal Liberalism, 1936–1945." *Studies in American Political Development* 25 (2): 162–89.

Schumpeter, Joseph A. 1950. *Capitalism, Socialism, and Democracy*. 3d ed. New York: Harper and Brothers.

Selinger, William, and Greg Conti. 2015. "Reappraising Walter Bagehot's Liberalism: Discussion, Public Opinion, and the Meaning of Parliamentary Government." *History of European Ideas* 41 (2): 264–91.

Sewell, William H. 1986. "Artisans, Factory Workers, and the Formation of the French Working Class, 1789–1848." In *Working-Class Formation: Nineteenth-century Patterns in Western Europe and the United States*, edited by Ira Katznelson and Aristide R. Zolberg, 45–70. Princeton, NJ: Princeton University Press.

Smith, Adam. (1776) 1991. *The Wealth of Nations*. New York: Knopf.

Soskice, David. 1990. "Wage Determination: The Changing Role of Institutions in Advanced Industrialized Countries." *Oxford Review of Economic Policy* 6 (4): 36–61.

Spence Michael A., and Sandile Hlatshwayo. 2011. *The Evolving Structure of the American Economy and the Employment Challenge*. New York: Council on Foreign Relations.

Starmans, Christina, Mark Sheskin, and Paul Bloom. "Why People Prefer Unequal Societies." *Nature Human Behaviour* 1 (2017): 0082.

Stephens, John D. 1981. "The Changing Swedish Electorate: Class Voting, Contextual Effects, and Voter Volatility." *Comparative Political Studies* 14 (2): 163–204.

Streeck, Wolfgang. 2014. "How Will Capitalism End?" *New Left Review* 87: 35–64.

Szreter, Simon, and Graham Mooney. 1998. "Urbanization, Mortality, and the Standard of Living Debate: New Estimates of the Expectation of Life at Birth in Nineteenth-Century British Cities." *Economic History Review* 51 (1): 84–112.

Temin, Peter. 1997. "Two Views of the British Industrial Revolution." *Journal of Economic History* 57 (1): 63–82.

Tingsten, Herbert. 1937. *Political Behavior: Studies in Election Statistics*. London: P. S. King.

———. 1955. "Stability and Vitality in Swedish Democracy." *Political Quarterly* 26 (2): 140–51.

Tomka, Béla. 2013. *A Social History of Twentieth-Century Europe*. London: Routledge.

Treisman, Daniel. 2018. "Is Democracy in Danger?: A Quick Look at the Data." UCLA. Unpublished manuscrit.

Trump, Donald. 2017. "Transcript: Donald Trump Inaugural Speech." *NPR Illinois*. n.d., accessed November 13, 2018. http://nprillinois.org/post/transcript-donald-trump-inaugural-speech#stream/0.

Tuorto, Dario. 2010. "La partecipazione al voto." In *Votare in Italia, 1968–2008: Dall'appartenenza alla scelta*, edited by Paolo Bellucci and Paolo Segatti, 53–79. Bologna: Il Mulino.

UNCTAD. 1992. *Trade and Development Report, 1992*. New York: United Nations.

———. 2005. *Trade and Development Report, 2005*. New York: United Nations.

———. 2016. *World Investment Report 2016*. New York: United Nations.

United Nations University-WIDER. 2015. World Income Inequality Database, version WIID3c. September. https://www.wider.unu.edu/project/wiid-world-income-inequality-database.

Ure, Andrew. 1835. *The Philosophy of Manufactures; or, an Exposition of the Scientific, Moral, and Commercial Economy of the Factory System of Great Britain, with Illustrations*. London: Charles Knight.

US Bureau of Economic Analysis (BEA). 2018. "Gross Domestic Product by Industry: 2nd Quarter 2018 and Comprehensive Update." BEA website. November 1, 2018. https://www.bea.gov/data/gdp/gdp-industry.

US Bureau of Labor Statistics. 2004. "International Comparison of Hourly Compensation Costs for Production Workers in Manufacturing, 2003." US Bureau of Labor Statistics news release USDL 04–2343. November 18, 2004.

———. 2018. "All Employees: Manufacturing (MANEMP)." FRED, Federal Reserve Bank of St. Louis. September, last updated October 5. https://fred.stlouisfed.org/series/MANEMP.

Van Biezen, Ingrid, Peter Mair, and Thomas Poguntke. 2012. "Going, Going, . . . Gone? The Decline of Party Membership in Contemporary Europe." *European Journal of Political Research* 51 (1): 24–56.

Van Parijs, Philippe. 2004. "Basic Income: A Simple and Powerful Idea for the Twenty-First Century." *Politics and Society* 32 (1): 7–39.

Volkens, Andrea, Pola Lehmann, Sven Regel, Henrike Schultze, and Annika Werner, with Onawa Promise Lacewell. 2012. *The Manifesto Data Collection. Manifesto Project (MRG/CMP/MARPOR)*. Version 2012a. Berlin: Wissenschaftszentrum Berlin für Sozialforschung.

Wallerstein, Michael. 1999. "Wage-Setting Institutions and Pay Inequality in Advanced Industrial Societies." *American Journal of Political Science* 43 (3): 649–80.

Wass, Hanna. 2007. "The Effects of Age, Generation and Period on Turnout in Finland 1975–2003." *Electoral Studies* 26 (3): 648–59.

Western, John, Mark Western, Michael Emmison, and Janeen Baxter. 1991. "Class Analysis and Politics." In *Class Analysis and Contemporary Australia*, edited by Baxter, Emmison and J. Western, 306–38. South Melbourne: Macmillan.

Wood, Adrian. 1994. *North-South Trade, Employment, and Inequality: Changing Fortunes in a Skill-Driven World*. New York: Oxford University Press.

World Bank. 2016. *World Development Report*. Washington, DC: Digital Dividends.

———. 2017. "Stock Market Capitalization to GDP for United States [DDDM01USA156NWDB]." FRED, Federal Reserve Bank of St. Louis. n.d., accessed May 1, 2017. https://fred.stlouisfed.org/series/DDDM01USA156NWDB.

World Top Incomes Database. Part of the World Inequality Database. http://wid.world/.

World Trade Organization (WTO). 2013. *World Trade Report: Factors Shaping the Future of World Trade*. Geneva: WTO.

Wrigley, Edward Anthony, and R. S. Schofield. 1989. *The Population History of England 1541–1871*. New York: Cambridge University Press.

INDEX

Ackerman, Bruce, 197, 226n14
Airbnb, 188–89
Alford, Robert R., 93
Alford index, 93–96
Allen, Robert, 38
AlphaZero, 20
Alt, James, 153
American Federation of Labor (AFL), 71
American Tobacco Company, 60
Apple, 101, 112–13, 186
Ariely, Dan, 193
Arkwright, Richard, 5, 26
Armstrong, S., 179
Arntz, Melanie, 225n3
Aron, Raymond, 89
artificial intelligence, 102, 178–80
assembly lines, 9, 51–54
AT&T, 103
Attlee, Clement, 92
Australia: class-based voting in, 93–96; concentration of income in, 10; earnings dispersion and creation of private employment in, 131; political trust, downward trend in, 148; rioters transported to, 41
authoritarianism/authoritarian regimes, 87, 91–92, 191–92, 202–4, 212
automation: demand for labor and, 180–81; the evolution of capital and, 184–89; impact of, the range of predictions regarding, 177–80; jobs that are automatable, percentage of, 225n3; outside the West, potential impact of, 210–14; politics and, the range of predictions regarding, 189–90; supply of labor and, 181–84.

See also computers; technological innovation
automation, responses to: human capital formation, 204–5; Luddite policy program blocking technological change, 225n23; socialization of capital ownership, 209–10; universal basic income (UBI), provision of, 205–9
Autor, David, 103–4
Ayres, Ian, 197, 226n14

Baroche, Jules, 44
Barro, Robert J., 77
Bartels, Larry, 195
batch-production system, 53–54
Bayard, Kimberly, 113
Beckman, Arnold, 98
Bell, Daniel, 88–89, 91, 96
Beramendi, Pablo, 74
BMW, 112
Bonsack, James Albert, 54
Bornholdt, Oscar, 51
Bresnahan, Timothy, 104
Bretton Woods system, establishment of, 8
Britain. *See* United Kingdom
Bryan, William Jennings, 82
Byrne, David, 113

campaign funding, 195
capital concentration/ownership, 209–10, 213
capitalism: automation and the evolution of capital, 184–89; barriers to becoming a capitalist, 185–86;

era, 134–35; employment structure
during Silicon Valley capitalism,
106–7; enrollment in secondary education, 76; evolution of productivity
and earnings in, 62–63; expansion
of the franchise, opposition to, 44;
labor productivity and earnings
under Silicon Valley capitalism, 119–
20; the Paris Commune, 42; political
representation in, 45–46; populism/
nationalism in electoral politics of,
171; populist/antiglobalist political
parties in, 172–75; private sector employment in the Silicon Valley era,
131; response to the employment-
equality trade-off, 132–33; the top
one percent in, 139; unemployment
in, 158; wage distribution in the
Silicon Valley era in, 123–25
franchise, the. *See* suffrage
Frey, Carl, 180–81, 183
Frost, John, 40

Gaitskell, Hugh, 92
General Agreement on Tariffs and
Trade (GATT), 8, 108, 167
General Motors, 60, 74, 186
Germany: absence of mass-production
techniques during the interwar
period, 56; democratic capitalism in,
7–8; disaffection of public opinion,
growth in, 1, 148; earnings inequality
ratio in, 67, 70; electoral behavior
in, 94–95, 149, 151, 153; employment by sector in the Silicon Valley
era, 133–35; employment-equality
trade-off, responses to, 132; employment structure during Silicon Valley
capitalism, 106–7; enrollment in secondary education, 76; evolution of
productivity and earnings in, 62–63;
income distribution in, 2; offshored
production by firms in, 114; political
institutions after unification, 46;
populist/antiglobalist political parties in, 172–75; the top one percent
in, 139; trade unions in, 71; wage
bargaining in, 71. *See also* Prussia

Gilens, Martin, 195–96
Gini, Corrado, 10
Gini coefficient, 10–11, 13
globalization: economic boom associated with, 114; job losses and, 116–18;
versus nationalism in electoral
politics, 166–76; political developments reinforcing, 112; positions on
in party platforms, 145–46; during
the postwar era, 108–10; production
operations, impact on, 15, 112–14,
220–21n7; Silicon Valley capitalism
and, 111–15; transportation and communications costs, impact of fall in,
14–15, 110–12. *See also* foreign direct
investment
Goldin, Claudia, 58–59
Google, 186
Great Depression, 12, 48, 66–67, 69, 84,
87, 109, 142
Great Recession, 17, 135, 148, 150–51,
164, 225n22
Gregory, Terry, 225n3
Guo, Terry, 185
Guvenen, Fatih, 221n15

Hanson, Gordon H., 113
Hargreaves, James, 26
Hatton, Timothy J., 37
Häusermann, Silja, 162
health outcomes, inequality of in
late-eighteenth to early-nineteenth
century Britain, 36–37
height, evolution of human, 36
Hitler, Adolf, 87
Honda, 112
human capital: increase in stock of,
77–78; investment in as a response to
automation, 204–5

IBM (International Business Machines),
100–101
ICTs. *See* information and communication technologies
ideology: convergence of in Europe
post-World War II, 88–89; end of,
91, 96; moderation of in the United
States under Detroit capitalism,

A NOTE ON THE TYPE

This book has been composed in Adobe Text and Gotham. Adobe Text, designed by Robert Slimbach for Adobe, bridges the gap between fifteenth- and sixteenth-century calligraphic and eighteenth-century Modern styles. Gotham, inspired by New York street signs, was designed by Tobias Frere-Jones for Hoefler & Co.